KHAROṢṬHI DOCUMENTS

THE LANGUAGE OF THE KHAROṢṬHI DOCUMENTS FROM CHINESE TURKESTAN

by

T. BURROW, M.A.
Research Fellow of Christ's College,
Cambridge

CAMBRIDGE
AT THE UNIVERSITY PRESS
1937

CAMBRIDGE UNIVERSITY PRESS
Cambridge, New York, Melbourne, Madrid, Cape Town,
Singapore, São Paulo, Delhi, Tokyo, Mexico City

Cambridge University Press
The Edinburgh Building, Cambridge CB2 8RU, UK

Published in the United States of America by Cambridge University Press, New York

www.cambridge.org
Information on this title: www.cambridge.org/9781107629486

First published 1937
First paperback edition 2011

A catalogue record for this publication is available from the British Library

ISBN 978-1-107-62948-6 Paperback

INTRODUCTION

The documents in the Kharoṣṭhi alphabet, recovered by Sir Aurel Stein from Central Asia, are written in a variety of Indian Prakrit that was used as the administrative language of Shan-Shan or Kroraina in the third century A.D. The texts range over a period of at least eighty-eight years, as is seen from Prof. Rapson's Table of Kings and Regnal Years, *Kharoṣṭhi Inscriptions*, pp. 326-8. The date is approximately fixed by a Chinese document, found in the same heap with a number of Kharoṣṭhi tablets, which is dated A.D. 269. Further than this it is not possible to go yet, because none of the kings has been found referred to in Chinese annals. The language of the documents is uniform throughout and there is no trace of evolution from the earliest to the latest.

The bulk of the texts comes from Niya, the ancient Caḍ́ota which lay on the extreme edge of the kingdom bordering on Khotan. For the rest there are a few from Endere (= Sāca) and about forty from the Lou-Lan area where the ancient capital of the kingdom Kroraina was situated. A single document from Endere (661) is written in a different dialect from the rest, and since it refers to a king of Khotan, it may be taken to represent the Prakrit used similarly for administrative purposes in Khotan at that time. (*B.S.O.S.* VIII, 430–34.)

For a variety of reasons the language has presented considerable difficulties of interpretation. In the first place it represents a variety of Prakrit not otherwise known; and secondly it contains a large number of non-Indian words from various sources. The general position of the language has already been dealt with in a series of articles ('Iranian Loan-words in the Kharoṣṭhi Documents', I, *B.S.O.S.* VII (1934), 511 ff.; II, *B.S.O.S.* VII (1935), 779 ff.; 'Tocharian Elements in Kharoṣṭhi Documents', *J.R.A.S.* (1935), pp. 667 ff.; and 'The Dialectical Position of the Niya Prakrit', *B.S.O.S.* VIII (1936), 419 ff.). Referring to the full discussions in these papers, it will be sufficient here to indicate the main conclusions arrived at.

The language was used for official purposes in the Shan-Shan kingdom. Its original home was N.W. India, probably in the region of Peshawar. It agrees closely with the (post-Aśokan) Kharoṣṭhi Inscriptions from N.W. India and (slightly less closely) with the Prakrit version of the Dhammapada. Further, it exhibits sufficient characteristics in common with the modern Dardic languages to be assigned definitely to that group (*B.S.O.S.* VIII (1936), 434 and Konow, *ib.* 605 ff.). Among the Dardic languages it would seem to be most closely allied to Torwali.

At the same time it differs from all other varieties of Prakrit preserved, in the degree to which its inflectional system has decayed and altered. There is no reason to impute this to the users of the language in Central Asia, because with them it was a stereotyped official language, whereas the phenomena observed are those of normal linguistic change. Moreover, the changes are actually found to occur over the rest of the Indo-Aryan field at a later date. For instance, they have ceased to distinguish between Nominative and Accusative. This became general in Indo-Aryan in the Apabhraṃśa stage. Other phenomena which occur (though less thoroughly) in Apabhraṃśa are the tendency to transfer all nouns to the *a*-declension (§§ 67, 70), extension of -*ī* as the general termination of feminine nouns (§ 74, cf. forms in Ap. (*Bhavisatta-kaha*) like *sampunnī*, *avainnī*, *khittī*, etc.), use of the Locative instead of the Accusative with verbs of going, sending, etc. (§ 123, cf. L. Alsdorff, *Kumārapālapratibodha*, Introd. § 43 (1) b).

Especially interesting is the formation of a new active past tense from the past participle passive (§ 105). This has not developed even in Apabhraṃśa, but is common in the modern Indo-Aryan languages (cf. J. Bloch, *L'Indo-Aryen*, p. 276). There is a precisely similar development in Modern Persian.

The question arises whether these tendencies to evolution developed unusually early in the home of this Prakrit (due to foreign invasion, influence), or whether they may not have been more general in India only obscured by the conservative tendencies of the literary Prakrits. We might ask, for instance, that since the Prakrit used by Kālidāsa remained the same for centuries after his time, to what extent may it not have been artificial and archaic even then? Anyway it is curious that our language, while usually the most conservative in phonetic preservation (*B.S.O.S.* VIII (1936), 422), is at the same time the most advanced of all in inflectional decay.

The dialect that had thus evolved in India is subjected to two kinds of foreign influence: (1) Iranian, (2) the native language of Kroraina.

The Iranian loan-words have been dealt with in my two papers (*B.S.O.S.* VII, 509 ff., 779 ff.). Further examples (discussed in Index) are *anada* 'carefully', *cojhbo* (name of an official), *namaṃniya, parāṣa, veǵa sujinakirta.* They total together some forty or forty-three words, which is quite considerable.

As regards the origin of these Iranian words, there is no reason to assume that they entered the language at the same time and from the same place. In the case of the word meaning 'treasury', for instance, we have two dialect forms *gañja-* (cf. *gaṃña* and *kañi*) and *ganza-* (cf. *kaṃjhavaliyana*). A very few words are specifically Saka, namely *anada, prahoni, lastana.* The title *cojhbo* appears in the Maralbashi dialect of Saka as *cazba. jheniǵa* is peculiar to Saka and Sogdian, although the same base appears in N.Pers. *zīn-hār* 'protection, security' and *zindān* 'prison'. If *draṃga* is connected with Avestan *θraxta-*, etc., it shows the typically Saka treatment of *θr-*. *aváana* 'village' occurs in both of the Saka dialects (having lost its initial *a-*), but also in Western Iranian, Arm. *avan.*

On the other hand, the mass of the words might equally well appear in a typically Western Iranian language, e.g. *kākhorda, guśura, divira, nac̄ira, tavastaǵa, s̄pura, veǵa, ṣada, stora.* Many of them have not, so far at any rate, turned up in Khotanese. *ṣada* 'pleased' definitely cannot be Kh. (*tsāta*), and *guśura* shows a treatment that is not Khotanese but typical of the eastern part of Iranian. There is some reason to believe that a large number of the words at any rate had been taken into the Prakrit in N.W. India before it came to be used in Central Asia.

(1) Quite a number of the Iranian loan-words here appear also in India in Sanskrit, etc., namely, *sthora, gañja,* (*aśva*)*vāra, divira, draṅga, kākhorda. saste* 'day' occurs in Kharoṣṭhi in-

scriptions from N.W. India; *namataka* 'felt' is used in Pali. In the case of these words we may be pretty sure that they had become part of the language in India itself.

(2) There are traces of the phonetic developments that occur in the languages of specifically those Iranians who occupied N.W. India in the centuries round about the Christian era. *Guśura* shows the same treatment of initial *vi-* as occurs in the proper name *Gudaphara* (Gondophernes). The change of *d* > *l* in *laṣni* 'gift' is paralleled by royal names in India beginning with *spala-* (= *spāda* 'army'). The same change is observable in Pushto, and may have been characteristic of the Iranian-speaking population bordering on N.W. India at quite an early date.

(3) Iranian proper names in the Kharoṣṭhi documents (*B.S.O.S.* VII, 789) are exceedingly rare, so that certainly there was no Iranian population in this kingdom. The solitary Khotan document (661) indicates a different state of affairs for Khotan, but there is no means of ascertaining its relative date. The differences between the two varieties of Prakrit are such that each must have its origin separately in India and not one depend on the other (cf. *B.S.O.S.* VIII (1936), 430 ff.).

We may conclude that the Prakrit already in India had a fair sprinkling of Iranian words, and that in Central Asia a smaller number (*cojhbo*, etc. above) were further introduced.

The second foreign element to which the Prakrit was subjected is the native language of the kingdom. It is represented by a wealth of proper names (over 1000) and about 100 words. Working on the phonetic structure and suffix formation of this material it is possible to demonstrate a strong affinity of this language with 'Tocharian' (Agnean and Kuchean, cf. H. W. Bailey, *B.S.O.S.* VIII (1936), 883–917). This point I have dealt with in detail in *J.R.A.S.* (1935), pp. 667 ff. We may term the language 'Krorainic' after the capital of the kingdom.

The pronunciation of the Prakrit was strongly affected by the phonetic structure of 'Krorainic'. It was devoid of voiced stops, consequently we find writings like *kilane* = *glāna* 'sick', *taṃḍa* = *daṇḍa*, *poǵa* = *bhoǵa*, etc. (§ 14). Similarly it was devoid of aspirates with like effects (§ 24). The solitary document from

Khotan does not show these tendencies, whence we may infer that the language there was of a different type.

Actual word-correspondences in the documents with Agnean and Kuchean are unfortunately few. Among the most certain are:

kilme 'district' = Agnean *kälyme* 'direction, district'.

kitsaitsa, a title (elder?) = Kuchean *ktsaitsañe* 'age'.

ṣoṭhaṃga 'tax-collector': Agnean *ṣoṣtäṅk-*, meaning the same.

amklatsa, epithet of *uṭa* 'camel': Kuchean *aknātse*, Agnean *āknats* 'ignorant', 'inexperienced'.

ṣilpoǵa (i.e. *ṣilýoǵa*) 'document': Agnean *ṣlyok* which translates Skt. *śloka*.

Considering the strong evidence (*J.R.A.S.* (1935), pp. 667 ff.) that Krorainic was a language closely akin to Agnean and Kuchean, it is surprising that there are so few obvious etymologies, but it may be due to difference of subject-matter: the texts in those languages are chiefly religious, whereas the Krorainic words in the Prakrit are mostly of a technical nature (official titles, crops and objects of local use, etc.).

Such briefly are the relationships and history of the language of the Niya documents. The present work is divided into two parts: first, a Grammar of the language; and secondly, a combined Index and Vocabulary, where the forms are referred to the paragraphs of the Grammar so far as they are treated there, while an attempt is made as far as possible to explain the meaning of individual words, with references to the existing literature.

Part I

GRAMMAR

VOWELS

§ 1. There is a slight tendency in the documents for *e* to become *i*: *ajiṣaṃnae* 419 (usually *ajeṣaṃnae* = *adhyeṣanayā* 'at the request of'), *ichiyati* 425 (usually *-eyati*), *c̄h́itra* = *kṣetra* 160, 255, etc.; *vitaṃna* 177 = *vetaṃnā*, but the reading is uncertain. Finally: *nic̄i* = *nic̄e* 'decision', *vaṃti* 'in the presence of' = *upāṃte*, *kiṃna* = *kena* 609, *tina* 532 (*tiṣu* 511). The change was regular in the dialect of Khotan: 661 *saǵaji* = *sakāśe*, *niravaśiṣo*, *kali*, *cudiyadi* = *codeyāti*, etc. But in the dialect of Niya the *e* is preserved in the vast majority of cases. In the Kharoṣṭhi Dh.p. instances are common, e.g. *viraneṣu averana* C^vo 28, *sarvi*, *uvito*, *etina*, etc. Likewise loan-words in Saka: *ajiṣ* 'to seek', *prracīya-sambuddha-*, *cīya* = *caitya*. It seems to have been a specifically Khotanese change, which had already taken place at the date of no. 661; but it cannot have been very much earlier, because the Saka loan-word *jheniǵa* always appears with *e* in the texts although *ī* in Saka *ysīnīya*.

§ 2. The treatment of *o* is parallel to that of *i*. It is preserved in the documents with the sole exception of *kuśava* 345 for usual *kośava*. *rucate* 585 is probably to be compared with Pali, Pkt. *ruccati* rather than with Skt. *rocate*. *paribhuchamnae* 579, 581 is probably for *°*bhuñjanae*, rather than *°bhojanāya*, because the infinitive is usually formed from the present base. *cudiyadi* in 661 shows that the change was established in Khotan, as is later borne out in the Saka texts (Konow, *Saka Studies*, p. 20).

§ 3. *e* occasionally appears for short *i*: *garbheni* 593, *Jeṭugha* 591 (usually *Jiṭugha*), *pac̄emakalammi* 332 (*pac̄ima* 165, etc.); *levistarena* 160 (usually *livistara* = *lipi-vistāra*) has probably been influenced by *lekha*.

§ **4.** *o* is written for *u* frequently after *h* and *pr*: *baho*, *amaho*, *prahoḍa*, *laho*, *ahono*, *gohomi* side by side with *bahu*, *amahu*, etc., *prochidavo* and *pruchidavo*. In all these cases the difference between the signs for *o* and *u* is very small, and it is more likely that *u* should everywhere be read than that there was really a change from *u* to *o*.

§ **5.** The regular treatment of the vowel *ṛ* is *ri*, which is written *ri*, *ṛ* and *rṛ*: *atripta* 390, *etriśa*, *krita*, *kriṣati*, *ghrida*, *grihasta*, *driṭha*, *triti*, *prichati*. It is written *ṛ* in *ṛna*, *kṛta*, *gṛha*, *gṛheyati*, *dṛṭhati*, *rṛ* in *drṛthaǵa*, *tadrṛśa*. The *rṛ* is also used to represent *ri*, *rī aśrṛta* 511, *Priyaśrṛ*, *Kutaśrṛae*. After *p* we get *ru* in *pruch-* (*proch-*), though also *pricha*, *pariprichati*. Usually after labials the vowel *ṛ* is written (probably = *ru*): *pṛchati*, *pṛṭheṣu*, *mṛga*, *mṛda* 'dead', *mṛduka* (*mṛyati* = *mriyate*), *vivṛdhi*, *vṛcha*, *vṛdha*, *samṛdhae*, *pravṛti*. It appears as *i* in *kica* = *kṛtya*, *kiḍa* = *kṛta*, *kiṣaṃnae* 'to plough', *giṃnaṃti* 'they take', *śiṃgavera* 'ginger'. As *a* in *praǵaṭa* = *prakṛta*, *anahetu* = *ṛnahetu* (unless *ana-* = *a-*, *an-* 'not'), *kataṃti*. As *u* in *huḍi* 703 = *bhṛti* *prahuḍa* = *prābhṛta*. A following dental is usually cerebralised when the *r* disappears: *praǵaṭa*, *kiḍa*, *huḍi*. The rule seems to be that *r* is preserved, but a number of forms have crept in from other dialects without *r*. In the Dh.p. examples are found where the *ṛ* becomes *r* and vowel: *vriḍha* C^vo 34, *driḍha* C^vo 17, *savruto* = *saṃvṛta*; but (as a result of its Prakrit original?) forms without *r* are more common: *diṭhi*, *kita*, *kica*, *alagito* = *alaṃkṛta*, *akitaña*, *amutu*, *mucuno*, etc.

§ **6.** *aya* = (1) *aya*: *svaya* 'self' 709, *vayaṃ* 663, 666, *ṣayati* 'gets hold of' (*śrayate*), *jayaṃta* 'victorious'.

(2) *eya*: *bheya* (*bheyidavya*), *veyaṃ*, *ubheya*, *treya*, *niceya*, *praceya* (*ṣeyita*), *jeyaṃtasa*, *sampreṣeyati* 288.

(3) *e*: *aneṃti*, *nice*, *prace*, *tre*, *sve* = *svayam*. Almost always in causative verbs: *taḍeti*, *dhareti*, etc.

The forms in *-aya* are certainly due to the influence of Sanskrit. It is more difficult to judge of the relation of the *-eya* and *-e* forms. We find *praceya* by the side of *prace*, *niceya* and *nice*, *treya* and *tre*. It would seem that *-aya* everywhere regularly became *-e*, but that final *-e* = *-aya* was readapted to the declensional system by the adding of *-a*. The process was applied also to native words and names ending in *-e*: *loteya* for *lote*, *Lṗipeya* beside *Lṗipe*, etc. Further, when the second *-a* formed part of a heavy syllable (e.g. *Jayaṃta*, *Jeyaṃta*) the disyllabic form was regularly preserved (never **Jenta*).

§ 7. *ava* becomes *o* in *vyochiṃnida*, *vyoṣeti*, *no* = '9', *omaǵa* = *avama*(*ka*) 'falling short', *ohara*.

ava is preserved in *avásiṭha* 'remaining', *avakaśa*, *avaśa* 'certainly'.

va alternates with *o* in the non-Indian *ṣoṭhaṃga* (an official), also *ṣvaṭhaṃga*, and in the name of the king, *Aṃgoka* and *Aṃkvaga* (*Aṃgvaka*, *Aṃguvaka*, *Aṃgoṃka*).

§ 8. Final *-āya* > *-ae* in infinitives: *deyaṃnae* 'to give', etc. Also written *-aya*, *-aye*; *karaṃnaya*, *karaṃnaye*; the suffix *-aǵa* = *-aka* is treated in the same way: *ditae* 'given', *thavaṃnae* (*-aǵa*) 'cloth'; also *-aǵa*: *ditaǵa*, *dharaṃnaǵa*.

The change is much more common in past participles than in ordinary nouns and adjectives. (Here perhaps the original Nom. Sing. *-ake* (cf. § 53) might be responsible, cf. § 74.)

§ 9. Final *-ya* and *-iya* become *-i*: *muli* 'price', *eśvari* 'ownership', *arogi* 'health'.

-ya is always preserved in *karya*. *Dhamapri* n.pr. = *Dharmapriya*. Then *-ya* comes to be written for *-i*: *ahumapya* 399 = *aham api*, *palṗiya* 42 = *palṗi* 'tax'. The treatment of gerundival forms is peculiar. Either the *-vya* is preserved or it becomes *-vo*: *dadavya* and *dadavo*. Both forms are found in about equal numbers, cf. §§ 53, 116.

§ 10. Svarabhakti occurs regularly between *r* and *h*: *garahati* 'complains', *arahaṃta* 'saint'. Also in *gilanaǵa* 'sick'.

An *i* is evolved before *stri* only in 231 *istriae*, but the regular form in the dialect is *stri* as in Sanskrit.

§ 11. A certain amount of vowel elision occurs in Sandhi: e.g. *ajuvadae* 'starting from to-day', *ceṣa* = *ca eṣa*, *emaceva* = *evam ca eva*, *ciśa* = *ca iśa*. That is to say in formulae that are regarded as one expression. For the rest hiatus is the rule: 324 *parihara oḍita aṃñeṣa*, etc.

§ 12. Final *-as* seems to have become *-e* as in the Mansehra version of Aśoka's edicts. It is preserved regularly in the ablative singular: *tade*, *Caḍodade*, *goṭhade*, *śavathade*, etc. = °*ātas*. The nominative and accusative have been confused and the *-a* which serves for both is the accusative *-am*. Only *se* = *saḥ* preserves the old nominative ending. In addition we often find *u* (*o*) or *a* in adverbial forms in *-tas*: *itu*, *ito* = *itaḥ*, *agratu*, *agrata* = °*taḥ*, *punu*, *puno*, *puna* = *punar*, *pratu* = *prātar*, *yatu* 52 = *yataḥ*.

J. Bloch (*B.S.O.S.* VI, 292) points out a similar occurrence of the adverbial *tato* in the Kalsi (and Mansehra) version of Aśoka's edicts.

Both *e* and *o* seem to have been current in the North-West. In Aśoka Shahbazgarhi has *o*, Mansehra *e*. In the later Kharoṣṭhi inscriptions the *e* seems to predominate in the districts west of the Indus. The Kharoṣṭhi Dh.p. has *o* or *u* (or *a*) in the nominative, which may be due to its Prakrit original.

§ 13. The elision of vowels is not infrequent: *Butsena* = *Buddhaṣena*, *Yoksena* = *Yogaṣena*, *Ṣamnera* = *Śrāmanera*, *Śamseṃna* = *Śamaṣena*, *vastarna* = (*u*)*pastarana*, *muṣka* = *mūṣika* 565. Often in non-Indian names: *Yilika* and *Yilǵa*, *V́apika* and *V́apǵa*, *Mañǵeya* and *Mañiǵeya*, etc. Finally: *cotaṃ* = *codaṃna* 425, *rotaṃ* 252, 272 = *rotaṃna*, *gamaṃ* 646 = *gamana*, *śramaṃ* 250 = *śramana*. It is worth while noticing that all these examples of the elision of final *a* come after *n*. Probably there was a general tendency to elide the final *a*, but except in the case of *-na* there was no temptation to express it in writing, since the *a*-vowel is not written and the *virāma* was not used in writing Prakrit. Only in the case of *-ana* was it convenient to write the shorter form by using the anusvāra under the preceding akṣara. No doubt *-aṃ* stands for *-an* as in Tocharian.

Final *-deva* in proper names seems to have been shortened to *-*dew*, and then this has further developed into *-deyu*. Examples: *Upateyu*, *Jivadeyu*, *Baladeyu*, *Budhadeyu*.

CONSONANTS

§ **14. Unvoicing.** The native language of Shan-Shan lacked the voiced stops *g*, *j*, *d*, *b*, as is evident from a survey of the proper names. As a result of this they tended to unvoice the Prakrit *g*, *d*, etc., and the fact is sometimes reflected in the spelling, e.g. *kilane* 'ill', *yokac̄hema*, *civarac̄hi* 460, *chaṃlpita*=*jalpita* 113, *caṃnma*=*janma* 180, *saracidati* 648=*sarajitaṃti* (usually), *canati* 590=*janati*, *taṃṭa*, *taḏima*, *taśavida*, *tita*, *tivajhi*, *tivira*, *tivya*, *tui* '2', *tura*, *toṣa*, *trakhma*, *traṃgha*, *triṭha*, *tharidavo*, *utaǵa*, *satriśa*, *mutra*, *prateja*, *coteyati*, *veteyati*, *Naṃtaṣena*, *poǵa*=*bhoga*.

Usually the forms are sporadic, the voiced forms being the usual ones, but in *palpi* (i.e. *palýi*), = *bali*, the *p* invariably occurs because that word had been adopted into the popular speech and was felt as a native word.

As will be seen the confusion is commonest with dentals. That is probably because the state of things in the Prakrit itself gave rise to confusion. The traditional writing of *dida* 'given' was *dita*, and so it was easy to write *t* in other positions, e.g. *tida*. In other cases a spirant, *ǵ*, *y*, (*s*), *w*, was produced and there was less tendency to confusion. Further, the *t* and *d* are often difficult to distinguish in writing.

§ **15.** Another result of pronouncing *d*, etc. as *t*, etc. was to write *d*, etc. instead of *t*: *dusya*, *daha*, *dahi*, *dumahu*, *dena*, *danu*, *danuvaka*, *daḏita*, *dac̄haṃna* 'carpenter', *jinida*=*ch°* 580, *jhorida* =*chor°*.

In native proper names: *Giraka* beside *Kiraka*, *Jimoya* beside *Cimoya*, *Jinaśa* beside *Cinaśa*, *Pideya* and *Piteya*, *Dhameca* and *Tameca*, *Bośarsa* and *Pośarsa*, *Buṃni* and *Puṃniyade*, *Parabulade* and *Paraṃpulammi*.

It is worth while noticing that most of the Prakrit examples are pronominal forms, and possibly the voicing has some foundation in the Prakrit itself. As unaccented forms their initial would be liable to be treated as intervocalic *t*, i.e. become voiced; although here again it should perhaps be attributed to confusion of writing.

§ 16. Intervocalic consonants *k*, *c*, *ṭ*, *t*, *p*, *ś*, *s*, probably *ṣ*, become voiced, and *k*, *c*, *ṭ*, *p*, also *g*, *j*, *ḍ*, *b* (?), further become spirants *ǵ*, *ś*, (*j́*), *ḍ̄*, *v*.

k, *g*: *avaǵaja*=*avakāśa*, *praǵaśita*=*prakāśita*, *aǵasita* 'carried off' from *ā* and *kas*; *pratiǵara*, *siǵata*, *yathaǵamaǵaraniya* 661 =*yathakāmakaranīya*, *aneǵa*, *bhaǵa*, etc.

The *k* is usually preserved in *eka*, which points to a double *k* as in Prakrit *ekka*. The pronunciation of this *ǵ* was very close to *y*, because they are occasionally confused.

ǵ is written for *y*: *aprameǵo*, frequently for *aprameyo*(*a*); *kośalǵa*, for *kośalya*; *vyaǵa*=*vyaya*-.

y is written for *ǵ* in *aṃña yala* 431=*aṃña kala*. The phrase has been treated as a compound. Also *viraya*=*viraǵa* 546, 622, *jheniya* 278 (usually *jheniǵa*) 'under the care of', *saṃvatsaraye* (=-*ake*) 186, 422.

The suffix -*aǵa* tends to become -*ae*, especially in past participles, *ditae* and *ditága*, etc. Similarly -*uka* becomes -*uv́a* in *agaṃduv́a* 33. The guttural was weaker in the suffix than in other places. -*ika*=-*i*, cf. § 75.

k and *g* are often preserved in writing: *akasida*, *agata*, *nagara*, etc.

Noteworthy is the title *ogu*, which never appears with the spirant, although that is otherwise the rule not only in Indian but in native words: *Caǵu*, *Moǵata*, etc. It is perhaps *oggu* with double *g*.

The state of things in the Dh.p. is exactly the same, although the writing is less clear. Intervocalic *k* and *g* both appear as *k*: *urako*, etc.; but that *k* is confused with *y* just as *g* in the documents *udaka* B 13, C^vo 18=*udaya*, *dhoreka* C^vo 37=*dhoreya*, so that it is plain we are dealing with a spirant.

§ 17. *c* and *j*. In the Dh.p. intervocalic *c* and *j* invariably become *y*: *śoyati*=*śocati*, *goyari*=*gocare*, *vianato*=*vijanato*, *parvaitasa*=*pravrajitasya*. In the documents the treatment is not so regular. We find *y* for *j* in *maharaya* (always), *vaniye* 'merchants' 35. *ni* contracted out of *niya*=*nija* 'own', and in the literary pieces *oya*=*ojas* 501, *bhoyaṃna*=*bhojana* 501.

In addition both *c* and *j* are represented by *ś*, *j́* (i.e. *ẑ*): *praśura*=*pracura*, *yaj́itaga*=*yācitaka*, *vaj́idesi* 'you read' 376 (so read instead of *vaṭ-*); *j*=*ś*, *j* in *bhija* 'seed', *vibhaśita* 'decided'. There is some difficulty in deciding between *y* and *ś*, and, in the last instance, *vibhayita* could possibly be read. Since both treatments are well attested it is impossible to decide on linguistic grounds. Perhaps *vibhayi-* is more likely because the alternative spelling *j* never appears. In that case *y* may be taken as the regular treatment of *j* because the *j* of *bhija* may be explained by the doubling of the consonant after a long vowel (common in Prakrit, Pischel, § 91), i.e. *bīja* > **bīya* > **biyya* > **b(h)ijja* > *bhija* (on *j*=*jj*, cf. *raja*, *aja* beside *raja*, *aja*). The same development appears in *iśa* 'here', Skt. *iha*, Aś. (Shah) *ia*, i.e. *iya* > *iyya* (by a natural emphasising which particles like this are exposed to) > *iśa*, *ija* (=**iźa*).

In Saka loan-words *j* and *c* usually appear as *ś* (=*ź*): *ttīśa* = *tejas*, *daśa* = *dhvaja*, *āśiria* = *ācārya*, *avīśä* = *avīci*.

§ 18. *ṭ* and *ḍ* become =*ḍ̂*: *kukuḍ̂a* 'cock', *koḍ̂i* 'crore', *kiḍ̂a* 'done', *vaḍ̂avi* 'mare', *taḍ̂ita*, *daḍ̂ima* 'pomegranate'.

Intervocalic *ṭ* is sometimes preserved: *aloṭa viloṭa* 'plundering and ravaging', *samghaṭi-davo* 106, 584, *paṭa* 'cloth'. Here we probably have *ṭṭ*. Not however in *viheṭa* 621 (usually *viheḍ̂-*) 'worries', *coṭaǵa* 317 = *coḍ̂aǵa*, *guṭa* 17, which obviously stands for *gūḍha*. With reference to these spellings it must be borne in mind that the difference between the akṣaras for *ṭa* and *ḍ̂a* is often very small.

At present in the North-West intervocalic *ḍ* is represented by *ṛ*, and that may have been the pronunciation at this time. There seems to be one instance of confusion between *ḍ̂* and *r*. In 574 *śaḍ̂a taṃmi* appears for *śaratamṃi* 'in the autumn'. Moreover in the Dh.p. B 43 *visara* = *visaṭa*, C^vo 39 *karu* = *kāṭuṃ*, *ajinaśaria* (Pet. Fragm.) = *ajinaśāṭyā*. Likewise in Tocharian loan-words we find *r* for *ṭ*, *ḍ*: *Cakravar* = °*vāḍa*, *kapār* = *kapāṭa*, *kor* = *koṭi*.

On the other hand loan-words in Saka usually appear with *l*: *alavi* 'forest', *kūla* 'crore', *gula* 'molasses', *nālai* = Skt. *nāṭaka*, *vīrūlīnaa* 'made of beryl', *palā* 'banner', which would seem to point to *ḷ*.

§ 19. *t*, *d*. There is no doubt that intervocalic *t* was voiced in the Prakrit, but matters are obscured by the fact that the natives of Shan-Shan pronounced everywhere *t* for both *d* and *t*. Further, the traditional system of writing was probably archaic, so that e.g. *dita* was written for what was pronounced *dida* by proper speakers of Prakrit and *tita* by the natives of Shan-Shan. As a result we find *t* and *d* used indiscriminately for intervocalic (and even initial, §§ 14, 15) *t* and *d*.

t is omitted in *caura* '4', side by side with *catu-* and *caturtha*. Similarly in the Dh.p. we find *cauri* '4', although intervocalic *t* is usually preserved. Further possible examples are *samao* (*samaho*) 'with' < *samataḥ* and *mahuli* 'aunt' < *mātulī*.

§ **20.** *p* = *v*: *avi*, *darśaveti*, etc.; *uṭavala*, *parivalitavya*, *vavaṃnae*, *mavida*, etc.

The *p* is often preserved in writing: *paripalitavo*, *upagata*, *apanaya*, etc.

Intervocalic *b* (*bh*) is usually preserved as such: *paribujiśatu* 'you shall understand', *vibhaśita*, etc. They may have pronounced *v*, which does turn up occasionally: *Śilaprava* n.pr. 519, 592, and possibly *parivanae* 214 = *paribhāṇḍa*(*ka*), *pivaṃnaṃnae* 586 = **pi-bandhanāya*. In 519 read *bahuve* not *vahuve*.

In the Dh.p. examples of *b* (*bh*) = *v* occur: *avalaśa* = *abalāśva*, *abhivuyu* = *abhibhūya* and vice versa *makabha* is written for *maghavā*.

In *supraudha*, *praujhati* the *v* (i.e. *v̄*) is not written. Similarly in Saka *aviṣīya* = *abhiṣeka*.

§ **21.** *ś* becomes *ź*, written *j*: *avaǵaja* = *avakāśa*, *kojalya*, *dajavita*, *pradejade*. This *ś* is often preserved in writing.

§ **22.** *s* becomes *z*, written *s̱* or *jh*: *ajhia* = *āsya*, *aǵajhidati* 'they seized', *tivajha* 'day', *dajha* 'slave'.

s̱ in *mas̱a* 'month', *das̱a*, *divas̱a*, *spas̱a*, *Budhas̱ena*, and always in names in *-sena*, *as̱i* 'was', *vis̱ajides̱i* 'you sent'.

The *-asya* (*-assa*) of the genitive singular also appears as *-as̱a* (cf. R. L. Turner, *J.R.A.S.* (1927), 227–39).

As in the case of the other consonants intervocalic *s* may be preserved in writing: *asi* (3 times) side by side with *as̱i* (3 times), *asita* 'sat' 339, etc., *ukasita*, *nikasiṣyati*, *prahitesi* 358, *denasi* 358, etc.

s̱ never appears when followed by *u* or the anusvāra, e.g. *śvasu* 'sister', *masu* 'wine', *vasaṃta* 'spring'. Probably this was a question of convenience of writing.

s appears initially in certain particles and pronominal forms which were unaccented, and consequently the *s* could be treated as intervocalic: *ṣ̱amao* and *ṣ̱adha* 'with', *ṣ̱aca* (particle introducing a quotation), *ṣ̱e* 'he', *ṣ̱arva* 'all'.

The two ways of expressing *z* probably arose independently. Perhaps *jh* was modified from the existing *jh* specially to represent the Iranian *z*, which there was no room for expressing in Kharoṣṭhi, because in the Iranian word *jheniǵa* we invariably find *jh* and not *s*. Similarly *ajhade* 'free-born', *Hinajha*= στρατηγός, whereas *s* arose as a modification of the *s* in the same way as *ǵ*, *j*, etc. were invented, to meet the developments of the Prakrit itself which had occurred by this time. On the whole question see the Account of the Alphabet, p. 310 of the edition.

§ 23. *ṣ* probably followed the analogy of the other sibilants, but trouble was not taken to express it: *darṣida*, which is no doubt = Av. *darəz* 'bind', must contain a voiced *ṣ*, i.e. **darẓida*.

§ 24. There is a tendency to drop the aspiration in the aspirated consonants *kh*, *gh*, etc. That was because the native language of Shan-Shan had no aspirates and consequently in pronouncing the Prakrit they neglected them: *nikaliṣyati* 188 (usually *nikhal-*) 'to remove', *gaṣa* 'fodder', *grida* 'ghee', *śigra*, *vyagra*, *saṃga*, *agacati* 122, *ciṃnita* 598 'cut', *jinida* = *chiṃnita*, *pratama*, *śavatade*, *śitilya*, *adicite*, *gaṃdarvena*, *goduma*, *daridavo*, *paṃda* = *pamthā*, *sada* 'with', *madya* 'middle', *tanana* = *dhanā-nām* 583, *vṛtaǵa* 399 'old', *uṭa* 'camel', *kuṃba* 'jar', *baǵena*, *bara*, *buma*.

§ 25. It was always correct to write the aspirated forms, and these more usually occur, e.g. *ghrida* (21 times), *grida* (3 times), *bhuma* (39 times), *buma* (7 times), *adhimatra*, *ghaṣa*, *ghrita*, *lekha* (never **leka*), *goṭha* (never *goṭa*), *jeṭha* (never *jeṭa*), *śavatha*, *bhaǵa*, etc., etc. *uṭa* 'camel' is invariably written without aspiration except in 422 (one of the earliest of the documents), where it appears with the modified *ṭh́*: *uṭh́a*.

§ 26. This state of affairs further results in the writing of aspirated forms where they do not belong: *aṃgha* 252, *draṃgha*

430, *śighavera* 'ginger', *Sachaṃmi* 159 n.pr. (usually *Saca-*), *paribhuchanae*=*paribhuñjanāya* or *paribhoj-*, *sarachidati* 591 'agreed' (usually *saraj-*), *uthiśa*=*uddiśya*, *vivatha* 'quarrel', *gaṃdhavo*, *dhaṃḍa*, *dhajha* 225, *dhaḍima* 617, *dhana*=*dāna*, *dhaśaṃmi* 401, *dhida* 'given', *dhivaṣa*, *dhura*, *durbhale* 392, *bhiti* 'second'.

§ **27**. Those aspirated consonants which had remained down to the time of the importation of the Prakrit into Central Asia are treated as stated above. But before this time the majority of intervocalic aspirates had become *h* (for those that remain, e.g. *śavata*, cf. § 24): *-ehi*, *-ahi* of the instrumental plural: *lihati* (also written *likhati*), *saṃmuha*, *pramuha*, *suha*, *nihan* (=*nikhan* or *nihan*?), *taha* 'so', *amahu*, *tumahu*=*asmabhyaṃ*, etc., *lahu*, *lahaṃti*=*labhante*, *parihaṣa* 'claim'=*paribhāṣā*, *prahuḍa*=*prābhṛta*, *gohomi* 'wheat' (also *goma* and *godūma*), *huḍi-*=*bhṛti-* 399, *hoti*, etc. 'is'. The change is regular in the case of terminational elements, the unaccented *hoti*, *huda*, and in the case of intervocalic *kh*.

In the examples of *h* in the Dh.p. we cannot be sure whether we are dealing with northern forms or forms from the original version, e.g. *oha*=*ogha*, *ohaseti*=*avabhāsayati*, *suhu*, *lahati*, *aśuha*, *uhu*=*ubho* B 2.

§ **28**. There is considerable irregularity in the treatment of *h*, owing to its absence in the native language.

(1) It is omitted: *mahanuava* for *mahanuhava* (once, 593)= °*bhāva*, *mayi* 661=*mahi* (Gen. not Loc.), *ara*=*hāra* 113, *svarna ara* (?), *danagrana* 577, 588 for usual *danagrahana* 'giving and taking', *goma* 'wheat', *giḍa*=*gṛhīta*, *Syabala* n.pr.=*Sihabala*, *ac̄hati* besides *hac̄hati* (only here *akṣ-* is the original form), *astama* besides *hastama* 'dispute', *astalekha* 414, *astaṃmi* 662, *paḍuv́aga* 'security'=**paḍihū-aǵa*=*pratibhū*, *paropiṃtsamānā* 510=**paropahiṃsamāno* (as required by the metre).

(2) It is transposed in *uhati* for *huati* 'is'.

(3) It is put in where it does not belong: *prihito smi* 140= *prītosmi*, *hadehi* 476 (usually *adehi*), *sahasrahani* 646 'thousands', *ṣamaho* besides *ṣamao* 'with', *Pugohasa* 511 (Gen. of *Puǵo*). Possibly *heḍi* 663=*eḍā* 'sheep'.

§ 29. Besides *v* there is a letter transliterated *v́* which was probably a *w*. It was characteristic of the native language which had no *v*. It occurs commonly in native names: *V́apika*, *V́arpa*, *V́uǵaca*, *V́ua*, and in the title *v́asu*.

In Prakrit words it is evolved between *u* and a following vowel: *hetuv́ena*, Instr. of *hetu* 'cause'; *tanuv́aǵa* 'own'; similarly in *vasuv́ana Lṗimsuv́asya*.

They are not however consistently used. We find *v* side by side with *v́* in native proper names: *Varpeya* beside *V́arpeya*, *vasu* besides *v́asu*. Further *Vukto*, *Vuǵaca* (also *V́uǵaca*), *Vuǵeya*, *Vuru*, *vuryaǵa*.

Also *v́* instead of *v* in the Prakrit: *uv́adae*, *kam̄av́eti*, *viṃñav́eti*, *mav́esi*, *v́amti*.

The explanation of this confused state of affairs is probably that they tended everywhere to say *v́*, which was the nearest sound in their own language to the Prakrit *v*.

§ 30. It was probably a characteristic of the local pronunciation that they tended to pronounce initial *u*- as *wu*-. We find *uryaǵa* side by side with *vuryaǵa* (some kind of profession or class) and in 399 *vulasi* seems to be for *ullāsa* 'wonder'. Also native names are common beginning with *vu*-, *v́u*-, practically non-existent with *u*- (see *Kharoṣṭhi Inscr.* Index Verb.).

§ 31. *l* was softened before *i* in the native language into what has been printed *lṗ* but should be written *ly* or *lý*, e.g. *Lýipeya*, *Lýimsu*, etc. In Prakrit words it does not often appear, though it was probably usually pronounced. We find *lṗihida* 575 for *lihita*, *vyalṗi* fem. of *vyala* 'wild'. In *palṗi* 'tax' = *bali* it is invariably written just as the initial *p*- always appears for *b*-, presumably because it had become part of the native language. In native names it is occasionally, though rarely, omitted to be written: *Lipe* 754 beside *Lṗipe*, *Livarajhma* beside *Lṗivarasma*, *Piṣaliyammi* beside *Piṣalṗiyaṃmi*.

§ 32. *yi*- probably developed in other positions too. Certainly at the beginning of words, just like *wu*- developed out of *u*-. There are no native names beginning with *i*-, plenty with *yi*-: *Yitaka*, *Yiliǵa*, *Yipǵe*, *Yiṣata*, *Yiruṃḍhina*. It affects Prakrit words only in *yiyo* = *iyam* 348, 410, *yima* = *ime* 237.

Possibly native *ni*, *ti* had also become *ñi*, *ci*. *ti* does not seem to occur in native names, *ni* only in *Kenika*, *Cinika* (which is probably derived from *Cina* 'Chinese' and so would keep its *n*); whereas *ñi* is common: *N̄imeya*, *Acuñiya*, *Apñiya*, *Kuñita*, *Kriñila*, *Mañigeya*, *Señima*. In the case of the last two changes, no influence on the Prakrit can be traced.

§ **33.** One of the chief characteristics of the North-Western Prakrit, and which is found in the Dardic languages to this day, is the preservation of the three sibilants as in Sanskrit:

ś. *śata*, *daśa*, *darśaveti*, *avakāśa*, etc.

ṣ. *teṣu*, *doṣa*, *eṣa*, *varṣa*, etc.

There are no instances of confusion.

śāsana becomes *śāśana* 310 in the same way as original **śasa* became *śaśa* in Sanskrit. It was the regular form in the North-West, as it occurs also in the Dh.p. and as a loan-word in Saka *śśāśana*. The Dh.p. also has *viśpaśa*, which is the same kind of assimilation.

§ **34.** The cerebral *ṇ* has ceased to be distinguished from *n* in the dialect. It is occasionally written, but irregularly. (See Account of the Alphabet, p. 305 of the edition.)

CONJUNCT CONSONANTS

§ **35. Stop + stop.** Assimilated in the same way as in other Prakrits: *anata* = *ājñapta*, *śata* = *śapta*, *satati* '70', *satamma* '7th', *bhata* = *bhakta*, *balakarena* = *balātkāreṇa*, *rataǵa* = *raktaka*, *satu* = *saktu*, *vuta* = *ukta* and *upta*, *saṃc̄hitena* = *saṃkṣiptena*, *upaṃna* = *utpanna*, *ukasta* = **utkasta*, *uc̄hivana* from *ut* + *kṣip*, *ladha* = *labdha*.

The conjunct consonants are preserved in writing sometimes: *vibhaktaǵa*, *vukta*, *prañapta*, *viṃñapti*.

In 511, *uktama* = *uttama*, a mistaken attempt at restoration is made.

§ **36. Compounds with *r*.** As a rule *r* is not assimilated.

(*a*) *r* comes first: *antargata*, *Arjunaṣa*, *varjavidavo*, *viṣarjida*, *artha*, *ardha*, *kartavo*, *kirti*, *vardhati*, *purva*, *sarva*, *garbha*, *karya*, *niryoǵa, durlāpa=durlabha, parvata, varṣa, darṣida* 'packed', *darśana*.

There do not seem to be any examples of Prakrit *rk*. In native names there seems to be a tendency for it to become *rg*, though voiced stops are otherwise absent from the language, e.g. *Argiceya, Argiya, Kargate, Cargayodae, Tsurgeya, Bargada*. *k* also appears: *Carka, Tsurkeya, Patirke*, etc. *g* never appears as a spirant in this position. The same change appears in Saka (*birgga* < *vṛka*, etc.) (Konow, *Saka Studies*, p. 23).

rm is written *m̄*: *dhāma, kam̄a, cam̄a, nim̄ala, Jivaśam̄a*. *rm* is occasionally written; *dharmiyaṣa* 579, 581, title of king Aṃgoka. Occasionally also the superscript line is omitted: *Jivaśaṃma* 611, *dhama* 228, *Dhamaśriae* 21, etc.

(*b*) Consonants + *r*: *agra, vyagra* 'tiger' 665, *citra, atra, tre, matra, kam̄akaritra, kriṣivatra, apramana, pra-, prati-* (also *paḍi-*), *prathama* (also *paḍama*), *bhrata*.

gr is represented by *kr* in *ajakra* 'up till to-day' and possibly in *akri* (*bhuma*) = *agrya*.

The *ṭ* which sometimes appears for *tra*, e.g. *Paṭaya* and *Patraya*, *Brahmacariṭa* 399 for *Brahmacaritra*, *kamakariṭa* 166 v.l. for °*tra*, is merely due to the fact that the two akṣaras are difficult to distinguish.

§ 37. Cases where *r* is assimilated.

(*a*) When placed first: *śakara* 702 'sugar', *vadhi* 264 n. 3 might be *vardhrī* 'rope', *viṣajidavo* side by side with *viṣarj-*, *parivaṭidemi* 'I exchanged' = *parivart-*, *kaṭavo* beside *kartavo*, *bhaṭaraǵa* 'master', *adha* 169 (usually *ardha*). At 589 also *aḍha* occurs. *ṣadha* 'with' (also *sardha*), *payati* = *paryāpti*, *aya* (409) = *ārya*, *sava* 565 (elsewhere always *sarva*), *tuṃbhicha* 589 (*trubhicha* 581) = *durbhikṣa*, *uṃna* 149 = *ūrṇā*.

The cases of assimilation are definitely in a minority; where both forms occur those with *r* are much more common (e.g. *sava* and *sarva*, *adha*, *aḍha* and *ardha*; the forms without *r* occur only once). Some forms may be borrowed from an Eastern dialect. That is certainly so in the case of *bhaṭaraǵa* 'master'.

Aṭhovaǵa 'serviceable' according to Prof. Thomas = *arthopaka*. The value of the *ṭh* is not certain (see the Account of the

Alphabet, p. 304 of the edition). No other example is found which contains an *r*.

(*b*) *r* comes last: *vakuṭha* = *apakruṣṭa* (doubtful), otherwise *kr* is always preserved, *krita*, *parikraya*, etc. The *r* is always assimilated in *uṭa* = *uṣtra* 'camel'; also *Rāṭhapala* n.pr. 660 = *Rāṣtrapāla*.

§ **38.** Apart from these it is only assimilated in the case of *śr*, which regularly becomes *ṣ*: *ṣayati* 'seizes' = *śrayate*, *maṣu* = *śmaśrū*, *ṣamaṃna*, *ṣamaṃnera* = *śramaṇa*, *śrāmaṇera*, *ṣunami* 695 'I hear'. *vyoṣeti* 'pays, hands over' probably = **vyavaśrayati* and perhaps Prakrit *vosirai*, which the grammarians explain as *vy-ava-sṛj*. *miṣi* (*bhuma*) may be *miśrya* 'mixed'.

The change is often neglected in writing, almost always in *śru-* 'to hear', also *śramana*.

This development was universal in the North-West. It does not occur in Aśoka, but is common in the later Kharoṣṭhi inscriptions, and in the Dh.p., e.g. *ṣavaka*, *ṣadhu* 'faithful', *ṣamano*, *ṣebha* = *śreyas*, *ṣutvana*. Also in loan-words in Saka: *ṣṣamana*, *ṣṣāvaa*, *ṣṣadda*. Note also Toch. *ṣamaṃ*, Sogd. *šmn* = *śramana*.

In the Dh.p. *sr* also seems to share this treatment in *anavaṣutacitasa*; *viśravatena* = **visravantena* represents an intermediate process or else *śr* is just written for *ṣ*. Compare also *śrotas* = *srotas*, etc. in the Divyāvadāna. The *Vinaya* of the Sarvāstivādins, from which this text is abstracted, is said to belong to the North-West.

§ **39.** A characteristic of the North-West was the transposition of *r* in forms like *dhrama* for *dharma*. It occurs in both the Kharoṣṭhi versions of Aśoka, e.g. *grabhagara*, *dhrama*, *krama*, *pruva*, *draśana*, side by side with forms that are not transposed, e.g. *savra* (written for *sarva*), *kiṭra*, *athra*, etc. Outside Aśoka it is common in the *MS. Dutreuil du Rhins*, e.g. *drugati*, *drumedhino*, *drugha*, *pravata*.

On the other hand there is practically no trace of it in the dialect of these documents. The only examples are *trubhicha* = *durbhikṣa* 581 and *śirmitra* n.pr. 117, etc. compared with *śrṃitra* 94.

Similarly, in most of the later Kharoṣṭhi inscriptions from N.W. India this change is absent, e.g. (Konow, *C.I.I.* II, p. cvi) *dirgha*, *dharma*, *°karmi*, *°śarma*, *°varma*, etc.

§ 40. *l* is usually not assimilated: *jalpita*, *jalma*, *śilpiǵa*, *alpa*. In this respect the dialect is more archaic than the Northern versions of Aśoka, where *l* is assimilated, e.g. *apa*, *kapa*, as also in the Dh.p. *apa*

§ 41. *y* is usually assimilated to a preceding consonant.

ky = *k* or *ǵ* in *osuka*, *°ǵa* = *autsukya*.

jy = *j*: *raja*, *jeṭha*.

ḍy = *ḓ*: *paḓeka*, *paḓuvaǵa*.

ty = *c*: *kica*. But always *nitya*.

dy = *j*: *aja*, *upajeśadi*, *khaja*.

dhy = *j*: *ajeṣaṃnae* = *adhyeṣanayā*, *jāna* 511 = *dhyāna*, *vijaṃti* = *vidhyanti*.

ny = *ñ*: *aña*, *puṃña*.

bhy = *b* in *abomata* = *abhyavamata* in the phrase *abomata kṛ-* 'to disregard, disobey'.

vy = *v* in gerundives: *dadavo* beside *dadavya* (cf. § 9).

śy = *ś*: *avaśa*, *udiśa*, *naśati*.

ṣy = *ś*: *kariśadi*, *maṃnuśa*, etc. The change had already taken place in Aśoka's time and was general in the North-West, e.g. (in Aśoka) *arabhiśaṃti*, *manuśa*, *anapeśaṃti*, etc. Similarly in the Dh.p. *devamanuśana* B 4. In the latter text the future seems usually to be in *ṣ*: *eṣiti*, *payeṣiti*. Presumably the *ya* of the future had become *i* before the change took place.

c̄ḧy = *c̄ḧ* in *śac̄ḧami* 188.

sy becomes *ṣ* in the termination of the genitive singular (§ 22): *goṭhaṣa*, etc.; *s* initially in *sali* 'brother in law' = *syāla*.

Sometimes *y* is written in connection with *ś*, *c*, *ch*, *ḓ* where it is not justified, e.g. *priyadarśyanaṣa* 152, *paripruchyaṃti* 690, *Sacyami* 436, *giḓya* = *giḓa* 215 'took'.

§ 42. Sometimes *y* is not assimilated. In many cases this is merely the archaic or Sanskritising way of writing, which we are continually meeting with. Certainly in the case of genitive singulars in *asya* and futures in *iṣyati*. (The assimilation had already taken place in Aśoka 500 years earlier.) Also in *osukya*, *madya*, *madhya* (curiously enough *j* is never written in this word, though it usually occurs in such forms as *aja*, etc.), *aṃnyatha*, *manyu*, *udiśya*. It is perhaps regularly preserved in the futures *stasyati*, *dasyati*; *syāt(i)* always becomes *siyati*.

The combinations *ry* and *ly* were probably regularly preserved: *kalyana*, *niryoǵa*, *viryavaṃda*, *karya*. *payati* in the phrase *bhijapayati* 'capacity for seed', which seems to be =*paryāpti*, is an exception, also *aya* in 419=*ārya*. Final *-ya* (i.e. *-iya*) usually becomes *-i* (§ 9). It is always preserved in *karya*.

Initial *vy-* and *sy-* stand for *viya-*, *siya-*, with which they alternate, e.g. *vyochiṃnita*, *vyoṣeti*, *vyartha*. Also *viyoṣ-*, etc., *siyati* and *syati* 'may be'. Note also *Syabala* n.pr. = *Sī(h)abala*.

§ 43. *tv* and *dv* tend to become *p* and *b*, e.g. *badaśa* '12', *capariśa* '40', *biti* 'second'.

We also find *dvadaśa* and always *dvi*, *dui* '2', which was disyllabic. Also *daditva*, *saṃpreṣitva* 204, *bhudva* 49. Always *dvara*.

The *v* is omitted in *diguna* 'double'. Presumably also in indeclinable participles in *ti* = Vedic *tvī*, *vajiti* 'having read', etc.

Similar forms are found in the Kharoṣṭhi inscriptions of N.W. India, see Konow, *C.I.I.* II, p. cviii, e.g. *sapana* = *sattvanaṃ*, *ekacapariśai* '41'.

The rule is that original *tuva-*, *duva-* as found in the Veda were not assimilated: *dui*, Vedic *duvā*, Lat. *duo*, etc., but *di-guna*, *bitī*, assimilated in different ways. Compare Vedic *dvi-* always monosyllabic, *dvara*, Vedic *duvā́rā*, e.g. R.V. 4. 51. 2.

§ 44. A nasal following another consonant is usually preserved. *n* is represented by the superscript line in *naǵa*, *viǵa* = *vighna*, *gr̥̄heyati* (usually *giṃn-*), *trṣa*, *tuṣi*, *laṣi* 'gift', *śatra*.

nm is preserved in *jaṃnma*.

khm in *trakhma* 'drachma'.

tm becomes *tv* in *mahatva* (an official title), if that is not = *mahattva*, and in *atvana* 510. The *tv* passes further into *p* in *apane* 139, which seems to = *atmanaḥ*.

Compare *atva* in the M. version of Aśoka (ed. 11), also *ata*.

Sh. has always *ata*. The Dh.p. has *anatma* and *atuma* with svarabhakti.

jñ is assimilated to *ñ* in *viṃñati, saṃñaveti, yaṃña.*

In *anati* = *ājnapti* we have to do with a borrowing. In Aśoka too we find *aṇap-* instead of the regular *añap-*. Similarly in Pali.

§ 45. The voiced stops *j, ḍ, d, b* tend to be assimilated to a preceding nasal. The process is most regular in the Dh.p.: *kuñaru* A² 4, *nivinati* A³ 1, *tunati* B 28, *kana* B 34, *china* B 37; *Ṇ, ḍ*: *kunala* Cᵛᵒ 31, *dana* B 39, *panita* Cᵛᵒ 26; *mb*: *avaramu* A⁴ 2, *udumareṣu* B 40.

In the documents we find *gaṃñavara* = *gañjavara, chiṃnati, bhiṃnati, baṃnanae* 'to bind', *amila* 655 (of uncertain meaning) besides *ambila* 33 (= *āmla*?), *hastama* 'dispute', an Iranian word = *ha-* + *stamba-*, *parivanae* 214 probably = *paribhāṇḍaka* 'the load of a horse, baggage', *bhana* 149 = *bhāṇḍa-* (?).

The change never appears in *daṃḍa, piṃḍa*, and we find for instance *baṃdhitaǵa* 660 side by side with *baṃnidaǵa* 346.

On this change and its occurrence in the modern languages, cf. J. Bloch, *J. As.* (1912), pp. 331–7.

§ 46. In the Dh.p. unvoiced *k, c, t*, etc. are voiced when preceded by a nasal, e.g. *paga* = *paṅka, paja* = *paṃca, sabaśu* = *saṃpaśyan.*

The documents do not present any consistent picture. We find *upaśaṃghidavo* = *upaśaṅk-, saṃghalidavo* = *saṃkal-, gaṃdavo* 14 times against *gaṃtavo* twice, *ciṃd-* and *ciṃt-* in about equal proportions; *c* never appears as voiced: *kiṃci, paṃca.* Probably the change was regular as in the Dh.p., but since the natives of Shan-Shan tended to unvoice all voiced stops, it has been considerably obliterated.

The loan-words in Saka show the same change: *arahanda, cambaa, saṃduṣti.*

§ 47. The anusvāra is often omitted in writing, e.g. *abhyadara, kaḍa, gadavo, Tajaka, traghade* = *draṃghade, śrigha* 585 'horn', *śighavera* 'ginger', *ṣoṭhaga* 422 (usually *ṣoṭhaṃga*), etc.

It is written where it does not belong, e.g. *muṃtra* = *mudrā, Jiṭuṃgha* (name of a king, usually *Jiṭugha*), *chaṃlpitaṃti* 113 =

jalpitaṃti, *kāṃlaṃmi* 98, *nagaṃraṃmi* 25, *Jiṃvamitra* 290, *manasiṃǵara*, *Saṃrpina*, *tuṃbhic̄ha* = *durbhikṣā*.

In *viśati*, *triśa*, *capariśa*, *siha*, the -*ṃ*- is omitted as in all the Prakrits, Pali *tīsa*, *sīha*, etc. *siṃgha* in 511 is due to a re-introduction of Sanskrit *siṃha*, as elsewhere in India, 'Singhalese', etc. It is also regularly omitted in *sarajitaṃti* 'they agreed' (*saṃrajyati*) and *viṣalavita* 295 = *visaṃlap*-.

An anusvāra is usually inserted before *n*, *m* after short vowels, e.g. *gachaṃnae*, *deyaṃnae*, and all the infinitives: *asaṃna* = *āsana*, *khaṃnitaṃti* 'they dug', *Khotaṃna*, *gaṃnana*, *jaṃna*, *jaṃnma*, *śramaṃna*, *sumiṃna* 'dream', *biṃnita*, *chiṃnita*, *karuṃñya*, *puṃña*; locatives in *aṃmi*: *agaṃmisyatu*, *navaṃma*, *sataṃma* '7th', *naṃmakurvati*.

Forms without the inserted anusvāra occur, but they are very much rarer, *gachanae*, etc., not more than one in seven.

The anusvāra is only rarely inserted in the case of long vowels. Never in the case of genitive plurals in -*ana*, instrumentals in -*ena*.

Examples: *aṃnitaṃti* 'they brought', *jaṃnaṣi*, *paric̄hiṃna*, *pramaṃna*, *siṃmaṣa*, *Bhiṃmaṣena*.

Nasals followed by the corresponding stop are always written with anusvāra, not *ṅ*, *ñ*, *n*, etc. The *ṅ* which appears printed is probably never correct. The combination *ṅǵ* should be read, as given alternately in the notes, *tǵ*. It occurs only in native names: *Katǵeya*, *Kutǵe*, *Kuritǵe*, *Catǵu*, *Cipitǵu*, etc. *ṅg*, where it is certain, is always represented by *ṃg*(*h*): *draṃga*, *aṃgha*, *saṃghalidavo*. Also *g* never became a spirant after the nasal. *ṅk* should be read as *ts* in *Ramṣoṅka*, etc. Similarly in the *MS. Dutreuil du Rhins* the akṣara transliterated *ṅs* by Senart should be read *ts*: *satsara* A² 6, *ahitsai* A⁴ 8, *bhetsiti* C^vo 3, for *saṅsara*, etc. There was no *ṅ* in Kharoṣṭhi.

§ 48. Groups with final sibilant.

kṣ is preserved in the form *c̄h*: *c̄hetra*, *yogac̄hema*, *bhic̄hu*, *trubhic̄ha*, *coc̄ha* 'clean', *c̄huna*, *c̄hira*, *dilic̄ha* = *titikṣā*, *dac̄hina*, *nac̄hatrami*, *pracac̄ha*, etc.

hac̄hati 'may be, will be' = Prakrit *acchai* shows that that form must go back to an original *kṣ*. The *kṣ* is also preserved in the

Kharoṣṭhi versions of Aśoka and in the later Kharoṣṭhi inscriptions of the North-West.

In Saka we find *kṣ* in loan-words: *kṣāndä* = *kṣānti*, etc. The writing of the Kharoṣṭhi Dh.p. does not preserve the distinction between *c̄h́* and *ch*, e.g. *chaya*, *bhichavi*, etc.

In the modern languages of the North-West original *kṣ* is distinguished from *ch*, e.g. Shīṇā *çeç* = *kṣetra* *açi* = *akṣi*.

It is of course not certain whether *c̄h́* stands for *kṣ* or some modification of it in the direction of the modern languages, but it is worth noticing that in Saka we find *kṣattra* written for *chattra*.

kṣ is simplified to *ṣ* before *m* in *suṣmela* = *sūkṣmelā* 'small cardamoms', which occurs frequently in the Bower Manuscript.

kṣ becomes *kh* only in *khoritaǵa* 'shaven', which must be borrowed. In 322 we find *bhighu* instead of the usual *bhic̄h́u*. *Khema* is a place-name and not = *kṣema*.

ts is preserved in *saṃvatsara*, *vatsa*. It is assimilated in *osuka* = *autsukya*.

A *t* is developed between *ṃ* and *s* or *ś*: *maṃtsa*, *paropiṃtsāmanā* 510 = *paropahiṃsamāna*. Similarly in the Dh.p. (printed *ṅs* by Senart): *satsara*, *ahitsai* A⁴ 8, *bhametsu* B 34. In loan-words in Saka: *saṃtsāra*.

ṃś becomes *ṃc* (i.e. *ntś*) in *saṃcaya* 31 = *saṃśaya* 'doubt'. The same form occurs in the Tocharian loan-word *sañce*.

Konow (*B.S.O.S.* VI, 465 ff.) wants to read *ts* as *tś*, both original *ts* in *saṃvatsara* and when it has developed as in *saṃtsara*. But it is difficult to see how this would differ from *c*, and in fact when *saṃśaya* develops into *saṃtśaya* it is written *saṃcaya* in 31. In 283, however, we find *saṃśaya*.

§ 49. Groups with initial sibilant.

śc is preserved in the form *c̄*: *pac̄a*, *nic̄e*, *kac̄i*.

ṣk becomes *ṣǵ* in *muṣǵeṣu* (Skt. *muṣka*-), *Puṣǵariyade*. In *muṣka* 565 = *mūṣikā*, where the *ṣk* has arisen more recently by the dropping of the vowel, it is preserved. The etymology and meaning of *haṣǵa* are uncertain. *truṣǵa* 581 seems to be made up of the prefix *dur*- and Iranian *huṣka* 'dry' (or read *v́uṣǵa*).

More remarkable, initial *sk* seems to become *ṣǵ* in *ṣǵabhanae* 'to prop' 586. The *ṣǵ* might have originated in forms of the verb compounded with a preposition. The treatment is confined to the language of the documents. In Kharoṣṭhi inscriptions from N.W. India we find forms like *pukarini*=*puṣkarinī*, and in the Dh.p. we find *puṣkara* (see Konow, *C.I.I.* II, p. cix). Exceptions are *nikhal*- 'remove'=*niṣkal*- and *śuka* (*śukha*) if that=*śuṣka* 'dry'; *nikasta* 'went away' is probably=*niṣ-kas*. In the two last words the aspiration is almost always dropped.

st is preserved as a rule except sometimes in forms of √*sthā*: *asti*, *hasta*, *astarana*, *vistara*, *viśvasta*, *grihasta*.

√*sthā* appears either as *stā* or *thā*, never *sthā*, e.g. *stasyati*, *stavidavo*, *stidaǵa*, *thanaṃmi*, *thavaṃnae*, *thida*, *vithida*. *aṭhi* 'bone' for *asthi* appears with the cerebral, as in the other Prakrits (Pischel, § 308).

ṣṭ is always assimilated to *ṭh* (*ṭ*): *aṭa*, *aṭha*, *avaśiṭha*, *kaniṭhaǵa*, *goṭha*, *jeṭha*, *uṭa*, *praṭha*. *kāṣṭha* becomes *kaṭh́a* in 511, and in 422 *uṭh́a* is written for usual *uṭa*. The value of *ṭh́a* is doubtful, but it is usually consistently separated from *ṭh*. It would seem to stand for *ṣṭh* also in *kuṭh́ac̄h́ira*.

In *prasaṃṭh́ita* 511 and *vaṭh́ayaǵa* if that=*upasthāyaka* it represents *sth*; cf. Saka *vaṭhāyaa*.

In *aṭh́ovae* it seems to stand for *rth* (cf. § 37).

ṣp is preserved in *puṣpa* 'flower'.

śm becomes *m* in *maṣu* 'beard'.

sm becomes *m* in locatives in *aṃmi*, *amahu* 'of us'. It is preserved in *vismaridaǵa* 'forgot'. This treatment of *sm* was by no means general in the North-West. It also tended to develop into *sv*, which might further be assimilated into *ss* or become *sp*. We find locatives in -*asi* in Aśoka and later Kharoṣṭhi inscriptions (Konow, *C.I.I.* II, p. cxi).

Locatives in -*aspi* are confined to Aśoka. In the Dh.p. we find *sm*, *sv*, *s*, e.g. *anusmaro*, *asmi*, *svadi* A² 5, *pratisvado* A² 9. *s* in locatives in -*asa* for -*asi*: *asmi loke parasa ca*, etc.

sn is preserved in the form *s̄* in *s̄ana* 647, etc.

ṣn is preserved in the form *ṣ̄*: *tuṣ̄i*, *kṛṣ̄aǵa*, etc.

śl becomes *l* in *leṣiśaṃti*, which according to Prof. Thomas is from *śliṣ*.

śv becomes *śp* (printed *ñs*) in *aśpa* 'horse', *śpedaǵa* 'white'; *śv* is preserved in writing in *viśvasta*. Similarly in native names we find *Leśpaṃna* written side by side with *Leśvaṃna*. The same change occurs in the Dh.p. *viśpasa*, *viśpa*, and in Saka loan-words *viśpasta*, *Viśpaśarmä* n.pr.

sv becomes *śv* in *śvasu* 'sister', *śvastic̄h̄emena*. This *śv* further develops into *śp* in *priyaśpasuae* 317. Compare Kalasha *išpoṣi* = *svasrīya*, Garwi *išpo* 'sister'. *sv* is always preserved in *svayaṃ*, *sveya*, *sve* 'self', and we find *svasti* written as well as *śvasti*. This development does not take place in the case of *sv̄a-* or *suv̄a-*. Instead we find *sp̄* in *sp̄eṭha* (title) beside *suv̄eṭha*, *sp̄arna* beside *svarna* and *suvarna*.

The *sp̄* is also developed out of *sp*(*h*) in *parosp̄ara* 'one another', *sp̄ara*, *sp̄ura* = Iranian (*u*)*spurra* 'complete', and *sp̄aṣa*, which may be connected with the Iranian √*spas* 'to keep watch', *Tamasp̄a* n.pr. This *sp̄* appears as *sv* in *svaṣavaṃniye* 471.

§ 50. Miscellaneous.

In *aṣimatra* = *adhimātrā* we find a quite unexplained *ṣ* (= *z*) for *dh*. A similar change seems to have taken place in *masu* = *madhu* 'wine', cf. Lüders, 'Zur Geschichte des ostasiatischen Tierkreises', *S.P.A.W.* (1933), p. 5. For further examples inside India, cf. Prof. Thomas in *B.S.O.S.* VIII, 791.

v is represented by *m* regularly in *gameṣ-* = *gaveṣ-* 'to seek', *ema* = *evaṃ*. Further *āmec̄h̄itā* in the Dh.p. verses 510; *cimara* 149 may = *cīvara*. The phenomenon also appears in the Kharoṣṭhi Dh.p. *bhamanai* = *bhāvanāya*, *nāma* = *nāvam* and in Apabhraṃśa (Pischel, § 261).

For *śithila* besides *śitila* there is a form *śiśila*, which seems to be due to some kind of assimilation.

In 510 *dilic̄h̄a* = *titikṣa*. The change *t* (*d*) to *l* seems to be due to dissimilation. The change *d* to *l* is not uncommon in the modern North-West languages (Grierson, *Torwali*, p. 14, e.g. *talā* = *taḍā*). In 565 *tric̄h̄a* is probably the same word, with dissimilation into *r*.

Tiṃpura and *driṃpura* = *Tāmbūla* quite irregularly, as is natural in a word borrowed from the vernaculars; cf. Pkt. *simbali* = *śālmali*.

DECLENSION

§ 51. The declensional system is considerably modified, compared with the literary Prakrits. As in Apabhraṃśa there is no distinction between nominative and accusative. The instrumental tends to be confused with the nominative. The neuter is lost. Feminines, except proper names and words denoting living creatures, are transferred to the *a*-declension. Except for these feminines that survive there is only one declension, the *a*-declension, nouns in *-i*, *-u*, *-ṛ*, etc. being adapted to it by the addition of *-a*.

§ 52. The case terminations are:

	Sing.	Pl.
Nom. Acc.	*-a*	*-a* sometimes *-e*
Instr.	*-ena*	
Dat.	(*-ae aya*)	*-ehi* (Instr., Dat., Abl.)
Abl.	*-ade* (*āde*)	
Gen.	*-asa* (*asya*)	*-ana* (*-anaṃ*, *-ānāṃ*)
Loc.	*-aṃmi*, occasionally *-e*	*-eṣu*

§ 53. Sing. Nom. Acc. The *-a* of the nominative accusative is the original accusative. Final *-aṃ* became *-a*, as in the Gen. Pl. *-ana*, whereas *-as* became *-e* (§ 12). The nominative must have originally been *-e* in the dialect, but such forms as do occur are merely irregularities of spelling, e.g. *durbhale* 40, *pačevare* 164, *parikreye* 401. Compare *avaśe* 345, 437 for *avaśa* = *avaśyam*.

A nominative accusative sign in *-o* occurs sometimes. Regularly in the case of gerundives: *dadavo*, *kartavo*. Forms in *-avya* and *-avo* are used side by side indiscriminately. The former is presumably due to Sanskritising. Possibly *-aṃ* became *-o* after *v*, instead of *-a*, as elsewhere. We also find *jivo*, and *tuvám* 'thou' becomes *tuo*. Other forms in *-o* occur sporadically which cannot be so explained. They are probably due to the influence of Sanskrit or another Prakrit: *laṃgho* 'lame' 106, *arogiyo* 161 (usually *arogi*), *vartamano* 164 (usually *vartamana*), *prathamadaro* 165, *rajadaro* 579, *ekaǵo* 296, *grahito* 359, *jivaṃto* 646, *putro*, *praputro*, *ñatiyo* 437 (but see Index, s.v.). Further forms which frequently have *-o* are *aprameyo* and *aprameǵo*, *namakero*

=*namaskārya*, *manasikaro*. As a variant of *-o* we find *-u* in *toṣu* 373=*doṣaṃ*.

The suffix *-aǵa* tends to become *-ae* in the nominative accusative (§§ 8, 16): *kiṭae*, *ditae*, *giṭae*, *thavastae*, *namatae*. *-aǵe* in *culaǵe* 117=Pali *cullaka* is presumably just a way of writing *-aye*, *-ae* (cf. § 16). Occasionally this *-ae* is further modified into *-e*: *spaṣavaṃne* 'scout'=*spaṣavaṃnae* (*aǵa*), *bhaṭare* 'master' 147, *aṭh́ove* 'serviceable' 367=*aṭh́ovae*, *-aǵa*, *kuḏe* 164 =*kuḏaǵa* 'boy', *namate* 476=*namatae* 'cloth', *śune* 17=*śunaka* 'dog', *vaṭh́aye* 189=*vaṭh́ayaǵa*.

§ 54. **Sing. Instr.** The instrumental presents no remarkable features. It probably never becomes *-ina* (cf. § 1) except in pronominal forms: *tiṃna*, *kiṃna*. *Parihaṣina* 279 can alternatively be read *parihaṣena*. Nor does it ever appear shortened to *-eṃ*.

§ 55. **Sing. Dat.** Except in infinitives the dative is rare. It had obviously died out in the popular speech. We find *posathakam̄aya* in 489 *yo bhič́h́u posathakam̄aya nanuvarteyati*, 'Whichever monk shall not conform to the rite of fasting', which is obviously imitated from the language of the religious texts. Also one or two compounds with *-artha*: *prahuḏarthaya* 'for the sake of a present', *maghalartaya* 221 'for the sake of good luck'; °*artha* and °*arthi* are used in the same way. *prahuḏartha*, *khadaṃnarthi* 212, *puṃñarthi* 345. *avamicae* 'on loan' is probably=*apamityaka*, *āpamityaka* (*Arthaśāstra*, II, 13. 1, 6) rather than *apamityāya*.

§ 56. **Sing. Abl.** is always in *-ade*=Pkt. *-āo*: *goṭhade*, *nagarade*, *bhumade*, *Caḏodade*, *Calmadanade*, etc. The long *a* is sometimes expressed: *Nināde* 637, *Puṣǵariyāde* 660. There are no forms in *-ama*=*asmāt*. The words *avasama* and *hastama* are nominative singulars (see Index, s.v.).

§ 57. **Sing. Gen.** The genitive is in *-aṣa*, perhaps=*-aza*, cf. § 22. But it is never found written *-ajha*; *-asya* is often restored in writing through the influence of Sanskrit: *Lpimsuasya* 163, *Taṃjakasya* 541, *Kolpiṣasya* 159, etc.

§ 58. Sing. Loc. The usual ending is *-aṃmi*: *avánaṃmi, kalaṃmi, c̄hunaṃmi, rayadvaraṃmi, goṭhaṃmi, thanaṃmi, hastaṃmi, divasaṃmi, hemaṃtaṃmi*, etc.

-e occurs in *saṃvatsare, maṣe, divaṣe* used in dating formulas, elsewhere very rarely: *haste* 117, 140; *-i*: *rayadvari* 46. (This may be adjectival, § 75.)

The non-Indian *saste* 'day' forms a locative in *sastehi* 442–656. The same form occurs in Kharoṣṭhi inscriptions from N.W. India.

It is also inflected in the usual way: *sasteyaṃmi* 329, etc. *tivasehi* 655 is written on the analogy of *sastehi.*

§ 59. Pl. Nom. Acc. There is no distinction between the nominative and the accusative plural. They are usually identical in form with the nominative accusative singular. Thus *-a* 46: *mahatva vivada pruchitaṃti* 'The magistrates examined the dispute', 506 *ede śramaṃna*, etc.; in *-ae*: 293 *avi ca yo paraṣitae Caḏotiye* 'The Caḏotans who were carried off', *Koǵitasasaṃmi Supiye gadaya maṃtreti* 'He says the Supis have come to K.', 506 *ede śramaṃna Kuhaniyāde na aidae huaṃti* 'These śramanas have not come from the capital'; *-aǵa*: 180 *potaǵa dui mṛtaṃti* 'two young (animals) died', 27 *catu kiśoraǵa* 'four colts'. Gerundives in *-o*: *ede uṭa cavala Lṕipeyaṣa hastaṃmi Calmadanaṃmi viṣajidavo* 'These camels must quickly be sent to C. in the hand of Lṕipeya', etc.

§ 60. There is a plural in *-e* which is regularly employed in the case of the suffix *-i* and the native suffix *-eṃci, -iṃci.* Examples: *rajiye jaṃna* 272 (Acc.), *gramiye* 271, *Caḏotiye* 326, *kilmeciye* 'belonging to the district of', 152, 271, etc., *Yaveáv́aneṃciye* 401, *klaseṃciye* (a kind of official) 562, *Saciṃciye* 160, *seniye* 'soldiers', I. 397, 478, *Supiye* 109, 119, etc. **vani* out of *vaṇij-* forms its plural in the same way, *vaniye agamiṣyati* 35. This plural is not applied indiscriminately to all bases in *-i.* We never find **sac̄hiye* for instance as plural of *sac̄hi* 'witness' but *sac̄hi* according to the general rule. Similarly *gavi*='cow' and 'cows'.

Sometimes we find *-i* in the plural instead of *-iye*, following the general rule, e.g. 305 *Calmataṃci aṃna darṣitaṃti* 'The people of C. packed the corn', *Tseǵeci* 505, *kilmeci* 632, *raji jaṃna* 272 side by side with *rajiye jaṃna*; also 639 *yatha atra ogu ajhurakaṣa kilmeci Caḓotiye imade gachaṃti* 'That there the Caḓotans belonging to the district of the *ogu* Ajhuraka go from here', 32 *tatra bahove Caḓoti Parvatiye sachi* 'There many Caḓotans from the mountains are witnesses'. The last two examples are illustrative of the rule that of nouns and adjectives in apposition only the last is inflected. Similarly *Kroraiṃci maṃnuśana* 370.

There is a plural *-iya* (=*i*, § 9) in 324 *Supiya*...*aǵataṃti* 'The Supi's came'.

Other plurals in *-e* occur without it being possible to make any definite rules. Most commonly when preceded by *r*: *goṭhadare* 362, 371, 475, 506, 528, 735, *draṃghadhare* 'officials' 554, *draṃghadare* 107, *lehare* 'letter carriers' 109, 376, *bhradare* 195, *prahare* 'blows' 209, 462, etc. (also *prahara* 187, 204).

The plural *avaśiṭhe* 'remaining' is always in *-e*. Similarly *śiṭhe* 305, 519.

Further examples are *uṭavale* 562 (side by side with *uṭavala*), *thamavaṃte* 468, *mahaṃte* 160, *bahuve caṃnme* 180 (=*j*- 'young ones'), *vṛdhe* 326, *śadavide* 580, *kilane* 'sick' 414, *nave* 338, *padatale* (*namasyati*) 696, *khaṃje* ('lame'?) 156, *maṃnuśe* (Acc.) 130.

The *-e* is now and again written *-eya*: *spaṣavaṃneya* 522, *mahatveya* 580, *rajadareya* 582.

Instead of *-e*, *-i* is sometimes written: *avaradhi* 358, *cori* 676, *avaśiṭhi* 63, *ṣarvi* 279, *mahaṃti* 303, *bahuvi* 351, *yatmi* (kind of official) 349, *purimi* 140.

§ 61. Traces of the neuter plural in *-āni* occur rarely, chiefly in introductory formulas of which the style tends to be influenced by Sanskrit, e.g. *bahukoḓiśatasahasrani*, *rajakaryani* 272, *śadani* 133, *karyani* 161; *vaḓaviyani* 212 looks like the erroneous application of this termination to a feminine stem.

§ 62. Plurals which have nothing to correspond to them in Prakrit occur in *-aṃca* and *-eyu*.

(*a*) The plural in *-aṃca* was pointed out by Prof. Thomas in *J.R.A.S.* (1927), p. 544. Examples: *aśpaṃca* 387, 681, *śaḓaṃca*

85, *dajhaṃca* 133, *paṭaṃca* 660, *bhumaṃca* 366, 713, *uṭaṃca* 681, *uṭaca* (with omission of anusvāra) 387, *mahatvaṃca* 696, *paśunaṃca* 683.

(*b*) The native word *paǩe* (= ?) forms its plural in *paǩeyu*. These two forms are explained out of Tocharian in *J.R.A.S.* (1935), p. 673.

§ **63.** The **Pl. Instr. Abl.** *-ehi* is rarely met with: *putradhidarehi* (*ṣadha*) 450, *sarvehi ṣadena bhavidavya* 702. There is no certain instance of its being used in an ablative sense. At 12 *taǵastehi varidavo* it might be an ablative, only the meaning of *taǵasta* is quite unknown.

§ **64. Pl. Gen.** *bhratarana*, *cojhboana*, *paśavana*, *manuśana*, etc. The sign of length is sometimes written °*śatāyukāna* 399, *cojhboāna* 107. Under the influence of Sanskrit we find it written *-ānāṃ*, *bhratarānāṃ* 162 and *-anāṃ*, *bhaṭaraǵanāṃ* 140, 162, °*pramananāṃ* 140, *priyadarśananāṃ* 126, 140, *saṃpujitanāṃ* 140, 162, *cojhboanāṃ* 576.

§ **65.** The **Pl. Loc.** presents no abnormal features: *uṭiyeṣu*, *goṭheṣu*, *draṃgeṣu*, *nagareṣu*, *nimaṃtreṣu*, *paśuv́eṣu*, *parvateṣu*, *pṛṭheṣu*, *muṣǵeṣu*.

§ **66.** Their knowledge of Sanskrit has induced the writers to put in a dual occasionally: *padebhyaṃ* (Dat.) 288 with the *e* of the plural, *pateyo* 722, *padayo* 34, 97, 133, *pādeyo* 498 = *pādayoḥ*.

§ **67.** Except for words denoting living creatures old feminines tend to be transferred to the *a*-declension. Examples: *ratraṃmi* 415 'by night', *velaṃmi* 637; *simaṃmi* 163, 367 may be from *sīmā-* or *sīman-*; *devataṣa*, *siǵataṃmi* 576. Similarly feminines in *-i*: *pritiyena*, etc. (§ 70).

The feminine terminations occur sometimes as well: *ratriyae* 370, *vela velaya* 'from time to time' 358, 371, *pac̄imadiśaya* 90 side by side with *purvadiśade*.

The form is always used in *dutiyae* = **dūtyayā* in the phrase *dutiyae gam-* 'to go as an envoy', and more commonly in *ajeṣaṃnae* = *adhyeṣanayā* 'at the request of' (also *ajeṣaṃnena*). Preservation is to be expected in fixed formulas.

§ 68. The suffix *-ī* has become the sign of the feminine. Of old feminines in *-ā* only *bharya* 'wife' is regularly retained as a feminine; Nom. Acc. *bharya*, Instr. Gen. Loc. *bharyae*. No plural forms are found. The only feminine from which quite a number of inflected forms occur is *uṭi* 'a female camel'. The forms are Nom. Acc. *uṭi*, Gen. Instr. Loc. *uṭiae*, Nom. Pl. *uṭi*, Gen. Pl. *uṭiyana*, Loc. Pl. *uṭiyeṣu*. As will be seen the masculine forms are attached in the plural. Other nouns in *-i* are *stri* (*striae*, *strie*, *striyana*), *bhaṭariyae* 756, *vaḏavi* 'mare', *vaḏaviyae* 600, *vaḏaviyana* 600, *kuḏi*, *kuḏiyae* 'girl', *devi*, *deviyae*, *dajhi* 'slave-girl', *mahuli*, *prithivi*. From adjectives and participles the feminine is always in *-ī* where Sanskrit and Prakrit have *-ā*. There is a similar tendency in Apabhraṃśa. Examples: *uniti*= *unnītā*, *gilani* 'sick', *śpeti* 'white'. The *-i* is perhaps partly out of *-ikā*, cf. § 16.

Feminine nouns in *-ṛ* are adapted to this declension, e.g. Nom. Acc. *madu*, Gen. etc. *maduae*, *śvasu*, *priyaśpasuae* 316, *dhitu*, *dhitue* 416. In the dvandva *putradhidarehi* 450 there is a different treatment.

Instead of *-ae* the genitive is sometimes in *-e* in nouns ending in *-i* and *-u*, e.g. *strie* 209, *madue* 450, *dhitue* 416. This is due to analogy, *strie* is to *stri* as *bharyae* is to *bharya*. But compare also the similar treatment of the suffix *-ae* (§ 53), which cannot be explained in this way.

§ 69. Feminine proper names are distinguished from ordinary nouns in that the *-ae* of the oblique cases is transferred to the nominative, so that there is no distinction of case at all, e.g. 39 *yatha edeṣa dajhi Cimikae nama* 'They have a slave-girl called Cimika'.

Nominatives in *-a* are found rarely: 415 *sa striya Tsina*; *Sarpina* 279, *Supriya* 621, *Konuma* 46. Very rare is the nominative in *-ae* other than in proper names: 157 *mahi bharya... jivaṃtiyae asti*.

As a result of this we even once or twice find genitives in *-aeṣa*: *Suḡaeṣa* 117, *Cataroyaeṣa* 399.

The *-ae* is appended to native names in *-o*: *Kuviñoae*, *Kacoae*, *Kroae*, *Camoae*, *Pitoae*, *Yaśoae*, *Laroae*, etc.

Corresponding to genitives like *strie*, *madue*, we find nominatives in *-oe*: *Koloe*, *Caṃtanoe*, *Tsordhoe*, *Pitoe*, *Suǵoe*. Similarly *Sarvaśrṛe*. Conversely we find *-aae* on the analogy of *-oae*: *Cakuv́aae* 279, *Tilutamaae*, *Namilǵaae*, *Puñalajhaae*, *Lṗipiṃtsaae*, *Saǵanāpaae*, *Saǵapcaae*, *Sarpiṣaae*, *Saluv́aae*. Or we may be dealing with native bases on *-ā* to which the termination was added, as always in native bases like *Yaśo-ae*, *Lṗipe-y-aṣa*.

§ 70. Nouns in *-i* are transferred to the *a*-declension by appending the terminations *-aṣa*, *-ena*, etc. to the stem in *-i*. Nom. *-i*, Instr. *-iyena*, Gen. *-iyaṣa*, Loc. *-iyaṃmi*, Nom. Pl. *-i*, Gen. Pl. *-iyana*, Loc. Pl. *-iyeṣu*. Nouns originally in *-in*, e.g. *sac̄h́i*, are treated in the same way. The nominative accusative (singular and plural) may also be written *-iya* though less frequently. The genitive singular may be *-iṣa* (as in Pali and Prakrit), but in the other cases the fuller forms are always used. Examples: *palṗi* (=*bali*), *palṗiyaṣa* 725, *palṗiṣa* 162, 508, *palṗiyena* 42, *diṭhi* (Nom. Pl. measure of length), *khi* (Nom. Sing. and Pl.; also *khiyi* 186), *Saṃgarac̄h́isya* n.pr., *sac̄h́i*, *sac̄h́iyena*, *sac̄h́iyana*. Originally feminine: *priti*, *pritiyena*, *anatiyade* (cf. the treatment of nouns in *-ā*, § 67). Occurring only in the nominative: *prahuni* ('garment'), *sali* 'brother-in-law' (but Skt. *syāla-*), *vacari* ('jar'?), *mukeṣi*, *viṃñati*, *saṃñati*, *pravṛti*.

Nouns originally in *-ya*, *-iya* are not distinguishable from nouns in *-i*: *muli*, *muliyena*, *muliyaṃmi*, *aṣiyade*, *aroǵi*, *Dham̄apri*, etc. Similarly *-īya* in *biti* '2nd', *bitiyaṣa* and *bitiṣa*. The proper name *Saṃgaśri* makes its genitive *Saṃgaśrṛṣa* in 419 (i.e. *Saṃgaśriṣa*, cf. § 5).

§ 71. Nouns in *-u* are treated in exactly the same way as those in *-i*. Examples: *masu* 'wine', *masuv́ena*, *masuṣa*, *masusya*, *masuaṣa*, *masuaṃmi*; *vasu* (a title), Gen. Pl. *vasuana*, *v́asuv́ana*; *bhic̄h́u*, *bhic̄h́usya*; *hetu*, *hetuv́ena*. Only in Nom. Acc.: *lahu*, *vastu*, *tanu* 'own', *manyu*, *vac̄h́u* (= ?). The nominative is never extended to *-uv́a*, as *-i* to *-iya*. The genitive in *-usya* is much more frequent than *-uaṣa*. The word *paśu* preserves some old forms. Quite according to type are Gen. Sing. *paśuṣa*, Loc. Pl.

paśuveṣu 568. But we find *paśava* in the Nom. Pl. (*paśu* is also plural 519)=*paśavaḥ*, whence further a Gen. Pl. is formed, *paśavana* 315, 584. *paśuna* 725 seems to be a Nom. Pl., cf. also *paśunaṃca*, § 62; *bahu* is sometimes plural, e.g. 430, but it also makes its plural in *bahuve* (*vi*) presumably out of *bahave*= *bahavaḥ*, with the *-u* from the singular. But perhaps the analogy of *sarve* is responsible for the *-e* here, since we never find **paśave*.

§ **72. Other bases.** On feminines in *-ṛ* see § 68. From *pitṛ* we have Nom. Acc. Sing. *pita*, more usually *pitu*, Gen. *pitusya* 109 (text *-vya*), Nom. Pl. *pitara*. From *bhrātṛ*, Nom. Acc. *bhrata* and *bhratu*, Nom. Pl. *bhatara* and *bhratare*, Gen. Pl. *bhratarana*, *bhratuana* 157, *priyabhratre* 159 (case?); *priyajamata*. There are no agent nouns in *-tṛ*.

From *-an* bases *takṣan* 'a carpenter' is expanded into *tac̄h̄amna*. Usually the *-n* is simply dropped and they are inflected as *-a* bases. *mahatva* 'magistrate'=*mahātmā*, Gen. *mahatvaṣa*. Neuters: *bhuma*, *-aṣa*, *-aṃmi*; *śirṣa*, *śirṣaaṣa* (589, cf. the proper names in *-aaṣa*, § 73); *namena*; *posathakam̄aya*.

-ant bases are enlarged to *-aṃta* except *mahā-* in compounds, *maharaya*, *mahacojhbo* 259 beside *mahaṃta cojhbo* 161, etc. Examples: *mahaṃtaṣa*, *jayaṃta* 'victorious', *jayaṃtaṣa*, *arahaṃta*, *Puṃñavaṃta*, *Viryavaṃda*.

Śiraṣa in the phrase *śiraṣa viṃñavemi* is an isolated example of the consonantal declension, no doubt due to the influence of Sanskrit. We get the regular treatment in *manasaṃmi*; *manasiyaṃmi* 399 is a result of confusion between *manasi* and *manasaṃmi*.

From *śarat* we have Loc. *śarataṃmi* 'in Autumn'.

Dhanuṣ 'bow' is declined as a *-u* base: *dhaṃnuena* 190.

§ **73.** Native names (and words) are treated in the same way as Prakrit words in *-i*, *-u*; e.g. in *-i*, *-u*: *Caḍhi*, *Caḍhiya*, *Caḍhiyaṣa*, *Tami*, *Tamiyaṣa*, *Piǵi*, *Piǵiṣa*, *Saṃghuti*, *Saṃghutiṣa*, *Suǵi*, *Suǵiya*, *Suǵiyaṣa*, *Suǵiṣa*, *Suǵiyena*, *Yonu*, *Yonuṣa*, *Yonuaṣa*, *Lṕimsu*, *Lṕimsuv́asya*, *Lṕimsuṣa*, *Larsu*, *Larsua*, *Larsuaṣa*, *Larsuṣa*. Similarly in *-o* and *-e*: *Taṃcǵo*, *Tamcǵoaṣa*, *cojhbo*, *cojhboaṣa*, *cojhboana*, *Cǵito*, *Cǵitoena*, *Ciǵitoyena*. In names in *-e* the extended form *-eya* of the nominative is more common than the simple *-e*: *Lpipeya* and *Lpipe*. That is no doubt because in the Prakrit they wrote *parikreya nic̄eya*, etc. for what they pronounced (and sometimes wrote) *parikre nic̄e*. No doubt *Lpipe* is the real native form. Examples: *Maṣḏhiǵe*, *-eya*, *-eyaṣa*, *-eyena*, *Caule*, *Cauleya*, *Caulesa*, *Parsuǵe*, *-eya*, *-eyaṣa*, *-eṣa*. As in nouns in *-i*, *-u* shorter forms occur for the genitive: *-eṣa*, *-oṣa*, *-iṣa*, *-uṣa*, beside *-eyaṣa*, etc., but not for the other cases. Names in *-a* declined *-aena*, *-aaṣa*, etc. possibly contain long *a* (cf. feminines in *-a*, *-ae*, § 69): *Cācāaṣa*, *Cramaena*, *Taṃcǵaaṣa*, *-aena*, *Tamaspaaṣa*, *Tuṣanaaṣa*, *Tsuǵeṣlaaṣa*, *Motekaaṣa*, *Śakaaṣa*.

SUFFIXES

§ 74. The suffix *-ka* is very common in the form *-aǵa*, *-ae* (§ 8): *bhaṭaraǵa* 'master', *pravaṃnaǵa* 'document', *saṃvatsaraǵa* (100), *kālaǵa* 86, *kiśoraǵa* 'colt', *potaǵa* 'young animal', *kuḏaǵa* 'boy', *phalitaǵa* 214, *parivanae* 214 (*paribhāṇḍaka*?), *tāvastaǵa*, *thavastae* 'carpet', *thavaṃnae* ('cloth'), *namatae* (coat or cloth), *tanuvaǵa*, *-ae* 'own'.

Adjectives: *śpedaǵa* (*śveta*), *coc̄haǵa* (*cokṣa* 'clean'), *puranaǵa*, *satavarṣaǵa*, *trevarsaǵa*, etc., *kaniṭhaǵa*, *dharaṃnaǵa* 'owing a debt', *avamicae* 'on loan', *jivaṃdaǵa* 'alive', *culaǵe* (cf. § 53) = *cullaka*. In words of obscure origin: *kicamaǵa* 'due, owing' (of tax, etc.), *laṃcaǵa* 'proper, properly'.

The feminine corresponding to *-aǵa* is *-i* (= *ikā*): *śpedaǵa*: *śpeti*, *bhaṭaraǵa* : *bhaṭari*, *jivaṃdaga* : *jivaṃti*, *kuḏaga* : *kuḏi*.

When added to past participles in *-ta* they have a passive meaning, while the simple *-ta* is used as the 3rd person of the preterite: *dita* 'he gave', *ditaǵa*, *ditae* 'given'.

The form *-ae* for *-aǵa* is much commoner in participles than elsewhere.

§ 75. The suffix -i. Adjectives are made from nouns by substituting *-i* for the *-a* of the nominative accusative: *Caḏoti* 'belonging to C.', *Khotaṃni*, *Parvati*, *saṃvatsari palpi* 'the year's tax', *masuv̄i ṣothaṃga* 272 'The *ṣothaṃga* (an official) connected with *masu* (wine)', *ghriti paśu*, *caǵali paśu* 613 'small cattle consisting of goats', *goṭhi kam̄a* 298, *rayadvari mahatva* 46, *upaśaṃghi śrava* 139, *paruvarṣi* 'belonging to last year', *para-*

rivarṣi 'belonging to the year before last', *catuvarṣi* and *caura varṣi* 'four years old', *vatsiya* 'possessing a calf' (*gavi*) 676.

The *-i* is derived from *-ika*; the guttural was weaker in suffixes than elsewhere and would disappear (§ 16): *saṃvatsari palpi* = *sāṃvatsariko baliḥ*. Such forms were originally vṛddhied, but vṛddhi has died out in the language except for one or two stereotyped or borrowed forms: *vevatuǵa* 'an object of (legal) dispute'.

§ 76. A suffix *-tra* is used three or four times to make abstracts from agent nouns: *brahmacaritra* (*-ṭa*) 399, *kam̄akaritra* (*-ṭa*) 106, 130, *kriṣivatra* 'cultivation' (from *kṛṣīva-la* or = *kṛṣivaptra*, cf. Index).

Formed with the same suffix is *jañatra*. It is used in the phrases *jaṃñatrena dā-*, *anī-* which seem to mean 'give, take in marriage', e.g. 21 *taṃ kalaṃmi eṣa Cato śramana Sundaraṣa dhitu Supriya nama bharya anita caṃñatrena* 'At that time this *śramana* Cato took as wife the daughter of Sundara called Supriya, *caṃñatrena*'. The sense seems to require 'with the proper marriage ceremony, in legal marriage' or something like that. There is considerable difficulty in establishing a uniform reading, but °*tra* seems to be the best attested. We find 474 *jañatriyena* v.l. *jaṃñav́iyena*, 418 *jañatv́ena* v.l. *jañatrena*, 555 *jañatrena* v.l. *jañav́ena*, 621 *caṃñatrena*.

§ 77. **Native suffixes.** *-e*(*ṃ*)*ci*, *-i*(*ṃ*)*ci*, *-ci* is used in making adjectives from place-names: *av́anaṃci*, *Kroraiṃci*, *Caḏodeṃci*, *Calmataṃci*, *Calmadaneṃci*, *Tsakeṃci*, *Ninaṃci*, *Potǵeci Bha-*(*tsa-*)*ǵaseṃci*, etc. Native words: *kilmeṃci* 'belonging to the district of', *klaṣeṃci* (some kind of official). It is rarely applied to Prakrit words: *paṃthaci masu* 637, *simici mahatva* 436.

-ina appears commonly in native words: *cuv́alaina* (title), *cilaṃḍhina* 'shared', *paṃcaraina*, *acoviṃna*, *koyimaṃḍhina* (an official connected with corn).

PRONOUNS

§ 78. First Person.

SING. NOM. *ahu*. The explanation of the *-u* is difficult; *-aṃ* usually becomes *-a*. We also find *-u* instead of *-a* in the Gen. Pls. *amahu* and *tumahu*.

ahaṃ is also written quite commonly, which is of course Sanskritising. Also *ahum* (*apya*) 399.

ACC. not found.

GEN. DAT. *mahi* (=*mahyam*), *mama*, 161. Elsewhere *mama* is used as Nom. or Acc., e.g. 139 *mama aroǵemi* 'I am well', 524 *yatha mama Śristeyaṣa paride srutemi* 'As I have heard from Śriste', 164 *iśa mama prochaṃti* 'Here they ask me'.

INSTR. *maya* 16, 328, 331, 661. At 329 it is used as Gen.: *maya maharayaṣa padamulammi*.

LOC. not found. *mayi* 661 =*mahi* (cf. § 28).

PL. NOM. *veyaṃ*, *veya*, *vayaṃ*. Acc. not found. Gen. *amahu*, *asmahu*=*asmabhyaṃ*. As in the Nom. Sing. the *-u* is unexplained.

There also occur *asmehi* 370 and *asmabhi* 585; *asmaǵa* 713 = *asmākam*. In 86 we find *asmaǵena*: *Casminena viṣajideṣi asmaǵena caragena* 'You have sent Casmina our spy'. The Instr. is often confused with the Nom. Acc. as here, so that *asmaǵena* has nothing to do with the Vedic inflected *asmāka* 'our'. Loc. and Instr. forms do not occur; *asmehi* 370 is Gen. from the context.

§ 79. Second Person.

SING. NOM. *tuo* (Vedic *tuvám*; for the *-o* cf. § 53). *tu* at 63 may be just careless writing.

The form *tuo* is used apparently as an Instr. with gerundives, e.g. 113 *tatra tuo piḋita cita kartavo* 'There by you expressly attention must be made' (cf. Index Verb.). The form *tuo* naturally cannot=*tvayā*. On the confusion of Nom. and Instr. cf. § 117.

INSTR. does not occur. *taya* 430 is taken as=*tvayā* in the Index Verb. Read probably *tapataya* 'immediately' for *ta*(*tha*) *taya*. The Loc. also does not occur. Gen. *tahi* on the analogy of *mahi*=*mahyam* (*tehi dahi*). Also *tusya*, *tuṣa* with the nominal

-*sya*. *tusya* is used as a Nom. at 157 *tusya...udaǵa baṃnideṣi* 'you blocked up the water'. *tava* occurs once: 161 *tava paride*. *tomi*=*tava...mi* (see Index). The enclitic forms *me* and *te* are not used.

PLURAL. Only Gen. forms occur: *tumahu* (cf. *amahu*) with *t*- from the singular as always in Middle Indian. Other forms are *tusmahu*, *tusmaǵa* 399, *tusmakaṃ* 140. The forms are of course artificial, otherwise we should have **tuṣmahu*, etc. Quite isolated is *yuṣme*: 519 *avi tusya pitu Suǵuta yuṣme agrata uṭa atha aspa pratiśruta* 'And your father Suguta in front of you promised a camel and a horse'. The reading is not certain: *yuṣmu* and *yuṣma* are given as variants.

§ 80. *sa*-, *ta*-.

SING. NOM. Masc. *se* with -*e* regularly developed out of -*as* (§ 12). It is sometimes written *ṣe*, which indicates that the *s* was voiced owing to its being unaccented; *so* occurs rarely, 198, 337. Fem. *sa*; Neut. *taṃ*. Since nouns do not distinguish masculine and neuter *taṃ* is only used when it stands by itself, e.g. 283 *taṃ vismaridavya* 'That must be forgotten'.

ACC. Masc. Fem. Neut. *ta*=*tam*, *tām*, e.g. 582 *ta bhuma praceya* 'concerning that land'; 415 *ta striya...aǵajhidaṃti* 'They carried off that woman'. Unlike nouns the pronoun distinguishes Nom. and Acc. but there are occasional confusions, e.g. 625 *se* is Acc.: *ṣe kuḏaga Lṗimiṃnaṣa goṭhade Khotaṃniye paraṣa kritaṃti* 'The Khotanese carried off that boy from the farm of Lṗimiṃna'.

INSTR. Masc. *tena*. Abl. *tade* 140. Usually the form stands by itself=*tataḥ* 'thereupon'; *tasma*- only in *tasmartha* 'for that reason'.

GEN. *taṣa*, *tasya*, with suffix -*emi*: *taṣemi* 'of the very...' 491, 578. Fem. *taya*: *tae* 415, *tayā* 383.

LOC. The Loc. seems to be in *te* in the phrases *te bhumaṃmi ...eśvari huda* (222) 586, *te masu śaṭaṃmi* 'in that vineyard'; cf. 571, 572, 582, 587, 654, 715. In the phrase *taṃ kalaṃmi*, which occurs frequently, *taṃ* may either be abbreviated out of the Loc. **taṃmi* or it may be a compound=*tatkāle*, which is more probable. Compare also *taṃ karaṃna* 335=*tatkāraṇāt* (also *tena karaṃna*). *tomi*, in 123 *tomi divasaṃmi* is used as the equivalent of the Loc. Sing., otherwise it seems to be = *tava*. *tatra*, *tatremi* are used instead of the Loc. Sing., e.g. *tatrimi deśaṃmi* 55, *tatremi rajaṃmi* 40.

PL. NOM. ACC. *te*.

GEN. *teṣa*, *teṣaṃ*, with suffix *-emi*: *teṣemi*. Also *tana* 579, 655. *taṣa* 514 is a mixture of *teṣām* and *tāsām*; in *tana* 655 the ordinary nominal termination is used.

LOC. *teṣu*.

§ **81.** *eṣa-*, *eta-*.

SING. NOM. *eṣa* for all genders.

ACC. *eda*. *eda* is rarely used as a Nom.: 140 *eda vikridavo*, 309 *eda aṃna na anidae* 'this corn has not been brought'. In the phrases *yahi eda kilamudra atra eśati* 'When this wedge-seal comes there' (*yahi eda anati lekha*... 272) and *eda vivada*...*pruchi-davo* 'This dispute is to be examined' *eda* always occurs and never *eṣa*. On the other hand in the common phrase heading legal documents, *eṣa lekha* (*lihitaǵa*, *pravaṃnaǵa*) ...*anada dharidavo* 'This document is to be carefully preserved', *eda* does not occur. So perhaps in *eda kilamudra* and *eda vivada* we have a kind of Tatpuruṣa compound, 'A wedge-seal about this (matter), the dispute about this'.

eṣa is used as an Acc. in 714 *eṣa Tsuǵeta atra viṣajidemi* 'I have sent this Tsuǵeta there', 721 *eṣa Danutreya atra viṣajidama*.

The pronoun is not inflected in the oblique cases when used attributively, e.g. 52 *eda parikrayade*, 140 *eda karyami*, 255 *eta bhumaṣa*, 431 *eda masuaṣa*, etc.

GEN. Masc. *etaṣa*, *edaṣa* (*-sya*); Fem. *etaya* 331.

PL. NOM. ACC. *ede* for all genders (*ede vaḍavi* 212). *eda* is plural at 195 *eda bhradare*. As in the singular *ede* is not inflected when used attributively, e.g. 55 *ede khula uṭana*, 310 *ede maṃnuśana*, 187 *ede bhradarana*, etc.

GEN. *edeṣa*, *eteṣa*; *edana* occasionally, 113 (?), 187. In 478 *edeṣana* has a double termination.

§ **82.** *i-*, *ima-*.

SING. VOC. *iyo*, *yiyo* (printed *śiśo*, see Index Verb.) = *iyaṃ*. This is more probable than *idaṃ* because intervocalic *d* is not omitted in the dialect. On the initial *yi-* see § 32. It is not common, being used only in the phrase *iyo* (*yiyo*) *pravaṃnaga* 'this document'. *itaṃ* = *idaṃ* is likewise in these phrases *itaṃca lihitiǵa* 355, etc. The *-ca* is always added without having any meaning of its own.

Acc. *ima* 345. *ṣe śramana ima cora maṃnusa...Larsuaṣa dita* 'The *śramana* gave this thief man to Larsu' 291, 506. The Acc. is not very common. Like *eda*, *ima* is used as a stem form in apposition with oblique cases: 162 *ima varṣami*, 236 *ima śaradaṃmi*. Also in compounds like *imavarṣi* 'this year's'.

Pl. Nom. Acc. *ime* 399, *yima* 237.

§ 83. *ka-*.

Only found in the Nom. Masc. *ko*, Neut. *ki*, *kiṃ*. It is not found used as an interrogative but only as a relative = 'whoever', e.g. 209 *ko...pac̄ima aṃnyatha icheyati karaṃnae* 'Whoever afterwards should wish to do otherwise', etc.; 541 *kiṃ tade paḏivati siyati* 'Whatever news shall be from there'.

kiṃna, which is Instr. in form, = Pkt. *kiṇa* (cf. Pischel, § 428), is used as a Nom. 609 *kiṃna atra na esati* 'Whoever shall not come there'. It has an interrogative sense in 86 *na taha janami kiṃna pravaṃnaǵa atra giṃnidavo* 'I do not know what document is there to be taken'. This is a case of the usual confusion of Instr. and Nom. Unexplained forms are *kamita*, 169 *kamita maṣa divaṣa ghrida prace anati lekha atra gachiśati taṃ kala...* 'On whatever month or day a letter of command shall come about the ghee, at that time...' (= *kāmita* 'whatever you please'?), and *k̄ema*, 160 *yo atra k̄ema hasta lekha udaǵa bhiśaṣa prace...hac̄hati, taha margidavo* 'Whatever hand-letter may be concerning seed and water, so you must seek'. *k̄ema* seems to = *kac̄i* in the common phrase *yo kac̄i* 'whoever'. Initial *k̄-* is certainly not different from *k*. All words with initial *k̄-* are variants of forms with *k* (cf. Index Verb.). *kema* occurs in Apabhraṃśa = *katham*, but that meaning does not suit here.

§ 84. *kaścit ko pi*, etc.

Sing. Nom. *kac̄i*, i.e. *kaści*. Once *koci* 437: 161 *yo tava kac̄i puna isa agamiṣyati* 'Whoever shall come...'; 437 *yo ca koci pac̄ima kalaṃmi maṃtra uthaveyati* 'Whoever at a future time shall upset this ruling'. Neut. *kiṃci*: 335 *nevi adehi kiṃci śrudama* 'We have not heard anything from there'; 106 *kaṃm̄akaritra na kiṃci kareti* 'He does not do any work'; 260 *puna vivada kiṃci siyati* '(If) again there shall be any dispute'; 31 *yeṣa saṃcaya kiṃci tatra maṃtra siyati* 'Of whom there is doubt (whether) there is any ruling on that point'; 17 *tade kiṃci kiṃci Maṣḍhiǵe Pǵeya ṣa ca giḋati* 'M. and P. took from that little by little'.

iṃci in the phrase *na iṃci* 'not at all' (also *ma iṃci*) is out of *kiṃci*. The omission of the *k* is due to its being attached enclitically to *na* (*ma*). On the liability of *k* to be dropped in certain positions of weak stress cf. § 16.

Gen. *kasya ci*: 709 *na kasyaci maṃtra asti.*

Pl. Nom. *keci* with the *c̄* erroneously adapted from the singular.

kiṃca, 377 *na kiṃca triṭha* 'nothing has been seen', is perhaps just miswritten for *kiṃci*.

kopi occurs only 198 *kopi varaǵa syati so...iśa anidavo.* The text should be read *ko pivaraǵa syati* 'whichever shall be fat'. *kikama* 'whatever' = **kiṃ kāmam* in the phrase *kikama karaniya syati* 'whatever is to be done'.

§ 85. *ya-*.

Sing. Nom. Acc. *yo* for all genders: 136 *yo aṭh̄ovaǵa palayaṃnaǵa maṃnuśa siyati* 'What serviceable fugitive man there may be'; 157 *yo mahi bharya iśa gilani* 'My wife who (was) ill here'; 106 *yo iśa kam̄akaritra vithidaǵa huati* 'The work that has been put off here'; 126 *yo adehi spaṣavaṃne Paǵo iśa viṣarjidetu* 'The scout Paǵo whom you sent here'; 140 (*aṃna*)...*yo iśa paṭichidama* 'The corn which we received here'. *yo* is also occasionally used for the plural: 271 *yo asmahu atra Caḋodaṃmi kilmeciye, tahi ṣarvabhavena jheniǵa* (*siy*)*aṃti* 'The people of our district who are there in Caḍota, let them be under your care by all means'; 165 *yo puna tahi karyani hac̄haṃti* 'What affairs of yours shall be again (= in the future)'.

When followed by *ca* we usually have *yaṃ* instead of *yo*, e.g. 140 *yo aṃna...yaṃ ca aṃna*, 370 *yaṃ ca viṃñavemi*; 621 *yo puna edaṣa putra dhidara yaṃ ca daṣi* 'What sons and daughters (there are) of him and what slave-girls' (*daṣi* may be either singular or plural).

Occasionally the *ca* has no meaning of its own, e.g. 517 *ede jaṃna tade omaǵa isa aniṣyatu, yaṃ ca teṣa jaṃnaṣa śiṭha, tuo paḍichiṣyatu* '(If) you bring these people here less (than the proper number), what penalty there is for those people, you will receive it'. Apart from this *yaṃ* is only used in the phrases *yaṃ vela, yaṃ kala, yaṃ kalaṃmi*; compare *taṃ kala, taṃ kalaṃmi* (§ 80).

yo is probably out of *yam*, rather than *yaḥ* or *yad*, because the *yaṃ* is preserved in the combination *yaṃ ca*, where it was treated as in the interior of a word. Final *-am* usually became *-a*. Exceptions have been noticed in the case of *-vam* (§ 53). Perhaps *am* tended to become *o* after *y* too. Compare *iyo* = *iyam*. Also we find writings such as *arogiyo* 152, etc. beside *arogi*. On the other hand *svayam* always becomes *sveya* or *sve*.

INSTR. *yena* as an adverb = 'so that': 272 *yena raja karyani na iṃci śiśila bhaviṣyaṃti*.

GEN. *yasya*.

PL. NOM. *ye* (also *yo* above).

GEN. *yeṣa*.

§ 86. *svayam* appears *sveya, sve* 193, *sveyam eva* 22, *svaya* 709.

From *ātman-* we have *apane* = *atmanaḥ*: 139 *tuo apane acovina paśidavo* 'You must yourself examine the *acovina* (= ?)'. Transferred to the *a*-declension, *apanasya*: 201 *apanasya kritaǵa* 'your own deeds'. But the passage is fragmentary and the reading doubtful.

The old reflexive *tanū-* 'self' has taken on the meaning of 'own'. The meaning belongs properly to the derivative adjective *tanuv́aǵa* 'belonging to the self'. The simple *tanu* is used in the same way, e.g. 165 *tuo ṣoṭhaṃga Lṕipeya tanu goṭhade vyoṣiśasi* 'You, *ṣoṭhaṃga* Lṕipeya, shall pay it from your own farm'. Most usually, however, *tanu* is a noun meaning 'property': 326 *Kam̄aya ni goṭha gṛhavaṣa amahu pitupitamaǵa tanu* 'Kam̄aya's farm and residence are inherited property of us', etc.

Tanuvaka is also found in the inscriptions of N.W. India (Taxila scroll, Kurram). It is preserved in the Dardic languages, e.g. Torwali *tanu* 'own'. Grierson (*Torwali*, § 127) is wrong in explaining it out of *ātman*.

§ 87. Pronouns expressing quantity are *keti*=Pkt. *kettiya* (Pischel, § 153). It is used in relative clauses, e.g. 17 *Maṣḍhiǵe Pǵeya ṣa ca śavatha śavidavya, keti edeṣa siyaṃti* 'M. and P. must swear on oath (stating) how many they have'; 73 *eda palpi, keti vithidaǵa siyati...iśa viṣajidavo* 'This tax, however much has been held back, must be sent here'.

eti=*ettiya*: 439 *pruchidavo bhutartha eṣa eti draṃga dharidae siyati* 'It must be enquired whether he has really held so many offices'. Skt. *tati* occurs once in the compound *tativarsi*: 570 *garbhini uṭi bhaǵena kirsoṣa uṭi tativarṣi Śaraṣenaṣa vyoṣidavo* 'Śaraṣena must pay back, in place of the pregnant female camel, a *kirsoṣa* (=?) female camel of as many years old'. With *-dṛś* are formed *etriśa, ketriśa* and *yadṛśa*. The *e-* instead of Sanskrit *i-* is the usual thing in Middle Indian (Pischel, § 121).

§ 88. Adjectives declined pronominally are *aṃña*: Gen. Sing. *aṃñaṣa* or *aṃñisya*, Pl. *aṃñe*. Gen. *aṃñesa, aṃñeṣana* 690 (cf. *edeṣana*, § 81), *amñano va* 590, *aṃñamaṃñana* 357='one another'; *pareṣa* 509, 713; *parosparasya, parosparena* 'one another'; *eka, ekisya* 272; *eke* 'some' 468; *ṣarvi* 'all'; *-i* is always used, not *-e*, in the Nom. Pl. Gen. Pl. *sarvina* 431–2. The same form occurs in the Wardak vase. Instr. *sarvehi* 702.

NUMERALS

§ 89. Figures are usually employed, but now and again the numerals, sometimes as well as the figures. The numerals that occur are:

1. *eka*, i.e. probably *ekka* as in Prakrit because the *k* is always written and not *ǵ* (except 709). In the plural *eke* means 'some'. The ordinal is both *prathama* (*pratama*) and *paḍama*, just as *prati-* and *paḍi* are both used.

2. *dui, dvi, due, tui, du*=Skt. *dve*; as in the Veda it is disyllabic (cf. § 43). Ordinal: *biti* and *dviti*. *diguna* 'twofold' with irregular treatment of *dvi-* (§ 43).

3. *tre, treya*=*trayaḥ*. Gen. Pl. *trina*; *tre-* and not *tri-* is used in compounds: *trevarṣaga* 'three years old'. Ordinal: *triti*.

4. *catu* and *caura*. The omission of *t* in the latter form is unusual (§ 19). *cohura* seems to be '4' in 637 *aṃña paśava* 4 *cohura*, but the passage is difficult. Ordinal: *caturtha*. The *t* is never omitted in this form.

5. *paṃca*, *paṃcama*.

6. *ṣo*. *ṣo* is perhaps out of *ṣva*, cf. Av. *xšvaš*, etc., like *ṣoṭhaṃga* and *ṣvaṭhaṃga* (§ 7). Otherwise we should expect *-a* as in the other Prakrits. The ordinal is *ṣodhama* 110, 637. The *dh* may be just written for *t* (§ 15), in which case it is a new formation instead of *ṣaṣṭha-*, made by adding *-tama* to *ṣo*.

7. *sata*, *satama*. 8. *aṭha*, *aṭhama*. 9. *no*, *navama*.

10. *daśa*, *daśama*, *daśaṃmi* (ordinal locative).

11. *ekadaśa* 341 (ordinal).

12. *badaśa*, *badaśi* 599 (ordinal).

13. *trodasa* = *trayodaśa*. Otherwise in Middle Indian we have *te* = *tre* (*terasa*).

15. *paṃcadaśa* 489. As an ordinal: *paṃcadaśaṃmi* 599 (locative).

18. *aṭhadaśami* (ordinal locative) 354.

20. *viśati*. 30. *triśa*. 40. *capariśa*.

42. *du caparisa*. 50. *paṃcaśa*. 70. *satati*.

90. *novati*, with *o* instead of *a* borrowed from *no* '9'.

100. *śata*. 110. *daśutara śata*. 1000. *sahasra*.

ADVERBS

§ 90. Any adjective may be used as an adverb: *śigra*, *cavala* 'quickly', *piḍita* 'taking pains', *samuha*, *dura*, *bhutartha* 'really'.

As elsewhere the instrumental is used in making adverbial expressions out of nouns: *adhaṃ̄ena* 'illegally', *ṣarvabhavena* 'altogether'. There is further a tendency to apply this termination to indeclinables compounded with a preposition, e.g. *anupurvena* 'in front', *ṣavistrena* 140. The correct Sanskrit forms are *anupurvam savistaram*, etc., but later and incorrect texts reflect the state of things in the popular language, e.g. *Matsya. P.* 148. 65. *sāvadhānena*; regularly in Apabhraṃśa, e.g. *saviseseṃ*, *savinaeṇa*, *saviyappeṃ*, etc. in the *Bhavisatta-kaha*. As a result of this *sa* appears practically as an independent word, e.g. *tahi ṣa madue bharyae putra dhidarehi iśa agaṃdavo* 'You must come here with your mother, wife and children'. Similarly *yatha dhamm̄ena*=*yathādharmam*. Whence *yatha* also is used almost like a preposition: 40 *yatha purva rayadvari mahatvana vibhaśitaǵena* 'According to the former decision of the magistrates at the king's court'.

§ 91. Individual Adverbs. *atra* 'here'. *avaśa*=*avaśyam*; *anada*='carefully'. It is common in certain set phrases: *eda vivada anada pruchidavo* 'This dispute is to be carefully gone into'; *avi s̒paṣa jivida paricaǵena anada rac̄hidavya* 'Watch is to be kept carefully even at the expense of your life'; *eṣa pravaṃnaǵa anada dharidavo* 'This document is to be preserved carefully'. In the last-mentioned phrase *suha* occurs as a synonym (569, 593) and *suha*=*su* 'well' (compare 419 *suha vikrida* with 587 *suvikrida*). For the etymology cf. the Index. *ahuno*=*adhunā*. The *o* might be due to an original particle *u*, i.e. **adhunā u*. *adehi* 'from there'; for the suffixed -*hi* cf. forms in Apabhraṃśa like *annettahi*=*anyatra*, *ettahi*=*itaḥ*. *aṃnyatha* 'otherwise'. *aṃña* is used as a kind of particle introducing sentences='again, another thing'. *ajakra*='up till to-day'. *itu* and *imade* 'hence', *iśa* 'here'. The word occurs also in Kharoṣṭhi inscriptions from N.W. India, instead of *ia*, *iha* in Aśoka. Aśokan *ia* (S. and M. 6), i.e. *iya* for *iha*, became *iźa* as described in § 17. *upari* 'above'. *tatra* 'there'. *pac̄a* 'behind'. *patama*='back' (i.e. **pattama*, cf. Torwali *pat* 'back' out of **patta*-). *patena* occurs twice in the phrase *patena stavidavo*: 58 *teṣa jaṃnaṣa sa stri tatiyemi patena stavidavya Puǵo Lp̒ipeyaṣa ca nidavo* (cf. 63). The woman had been killed, so it cannot mean simply 'restore'. We must translate then: 'By those people that woman is to be made recompense for to such an extent (i.e. to the amount of her value) and (it) is to be taken by Puǵo and Lp̒ipe.' *puna*, *punu*=*punaḥ*. *praṭha* 'forthwith'= **praṣṭham*. *prata*=*prātar*. *bahi*, *bahiyade* 'outside'. *bhuya* 'again', also *bhui*, *buo* 377, and *bhiyo*=Pali *bhiyyo* 579. *suṭha* 'well' (*suṣṭhu*), but it must be out of **suṣṭham*. *sudha*='only', e.g. 272 *sudha nagara rac̄hidavya*, *avasiṭhe raji jaṃna oḍidavya*

'Only the city is to be kept, the rest of the people of the kingdom are to be abandoned'.

The suffix *-mi*, *-emi* is found commonly in adverbs (also after genitives of pronouns: *tasyemi*, *teṣemi*). Examples: *tatremi*, *atremi*, *iśemi*, *tatiyemi* (see above under *patena*), *iṃthuami* 'so' beside *iṃthu*.

PREPOSITIONS

§ 92. *a* = *ā*. 419, 549 *ko a pac̄ima kalaṃmi codeyati*. Against the explanation *ko ca* (*Kharoṣṭhi Inscr.* Index Verb.) *c* is never otherwise omitted. On the analogy of *acaṃta*, *yava* (see below), *ā* would take a locative, not an ablative, in this dialect. *agratu* (*ta*) = *agrataḥ* only 519, with the same meaning as *puraṭhida* (see below). *Sucamaṣa agratu*, *yuṣme agratu*; *yuṣme* only occurs here, and what case is meant is uncertain (cf. § 79).

acaṃta. 253, 367 *acaṃta Khotaṃnaṃmi* 'as far as Khotan'.

abhyadara. 291 *abhyadara kuhaniyaṃmi aniṣyaṃti* 'They will bring into the capital'.

karaṃna. 207 *ima Aputaṣa karaṃna iśa ichitaṃti marganae* 'They wanted to search this (man) on account of Aputa'.

pac̄a. 144 *taḏitaǵade pac̄a* 'after the beating'.

patama = 'back'. 64 *caṃkura Vajeśasa imade aṃtaǵi uṭa* 4 *Samarsade patama nikhalidavo Samarsade uṭa* 4 *dadavo S̄unade patama nikhalidavo S̄unade uṭa* 4 *dadavo Piṣaliyade patama nikhalidavo* 'From here the *caṃkura* Vajeśa has 4 *aṃtaǵi* camels, they are to be sent back from Samarsa (and) 4 camels are to be given from Samarsa, (these) are to be sent back from Snuna (and) 4 camels are to be given from Snuna, (these) are to be sent back from Piṣali'. The base **patta* is common in the modern Dardic languages, cf. Torwali *pat* 'back, behind'.

puraṭha, *puraṭhida* 'in the presence of' (as witnesses). 322 *eṣa lihitaǵa cojhboana Śitaka* (*Yi-*) *Vuktoṣa ca puraṭha* 'This was written in the presence of the *cojhba*'s Ś. and V.'; 592 *eṣa lihitaǵa puraṭha mahatvana* 'In the presence of the magistrates'.

paride 'from'. 11 *edaṣa Apiṣae nama uneyaǵa prace Kunǵeyaṣa paride vivada* 'He has a dispute about an adopted girl called Apiṣae (adopted) from Kunǵe'. *paride*, which is very common always, takes the genitive and not the ablative.

prace 'concerning' = *pratyayam* takes either the stem or the genitive, e.g. 582 *Yipiya ni bhuma prace* 'concerning Yipi's land' and 579 *Moǵata ni bhumaṣa praceya.* The word is borrowed into Saka in the form *prracai*. *bhaǵena* 'in place of', 'on behalf of': 30 *yatha Apiǵoaṣa bhaǵena Tseǵeyaṃmi Tuṣana thida taṣa bhaǵena Khotaṃni Kanasaǵa thida* 'That Tuṣana stayed at Tseǵe instead of Apiǵo and in place of him Kanasaǵa of Khotan'. It is also used without a case meaning 'as a substitute': 19 *iśa stri Tamaṣyanae bhaǵena Yitaṣenaṣa khulona* (= °*ana*) *vaṃti thida* 'Here the woman T. stayed with the herds of Y. as a substitute' (or 'taking her turn').

yava 'as far as'. 214 *yava Khemaṃmi*, 506 *yāva Tatiǵa Bhatraṣa ca agamanaṃmi* 'Until the arrival of Tatiǵa and Bhatra'.

It does not take the locative in the expressions *yava ajakra divaṣa*, *yaṿa jivo*.

vaṃti = *upānte*. It is borrowed into Saka in the form *bendä*: 5 *khulana vaṃti thidavo* 'Must stay with the herds, in charge of the herds'; 621 *eṣa*...*Aśoǵa ni kilmeci Catoṽeṣa vaṃti bala simaya āsiṣyati* 'He used to dwell when young next door (*sīmāyām*) to Catoṽe who belonged to the district of Aśoka'; 39 *teṣa vaṃti unida vardhida* 'She was brought up with them'. It is frequently used in expressions of legal transactions: 579 *tivira Ramṣotsaṣa vaṃti bhuma vikrida* 'He sold land to the scribe *Ramṣotsa*', etc.; 546 *ogu ṽasu Bhimaṣenaṣa vaṃti garahiṣyama* 'We will complain in front of the *ogu ṽasu* Bhimaṣena'. *vaṃti* is more frequently used of the person against whom an action is taken: 212 *ahuno ede vaḍavi praceya edaṣa vaṃti parihaṣaṃti* 'Now they are making a claim against him about these mares'. Further examples of legal transactions: 551 *eda kuḍi Pǵiṣena Bhaṣḍhaṣa vaṃti parivaṭida* 'Pǵiṣa made an exchange with Bhaṣḍha of this girl (for another)'; 24 *yatha edaṣa dajha Sarpiǵaṣa vaṃti Caule aśpa ṛna nikhalati* 'That Caule has a horse out on loan with his slave Sarpiǵa (or 'wants to take away a horse he has lent to...'). Frequently with the phrase *asaṃna gam*, which seems to mean 'take possession of': 425 *eka bhitiyaṣa vaṃti nasti danagrahana asaṃna na* [*gaṃdavo*] 'There shall be no giving or taking one from another and no assumption of ownership'; cf. 260, 436, etc. *ṣamaho*, *ṣamao* = 'with'; compare Apabhraṃśa *samau* = *samatas*. The omission of the *t* is unusual (§ 19), but might occur in a word like this which was weakly stressed. In that case the *h* must be regarded as simply indicating a hiatus: 326 *tena ṣamao*, 164 *ṣada storena jaṃna ṣamaho* 'With our beasts and our men'. *sardha*, *sadha* (*ṣ°*), the usual word for 'with', may be used with the instrumental, genitive, or simple stem. In the plural it is not found with the instrumental. It may be placed before or after its noun, more often after. Examples: 82 *sardha valaǵena* and *valaǵena sardha* 'with a guard', 425 *kala Cuǵapaṣa sardha*, 516 *Khotaniyana sardha*, 632 *bharya sadha*, 83 *Naṃtaśrṛma ṣadha*, etc.

VERB

§ 93. The personal endings are the same as in Prakrit except that side by side with the *-ṣi* of the 2nd singular there is a form in *-tu* which is used in all the three tenses, e.g. 399 *suṭha na laṃcaǵa karetu yadi kālihari karetu* 'Certainly you do not do rightly if you make a quarrel'; 439 *puna ahuno rayaka gavi picavidetu* 'Now again you have put the royal cattle in his charge'; 114 *puna ahuno bhuya palpi omaǵa viṣajiṣyatu avaśa tanu goṭhade puna vyoṣisatu* '(If) again now you send the tax less (than the proper amount) certainly you shall pay from your own farm'. The forms occurring are:

Present. *aroǵetu* 'you are well', *ichatu*, *karetu*, *choretu* 134, *darsav̆etu* 761, *denatu*, *picavetu* 439, *prasavetu*, *margetu* 399, *viṃñavetu*, *viṣajetu* 247, *ṣayatu* 'you seize, take'.

Past. *achimnidetu* 714, *ukastetu* 320 'went away', *picavidetu* 439, *lihitetu* 157, *viṣarjitetu* 126, 399.

Future. *agachiśatu* 634, *dāsyatu* 507, *aniṣyatu* 517, 554, *oḏiśatu* 'you will let go, allow', *kariṣyatu*, *nivartiṣyatu* 634, *paḏichiṣyatu* 517, *paribujiśatu*, *labhiśatu* 635, *vikriśaṃtu* 633, *vithiṣyatu* 165 'you will keep back', *viṣajiṣyatu* 68, 145, 714, *vyoṣiśatu* 714.

From a survey of the passages in which these forms occur it can be seen that they are always used of the actions of the person to whom the letter is addressed.

The *-tu* is probably taken from the 2nd person of the pronoun.

§ **94.** The middle is not used except occasionally artificially: *rucate* 585 = S. *rocate* or Pali *ruccati*, *vaṃtade* = *vandate* 669.

The passive is quite rare. It is used commonly in *śruyati* 'it is heard' and *vucati* 'it is said'. The only other examples are *pariniyaṃti* 399, *lihyati* 224, *niyati* 364 (possibly optative = *neyati*), *nikhalyati* 743.

§ **95.** Outside *asti* the only remnant of athematic conjugation is *śakoma* 161, 646, which is used as a 1st person singular (= *śaknomi*). *asti* is used as a strong affirmative and *nasti* as a strong negative: 315 *yava asti siyati* 'As much as there is'; 272 *yaṣa asti st(o)ra hac̄h̄ati tade nikhalidavo* 'Of whom there shall be a horse from him it is to be taken'; 714 *yo asti palpi kareti*, *yo nasti dura nikhalidavo* 'He who pays his tax (well and good), he who does not must be removed'; *nasti*: 124 *sac̄h̄i iśa nasti hutaṃti* 'There were no witnesses here', cf. 161, 166, 326, 431.

§ **96. Verbs in** *-ati*. It is not possible to tell whether verbs like *janati* keep the long *ā* or have been fully adapted to the *bhū* class; *janati* may be either *jānāti* or **jānati*.

Of interest is *denati* 'give' for *deti*, which also occurs. The *na* is probably borrowed from the verb with the opposite meaning *gr̥hṇāti*.

sthā makes its present *thiyaṃti* 358, compare Pali *patiṭṭhīyati* 'stands against, resists'.

The old perfect *āha* receives the terminations of the present *ahati* 345 'says'.

bhavati regularly became *hoti*. But more common is *hoati*, which has been readapted to the system.

List of forms: *avajaṣi* = *āpadyase*, *ichati*, *gameṣati* (*gaveṣate*), *garahati*, *codaṃti*, *jivama*, *naṃdati*, *namasyati*, *naśyati*, *naśati*, *nikasati*, *nikhasati* 'goes away', 'is spent', *paḍichati*, *paripruchati*, *parihaṣati* 'claims' (*pari-bhāṣ*), *pr̥chati*, *bhavati*, *marati*, *mr̥yati*, *maṃñati*, *margaṃti*, *rucati*, *lahati* (*labhate*), *likhami*, *lihati*, *vakośaṃti*, *vardhati*, *vahaṃti*, *vijaṃti* (*vidhyanti*), *saṃc̄h̄ivati*, *saṃtiśaṃti* (*sam-diś*), *harami*, *haradi*.

§ **97. Verbs in** *-eti*. As in the rest of the Prakrits *-eti* is no longer a specifically causative suffix, its place having been taken by *-aveti*. The regular terminations are *-emi*, *-eṣi*, *-eti*, *-ema*, *-eṃti*, but fuller forms also occur, presumably in imitation of Sanskrit: Sing. 1. *viṃñaveyaṃmi* 663, *preṣeyami* 269; Sing. 3. *preṣeyati* 25, etc., *saṃpreṣeyati* 288; Plur. 1. *saṃñaveyama* 288, *viṃñaveyama* 259. These forms are identical in spelling (but not in pronunciation; the *e* must have been *ĕ*) with optatives formed from the same verbs and can only be distinguished by the context.

kṛ, as usually in Prakrit, is conjugated in this class: *karemi*, *kareṣi*, *kareṃdi*. Beside *janami*, *janaṣi*, we find *janemi*, *janeṣi*, as occasionally in Prakrit (Pischel, § 510).

ārogya makes a denominative in this class: *aroǵemi*, *-etu*, *-ema*; also *-ama* 721, *-eṃti*; *arogyosmi* 399 is an attempt to Sanskritise it, like *gatosmi*, etc. for *gademi*.

Further examples: *aǵaseṃti* 'they carry off' 304, *oḏemi*, etc. 'let go, allow', *choreṃti*, *taḏeti*, *dhareti*, *nikhalemi* 'I remove, take out', *poḏeti* 'rubs', *preṣemi*, *viṃñaveti*, *viṃñavema* 164, 702, *viyoṣeti* 'pays', *viṣajeti*, *viheḏeti* 'oppresses, worries', *saṃpreṣeti*, *sthaveṃti*.

Cases of confusion between the two classes are rare: *saṃtiśemi* 127 (*saṃtiśaṃti* 703) = *saṃ* + *diś*, *nikhalati* 24, *nikhalamana* 189; *viṃñavatu* 292. Probably the vowel-stroke has been omitted by carelessness.

§ **98**. Practically no imperative forms occur. Outside *hotu* there is only *davyatu*, 3rd passive, 399 *ma iṃci vṛtaǵa uṭa davyatu* 'Let not an old camel be given'. *hotu* (*hutu*) is common and is used for both singular and plural, e.g. 10 [*ṣarvi*] *pruchitae hotu* 'Let all be asked' and 244 *avi Pǵeca uṭa* 3 *nita avaśa jheniǵa hutu* 'And P. brought 3 camels, by all means let them be under your care'.

The reason for the practical loss of the imperative is that its place has been taken by passive constructions with gerundives in *-avya*.

§ **99**. Future. *seṭ* forms are practically universal. The only *aniṭ* forms are *śac̄h̄yami*, *śac̄h̄e* 311, *stasyati* and *dasyati* (also *deyiśati*).

The *a* of *iṣyati* is sometimes marked long, so that possibly it had been lengthened on the analogy of the optative: *asiṣyāti* 621 (*ās*-), *gachiṣyāti* 223, *dasyāti* 677.

Beside *-ami* of the 1st singular there are a few forms in *-a*: *gameṣiśa* 372, *parimargiṣya* 368. They are not = Śaur. *-issam* but mistakes; cf. *bhaviṣya* 109 = *bhaviṣyati*.

The ending *-iṣyati* (*iśati*) is usually added to the present base, but we find *gamiśati* beside *gachiṣyati*. There is no distinction as a rule between verbs in *-eti* and verbs in *-ati*, e.g. *anaviṣyati* from *anaveti* 'commands', *oḍisyati* from *oḍeti* 'lets go'. At the same time forms corresponding to *-ayiṣyati* are found. These are no doubt artificial: *preṣeyiṣyasi* 399 (*preṣiśama* 288), *śodheyiṣyati* 'will pay' 635, *śodheṣyaṃdi* 272.

nī and *dā* make their future in various ways: *aniśati* 159, *aniṣyami* 696, *aneṣyati* 125, 399, *niyiṣyati* 362, *dasyati*, *deyiṣyaṃti* 182, *dheśati* 348.

hac̄hati, = Pkt. *acchaï*, is generally used as an optative, more rarely as a future: 352 *nic̄e hac̄hati* 'There will be a decision'.

Further examples: *ichiṣyati*, *kariṣyami*, *-atu*, *-ati*, *-ama*, *-aṃti*; *gachiśati*, *garahiṣyama*, *giṃniṣyasi*, *chiṃniṣyati*, *choriṣyaṣi*, *janiṣyami*, *thaviṣyati*, *nikaliṣyati*, *-iśati*, *nivartiṣyati*, *paḍichiśama*, *patiṣyati*, *paribujiśasi*, *-tu* (*pari-budh*), *pariśamiśati* 130 (= ?), *picaviṣyati*, *pranaśiṣyati*, *pruchiṣyati*, *preṣiśama*, *bhaviṣyati*, *mariṣyati*, *rac̄hiṣyati*, *labhiṣyati*, *lihiṣyaṃti*, *leṣiśaṃti* (*śleṣaya*- ? cf. § 49), *vaviśati* 'will sow', *viṣajiśasi*, *vyoṣiśati*, *saṃghaliṣyati* 'will collect', *sarajiśaṃti* 'will agree'.

§ 100. The optative has always the primary endings: (*-eyami*), *-eyaṣi*, *-eyati*, (*-eyama*), (*-eyatha*), *-eyaṃti*. The long *ā* is sometimes written: *gṛheyāti* 320, *coteyāti* 582, *bhaveyāti* 678, *deyāṃti* 437. From the last example it appears that contrary to the usual Prakrits *-ā-* can occur before the group *-nt-* in this dialect.

praviśayati 489 is a mistake for *praviśeyati*. *hac̄hati* is to be classified as an optative. In the majority of cases it occurs in subordinate clauses with *yadi*, etc., where the optative is the rule. Parallel with *syati*: 160 *yo atra hasta lekha udaǵa bhiśaṣa prace syati athava levistarena anati lekha hac̄hati* 'What hand-letter may be there concerning water and seed or what letter of instruction with a detailed account there may be'.

Other examples: *anuvarteyati*, *avarajeyaṃti* (*aparādh-*), *ichiyati* (cf. § 1), *uthaveyati*, *-yaṃti*, *kareyaṣi*, *-ati*, *coteyati*, *taḏeyati*, *deyati* and *deyeyaṃti* 345 (cf. *dey-iṣyati*), *prabhaveyati* 437, *praśameyaṣi* 373, *bhaveyati*, *maṃtreyati* 100, *viṣarjeyasi* 696, *veteyati*, *sajeyati*.

As in the future no difference is made between verbs in *-eti* and verbs in *-ati*.

§ 101. Present participles are rare. There is a tendency to generalise the middle forms in *-māna*, as in later Ardha-Magadhi. Examples are *achiṃnamana* 'encroaching on', *gachamana*, (*kathamana* 514), *karemana*, *nikhalamana*. *vartamana* is used as a kind of noun in the phrase *yahi Khema Khotaṃnade vartamana siyati* 'If there be any news (events, happenings) from Khema and Khotan', =*pravṛti*, *paḏivati*. The participle is used to make a circumscribed tense with *siyati*: 235 *pruchidavo bhudartha ṣe miṣi edaṣa tanuv́aǵa siyati anahetu Suǵika achiṃnamana siyati* 'You must enquire whether this *miṣi*-(land) really belongs to him (and whether) Suǵika is encroaching on it, (taking if off him) on account of a debt (or without cause *ana*=*a*, *an-* ?)'; cf. *nikhalamana siyaṃti* 189.

The active participle is only used in certain stereotyped phrases and in words that have become adjectives, e.g. *jivaṃdaǵa*, Fem. *jivaṃti*, 'alive'; *jayaṃta*, *jeyaṃta* 'victorious' (a title of kings). Used participially are *saṃta*: 482 *purva dhaṃ̄a vibhaktaǵa yena samula vṛc̄ha chiṃnaṃti tatra saṃta vṛc̄ha varidavo aśpa aviṃdama* 'The former law was that when they cut down trees with the roots—the trees which are there (still)—they must be stopped, a horse is the recompense', and *janaṃda*, frequently in the phrase *janaṃda bhavidavo* 'you must know'.

§ 102. Indeclinable Participle. The regular dialectical form is in *-ti*. It is not frequent: *śruniti*: 341 *ede śruniti Piṣaliyade iśa viṣajidavo* 'These, having heard them are to be sent here from Piṣali'. *apruchiti*: 39 *edeṣa dajhi Cimikae nama, edeṣa ana apruchiti dhitu Kapǵeyaṣa dajhana uniti dita* 'They have a slave-woman called Cimikae; without asking their permission (*ājñām* *apṛṣṭvā*) she gave her daughter to slaves of Kapǵe as a foster-child' (cf. 492). *vajiti*: 376 *eda lekha vajiti cavala kara* (...) *kartavo* 'Having read this letter, immediately...is to be done' (cf. 152, 725). *palayiti*: 491 *adehi palayiti agada* 'Having fled from there he came' (cf. 540).

The form was characteristic of the North-West. It is found in the Kharoṣṭhi Dh.p.: *upajiti* C^vo 44, *pramayiti* A² 3, *parivajeti* A² 8. Also in the two North-Western versions of Aśoka.

It is presumably out of Vedic *-tvī*, although this is not the regular treatment of the group *-tv-* (§ 43).

Apart from literary pieces (*kṛtva* 647, *saṃpreṣitva* 204, *Khatva*, *pitva* 565, which is influenced by the Literary Language) the only forms in *-tva* that occur are *śrutva* 399, *bhudva* 49, where the reading and interpretation of the whole text are difficult, and *daditva*, which occurs twice in the same phrase: 345 and 437 *yo ca koci...aṃñatha icheyaṃti karaṃnae...muha codana apramana ca bhaveyati taṃḍa praptaṃ ca deyaṃti catuvarṣaǵa aśpa paṃcaśa prahara sarva eta daṃḍa daditva avaśe ca eda yatha uvari lihitaǵa*. Here an indeclinable participle hardly seems to suit the context and we have perhaps an example of the Vedic gerundives in *-tva* (cf. Macdonell, *Vedic Grammar*, § 581). 'Whoever shall want to make it otherwise, attacking (the agreement) again shall have no authority, and they shall give the ensuing penalty (namely) a 4-year-old horse and fifty blows, *all this penalty is to be given*, and certainly (the agreement) shall remain as written above.'

With *-ya* are formed *uvadae* = *upādaya* 'starting from', and *utiśa*, *udiśa*, which presumably = *uddiśya*, although its usage does not tally with Sanskrit and Prakrit. It is used not with an accusative (*tam uddiśya* 'with reference to him'), but by itself at the beginning of clauses, apparently meaning 'with reference to this matter', e.g. 159 *adehi tusya mahahvana paride na kiṃci śrunaṃmi udiśa ahuno śadavida Kolṕiṣaṣa hastaṃmi vacari* 2 *prahidemi* 'From there I hear nothing from you and the high officials, with reference to that (fact), (considering that), I have sent 2 *vacari* ('jars'?) in the hand of the *śadavida* Kolṕiṣa', etc. etc.

vacitu: 399 *yahi eṣa stovaṃna atra eśati lekha vacitu, tomi stovaṃnaṣa haste uṭa iśa prahadavya.* It may be explained either as a passive *vacitu* = *vācyatu* for *vācyatām* (cf. *davyatu* below and § 98) or as an indeclinable participle like the Ardha-Māgadhi forms in *-ittu* (*chindittu*, *jinittu*, etc.). 'Having read the letter, thereupon the camel is to be sent here in the hand of Stovaṃna.'

§ **103. Infinitive.** The infinitive is regularly in *-aṃnae* = *-anāya* (*gamanāya*, etc.). The form is also found in the North-West versions of Aśoka, e.g. *kṣamanaye* S. 13 (where the other versions have *-tave*). The forms are always made from the present tense, not from the root as in the corresponding Sanskrit verbal nouns, e.g. *giṃnaṃnae* 'to take', not **grahaṃnae*. Examples: *ayaṃnae* 'to come' (*ayida* 'came'), *karaṃnae*, *-aya*, *-aye*, *asadhaṃnae* 'to settle' (*sad*), *ukasaṃnae* 'to depart', *kaṁavaṃnae; kiṣaṃnae*, *kriṣaṃnae*, *kriṣivaṃnae*, all meaning to 'plough', *khayaṃnae* 'to eat', *gachaṃnae*, *garahaṃnae*, *chiṃnaṃnae*, *taḋaṃnae*, *thavaṃnae*, *deśaṃnae*, *dhamanaye* 'to tame, break', *dharaṃnae*, *nivartanae*, *nihaṃñaṃnae* 331 = *nihananae* 586, *paribhuchanae* = *paribhuñj-*, *paśaṃnae* 'to inspect', *picavaṃnae*, *prichaṃnaye*, *preṣaṃnae*, *baṃnanae* (*bandh-*), *pivaṃnaṃnae* 586 (*pi-bandh-*), *maraṃnaya* 'to kill' (*mareti*) 420, *amaraṃnae* 'not to die' 703, *marganae* 'to seek', *raċhaṃnae*, *vikrinaṃnae*; beside *vikrinaṃnae* occurs *vikranaṃnae* 586–7, 590, 592, *vyoṣaṃnae* 'to pay', *viṣarjanae*, *śrunaṃnae*, *ṣ́gabhaṃnae* (= *skabh-*, cf. § 49), *sajavanae* 'to make ready', *śavaṃnae* 'to swear', *aniyanaye* 'to bring', *thiyaṃnae* 'to stay', *deyaṃnae*.

Forms in *-tu* = *-tum* are very rare: *kartu*, *aǵantu* 646 and probably *viṣajitu*, 262 *dviti vara imade anati kilamudra atra gachati adehi hastagada viṣajitu na iṃci iśa agachati* 'A second time a wedge-seal of command goes from here (with orders) to send him here under arrest, he does not come'. Compare *viṣarjanae* in 4 *anadi lekha gada adehi uṭa* 4 *Calmadanaṃmi viṣarjanae*.

The infinitive is used as a verbal noun in 376 *sajavanae prace* 'about getting ready'.

§ **104. Causative.** The causative is in *-aveti* = *āpayati* as in the rest of the Prakrits. The long *ā* is written in *śavāvitavya* 358 'to be caused to swear'. Examples of causative verbs are *aǵasavida* (*ā*+√*k̄as* 'to carry off'), *anaviṣyati*, *anavidavo* 'command', *asavidavo* (from √*ās*, 'to settle somebody'), *uthaveti*, *uthaveyati*, *thavita*, *darśav́eti*, *davidaǵena* 'with a gift' 749, *nivartavidavo* 'cause to turn back', *baṃdhavita*, *varjavidavo*, *viṃñaveti*, *vithav́esi*, *vithavida*='keep back', *vyavasthavidaǵa*, *sajavaṃnae*, *sthaveṃti*.

paric̄h̄inavitaṃti 'They caused to perish, used up' 272 is formed from the past participle passive.

From *karma* a denominative is made by this suffix *kam̄aveti*, meaning 'to cause to work'. It also means simply 'to work' in 107 (cf. Pischel, § 559).

PAST TENSE

§ 105. As in the modern Indo-Aryan languages and in Persian, a new past tense is formed by attaching the personal endings to the past participle passive. The paradigm from *dā* 'to give' would be:

ditemi	*ditama*
diteṣi	*ditetha*
dita	*ditaṃti*

The 3rd singular has no termination, the simple stem being used both for the masculine and the feminine 'he or she gave'. The forms in *-ta* are practically never used as participles, their place being taken by the extended forms in *-aǵa*, in the feminine by *-i* (cf. § 74). The development must have started from the intransitive verbs, *gataḥ*+*asmi* would give *gademi* in this dialect (§ 12). In the plural *gatāḥ*+*sma* would give *gadama*. These are the forms that actually occur, and this difference of vowel in the singular and plural shows that we are actually dealing with the nominative singular and plural of the participle and the verb 'to be' and not simply the addition of personal endings borrowed from the present. This is the only place where a trace of the old nominative singular in *-e* is preserved. The 3rd singular *dita* represents the neuter singular, to judge from the form *-u* in the Khotan dialect (661), where *-u*<*am*. Cf. *B.S.O.S.* VIII, 432.

The result of this (purely phonetic) development into *-emi*, *-eṣi* was that these terminations were felt as being the same as those of the present in *-emi*, *-eṣi*, and the transition into a purely verbal form was facilitated. In the 2nd plural *-etha* is due entirely to analogy instead of *-astha*. Forms in *-atha* probably never occur. The only example is *kiṭatha* 213 which is doubtful. The 3rd plural is always in *-aṃti* for *-āḥ saṃti*. Curiously enough forms in *-eṃti* never occur. There seems to be a rule that the anusvāra is never written when *d* takes the place of *t* in the past participle, e.g. *aitaṃti* and *ayidati* 'they came'. This is more likely to be a habit of writing than really phonetic, especially since we know that the people did not distinguish between *t* and *d* (§ 19). Compare *ida ca* 573 for the usual *itaṃ ca* (§ 82).

§ 106. The writers seem to have been aware of the origin of these forms because in the 1st person singular we find *-osmi* occasionally instead of *-emi*. It is of course Sanskritising. It is usually found in intransitive forms: *ṣadosmi* 'I am pleased' beside *ṣademi*, *prihitosmi* 'I am pleased' 140, *gatosmi* 146. In a transitive verb only *prahidasmi*=*prahidemi* 'I sent' 316. The same thing happens to the denominative *aroǵemi* 'I am well', for which *arogyosmi* appears in 317.

§ 107. As in the future (§ 99) the past participle and its derivatives are as a rule formed from the present with the help of the vowel *i*. But a greater number of original forms are preserved. Often both forms occur. Examples: *anatemi* 'I commanded' (also *anavideṣi*), *abomata*=*abhyavamata*, in the phrase *abomata kar-* 'disregard, disobey', *ukasta* 'went away' (also *ukasita*), *upaṃna*=*utpanna*, *kiṭa*, *kiḍa*, *kṛta* and *kata* from *kṛ*; *giṭa* also *giṃnita* 'took' (also *grahita*), *dṛṭha* (*tṛṭha*) 'saw', *thida*, *naṭha* 'perished', *nikasta* 'went away', *nikraṃta*, *nigada*, *parič̄hiṃna*, *parimugta* 702 (written for *parimukta* which is Sanskrit; the real dialectical form occurs in *mutaṃti* 'they released' 63), *praviṭha*, *prahita* 'sent' (**pradhita* rather than *prahita* from *prahinoti* on account of *prahatavya*=*pradhātavya*; perhaps the two verbs have been confused), *prasṛtaṃti*, *bhuta*, *mṛta*, *ladha*, *vakuṭha* (also *vakośida*), *vikrida* 'sold' (also *vikrinita*), *vinaṭha*, *viśvasta*, *vyochiṃna* 506 (usually *vyochiṃnita*), *śruta*, *śata* 'swore', *śiṭha* (a noun = 'punishment'), *śudha*, *samṛdhae* 'flourishing', *stita*, *huda*.

§ 108. Other forms are: Singular. 1. *agatemi*, *ayidemi* 'I came', *oḍidemi* 'I let go', *giṃnidemi*, *coridemi*, *jalpidemi*, *tidemi* 'I gave', *triṭhemi* 'I saw', *nitemi* and *niyidemi* 'I led', *parivaṭidemi* 'I exchanged', *picavitemi*, *preṣidemi*, *vavidemi*, *vikridemi*, *vithitemi* 'I kept back', *vyoṣidemi* 'I payed', *viṣarjidemi*, *śrutemi*, *ṣayidemi* 'I got hold of', *hudemi*.

The bahuvrihi *ñadartha* = *jñātārtha* is treated like a participle and we get *ñadarthemi* 'I have learned'.

2. *anavideṣi*, *kiḍeṣi*, *krideṣi* 'you bought', *gadeṣi*, *gameṣideṣi*, *giḍeṣi*, *giṃnideṣi*, *thaviteṣi*, *diteṣi*, *nikhaliteṣi*, *parimargideṣi*, *picavideṣi*, *prahiteṣi*, *baṃnideṣi* (*bandh*-), *vajideṣi* 'you read', *vikrideṣi*, *vithavideṣi*, *vibhaśiteṣi*, *viṣajideṣi*, *sajavideṣi*, *saṃtiṭheṣi*, *hudeṣi*. For the forms in -*tu*, cf. § 93.

3. *ayita* 'came', *akasita* 'carried off', *anita*, *anavida*, *ichita*, *ukasita*, *uthavida*, *oḍita*, *garahita*, *giṭa* and *giṃnita*, *govita* 225 (? *corita*), *ciṃtita* 'reckoned', *ciṃnita* 'cut' (*chiṃnita*), *jalpita*, *jhorida* (= *chorita*), *taḍita*, *thavita*, *darṣita* 'packed, loaded', *dahita* 666 (= *dagdha*), *naśida* 'disappeared', *nikhalita*, *niyida* 'took', *nivartita* 'returned', *paḍichida*, *pratilikhida*, *payita* 763 (from *pāyayati*), *parakramita*, *parivaṭida*, *palayita*, *poṣida*, *praǵaśida*, *praṣavita* 'let have, granted', *praharita* 'struck', *preṣida*, *biṃnita* and *bhinita*, *maṃtrita* 'said', *marita* 'killed', *mavita*, *likhida*, *lihita*, *leṣita*, *vakośida*, *varita* 'stopped', *vardhida*, *vikarida* 419 (passive), *vikrinita*, *vijita* 'wounded', *viṃñavita*, *vitita* 'known' (passive), *vyoṣita*, *viṣajita* and *viṣarjita*, *śavita* 'swore', *ṣayita* and *ṣeyita* 'seized', *saṃghalita* 'collected', *sargita* 49 'flooded'.

§ 109. Plural. 1. *ayitama*, *kiḍama*, *kridama*, *giḍama*, *chiṃnidama*, *tidama*, *triṭhama*, *nikhalidama*, *nitama*, *nivartavidama*, *paṭichidama*, *pariċhitama*, *prahitama*, and *prehidama* 'we sent', *leṣitama*, *varidama*, *vibhaktama*, and *vibhaśitama* 'we gave a (legal) decision', *viṣajidama*, *vyochiṃnidama*, *śakidama* 'we were able', *śrutama*, *hutama*.

There are probably no 1st plurals in -*ema*. Those forms which occur seem to be mistakes for the 1st singular in -*emi*. In 164 *gatema, śrutema, apruchitema, aroǵema*, are mistakes for *gatemi*, etc., as also *ṣatosma* for *ṣatosmi*. So probably *prahidema* 77 and *śrudema* 399.

2. *achiṃnidetha, asidetha, ichidetha, picavidetha.*

3. *aitaṃti, aǵajhitaṃti* 'carried off', *agataṃti, ichitaṃti, ukastaṃti* 'departed', *uthitaṃti, oḍ̄itaṃti, kataṃti, kritaṃti* and *kiḍ̄amti, khaṃnitaṃti, khayitaṃti* 'ate', *gataṃti, garahitaṃti, giḍ̄aṃti* and *giṃnitaṃti, chiṃnitaṃti, taḍ̄itaṃti* and *daḍ̄itaṃti, darṣitaṃti* 'they packed', *nikastaṃti, nikhalitaṃti, nikhastaṃti, nitaṃti, nivartavitaṃti, nihaṃñitaṃti, paḍ̄ichitaṃti, paraṣitaṃti* 'plundered, overpowered, took possession of', *paric̄h̄inavitaṃti, parivaṭitaṃti* 'exchanged', *palayitaṃti, picavitaṃti, prasṛtaṃti* 383, *prahitaṃti, pruchitaṃti, biṃnitaṃti* (*bhind-*), *maṃtritaṃti* 'said', *maritaṃti* 'killed', *mavitaṃti, mutaṃti* (*mukta-*) 63, *mṛtaṃti, varitaṃti, vavitaṃti, viṃñavitaṃti, viṣajitaṃti, viheḍ̄itaṃti* 'oppressed, worried', *vutaṃti, vyochiṃnitaṃti, śataṃti* 'swore', *śrutaṃti, ṣayitaṃti* 'took hold of', *sarajitaṃti* 'agreed', *stitaṃti, hutaṃti.*

With *d* for *t*: *gadaṃti, paḍ̄icidaṃti* 589 and *paḍ̄ichidaṃti, sarajidaṃti* 586.

As stated above (§ 105) the anusvāra is not usually written when *d* takes the place of *t*. Examples: *ayidati, uthavidati, uthidati, garahidati, chiṃnidati, nidati, niyidati, parajhidati* (beside *paraṣitaṃti*), *vikridati. paḍ̄iciṃtati* 598 = *paḍ̄ichitaṃti.*

§ 110. Passive forms in *-aka.*

Forms in *-aǵa* and *-ae* are used indiscriminately. Compare for instance 581 *eṣa hasta lekha likhidaǵa*, with 715 *eṣa pravaṃnaǵa hasta lekha likhidae.*

Forms in *-ae* and *-aya* are: *kiḍ̄ae, kiḍ̄aya* 593, *gadaya* 133, *coridae, asitae, giṭae, ciṃtidae* 'reckoned', *ditae, didaya, didae,* 'given', *dharitae, naṭhae, nikasitae, nidae, nidaya, patitaya* 414, *paraṣitae -aya* 'plundered, carried off', *palayitae, praviṭhae* 333, *praṣavidae* 'granted', *pruchitae, bhiṃnitaya* 633, *likhitae* and *lihitae -taya, varidae, vithitae, viṣajidae, saṃghalidae, sarajidae, hudae.*

On the ending *-ae*, see further, §§ 8, 74.

§ 111. Forms in *-aǵa* are: *avyochiṃnidaǵa* 471, *asitaǵa, kritaǵa* (*kṛ* and *krī*), *kriṣitaǵa, khayidaǵa* 'eaten', *khoridaǵa* 'shaved', *gachidaǵa* 388, *ciṃditaǵa* 'reckoned, assessed', *coritaǵa -daǵa, taḍitaǵa, tidaǵa, thavidaǵa, thidaǵa, ditaǵa, naṭhaǵa, nikastaǵa, nikhastaǵa, paḍichitaǵa, palayidaǵa, picavitaǵa, praṣavitaǵa -daǵa, prahitaǵa, baṃdhitaǵa* 660 and *baṃnidaǵa, biṃnidaǵa* 'broken', *muṃtritaǵa* 'sealed' 247, *mṛtaǵa* and *mṛdaǵa* 'dead', *yajitaǵa* 'borrowed' (cf. S. *yācitaka*), *ladhaǵa, likhitaǵa, vavitaǵa* 'sown', *vikaritaǵa, vititaǵa* 343, 544 'distributed', *vithitaǵa* 'kept back, withheld', *vinaṭhaǵa, vibhaktaǵa* and *vibhaśitaǵa* 'decided' (of a lawsuit), *viṣajidaǵa, vismaridaǵa, vyochiṃnidaǵa, vyavasthavidaǵa, saṃgalitaǵa, stitaǵa, hodaǵa.*

§ 112. A number of these forms are used substantivally, and as such may occur in the oblique cases. *coridaǵa prace* might mean 'about a theft' or 'about a thing stolen', but e.g. *taḍitaǵade pača* 'after a beating' is definitely an abstract noun. This is the only example of the ablative. Instrumental forms are quite common: *taḍitaǵena* 'through a beating', *darṣidaǵena*, 40 *yadi ...darṣidaǵena mariṣyati* 'If it shall die through being (over) loaded', *davida(ǵena)* 659, *vijitaǵena*, 190 *tena vijitaǵena mṛyati* 'dies owing to that wound', *vibhaśitaǵena* 'decision', *vyochiṃnidaǵena* 297, 339, *yatha purva vyochiṃnidaǵena* 'as formerly decided' (cf. § 90), *śrutaǵena* 399.

viṣajidaǵena in 732, *maṃnuśa viṣajidaǵena prace* is simply the instrumental written for nominative accusative (§§ 117, 118).

§ 113. Feminines in *-i*. The proper feminine form in the passive is in *-i*. In the active no distinction is made between masculine and feminine. Compare for instance in 39 *edeṣa dajhi Cimikae nama edeṣa ana aprochiti dhitu Kapǵeyaṣa dajhana uniti dita* 'A slave-woman of their's called Cimikae without asking their permission gave her daughter as a foster-child to the slaves of Kapǵe' with *pruchidavo bhutartha edeṣa dajhi Kapǵeyaṣa dajhana uniti diti edeṣa ana aprochiti siyati* '(You) must enquire whether really their slave (i.e. the child) was given to slaves of Kapǵe without asking their permission'; cf. further 279 *Yaśe aśanaṃmi kilmeci kala Acuñiyaṣa śvasu Cakuśaae nama Ajiyama aśanaṃmi kilmeci Pǵenasa bharya aniti huati* 'Cakuśaae sister of *kala*, Acuñi of the district of Yaśe *aśana*, was taken to wife by Pǵena of the district of Ajiyama *aśana*'; 4 *pruchidavo bhutartha kriti* *siyati* 'whether she has really been bought', etc. Compare the Apabhraṃśa forms like *avainnī, palittī, diṭṭhī, samjuttī, uppannī,* etc. (*Bhavisatta-kaha*) and § 74.

These forms have to be distinguished by the context from indeclinable participles in *-ti* (§ 102).

The distinction between masculine and feminine is occasionally neglected. We find feminine forms in *-ae* at 45 *edaṣa dajhi Cimikae dhitu Rutrayaṣa uniti giṭae* 'The daughter of their slave-woman Cimikae was taken as a foster-child by Rutraya' (cf. 434). On the other hand *-i* instead of *-ae* in 473 *yatha edaṣa śramana Saṃgaśira masuśaṭa bhumac̄ĥetra baṃdhova thaviti siyati* 'That the monk Saṃgaśira mortgaged a vineyard and a field of (ploughing) land with him'; 327 *muli huti.*

§ 114. There is one exception to the rule that the forms in *-taǵa, -tae* are passive, and that is the compound past tense *ditae siyati* 'he should have given' and *ditae huati* 'he has given'. Examples: 439 *bhutartha eṣa eti draṃga dharidae siyati* 'Whether he has really held so many offices'; 33 *yadi bhudartha eva hac̄ĥati, eṣa Suǵi giḋaǵa hac̄ĥati* 'If it is really so, (if) this Suǵi has taken (them)'; 345 *bhudartha śramamna Anaṃdasena Cuǵopaṣa paride aṃna avamicae giḋaka hoati* 'Really the monk A. has taken corn on loan from Cuǵopa'; 545 *yati bhudartha cojhbo Kaṃci edaṣa aśpa nidae siyati* 'If really the *cojhbo* Kaṃci has taken his horse'.

The auxiliary verb may occasionally be omitted, e.g. 144 *yati Soǵanaṣa taḋitaǵade pac̄a Kacana na karya kiṭae* (for *kiṭae siyati*) 'If Kacana did no work after being beaten by Soǵana'.

§ 115. In intransitive verbs there naturally cannot be the usual difference between active and passive. Here the difference is that the forms in *-taǵa* have a participial, those in *-ta* a verbal sense, e.g. *mṛtaǵa* 'dead', *mṛta* 'died', *gataǵa* 'gone', *gata* 'went', etc. As usual the form in *-taǵa, -tae* is used in making the compound past tenses, e.g. 637 *yaṃ kala kāla kirteya Khotanaṃmi dutiyaya gataǵa āsi* 'When *kāla kirteya* was gone on a mission to Khotan'; 19 *bhudartha Tamaṣyanae bhaǵena Yitasenaṣa khulona vaṃti thidaǵa siyati* '(Whether) really T. stays with the herds of Y. in her turn'; 370 *asitae huaṃti.*

§ 116. Gerundive. The gerundive is the most common of the verbal forms. It is practically always made with the help of the vowel *i* from the present: *giṃnidavo*, *krinidavo*, etc. Original forms preserved are *martavya*, *gaṃdavo* (never **gachid-*), *vikridavo* (beside *vikrinidavo*), *kartavo*, *nidavo* (beside *niyid-*), *prahatavya*=*pradhātavya*. There is no difference as a rule between verbs in *-eti* and verbs in *-ati*: *vyoṣidavo*, *viṣajidavo*, etc., but we find *uthavedavo* 575 besides *uthavidavo*.

Curious forms made from the past participle are *nikhastidavo* 612, *śiṭhidavya* 'to be punished' 482, *ṣaṃdedavo* 721 (from *ṣada* 'pleased').

Forms in *-vo* and *-vya* alternate indiscriminately (§ 53), as do *t* and *d* (§ 19). Thus there are four spellings: *-tavya*, *-tavo*, *-davya*, *-davo*.

Of the three forms *-avya*, *-ya* and *-anīya*, *-avya* is the only one that remains as a living suffix. *-ya* is found in *kica* and *uneya* 'foster-child'; *-aniya* in *karaṃniya* in the phrase *yatha kama karaniya* 'to be done what one likes with'.

SYNTAX

§ 117. The instrumental tends to be confused with the nominative accusative. This process is closely associated with the development of the past participle into an active past tense (cf. § 105). *tena dita*, 'given by him', began to be felt as active 'he gave', and finally the nominative was used as well, *ṣe dita*. This is exactly the same state of affairs as occurs in many of the modern languages. Compare for instance Grierson, *Torwali*, § 21. The subject of tense formed from the past participle is put into the 'agentive' case, which corresponds to the old instrumental. At the same time, as in these documents, the nominative is more frequently used. Examples of the instrumental=the modern agentive are 47 *edeṣa goṭha gṛhavaṣa Apǵeyena udaǵena sargita* 'Apǵeya flooded their farm and habitation with water'; 506 *Tatiǵena Śaṃcaaṣa dajha picavida kam̄avaṃnae* 'Tatiǵa sent a slave to Śaṃca to work'; 574 *kori Muldeyaṣa dajhana paride Ramṣotsena bhuma krida* 'Ramṣotsa (*-ṅka*) bought some land from the slaves of *kori* Muldeya', etc.

Of course these constructions correspond exactly to the ordinary Sanskrit passive constructions, but there is no doubt that they are translated as active because (1) exactly the same state of affairs is found in modern languages such as Torwali, where the construction with the agentive = instrumental is translated as active, (2) in the vast majority of cases the past participle in *-ta* is construed with the nominative where it must be active, (3) the instrumental is used as the subject of the present tense (§ 118), (4) in practically all definitely passive constructions, i.e. with participles in *-taǵa* and with gerundives, the genitive, not the instrumental, is used to express the agent.

§ 118. As a result of the development sketched above, the instrumental is confused with the nominative in all positions, and since the nominative is not distinguished from the accusative also with the accusative.

As nominative: 494 *yatha Paǵinena aloṭa viloṭade purva Moc̄hapriyaṣa vaṃti suvarna ṛna nikhaleti* 'That Paǵina has some gold lent to Mokṣapriya before the plundering (of the realm)'; 622 *Maharayaputra kala Puṃñabalena lihati* 'The king's son *kala* P. writes'; 106 *śigra Suǵitena tui uṭena iśa viṣajidavo* 'Quickly Suǵita and two camels are to be sent here'; 283 *tade ahaṃ maharayena sarva karya krida ñadartha hodemi* 'From that I the king have learnt all about what has been done'; 399 *Cinaṣenena mṛtaǵa* 'C. is dead'.

More rare is *-ena* in the 3rd singular of the preterite: 431 *suveṣṭha Mareǵa paḍichitena* for *°ta* 'The *suveṣṭha* Mareǵa received'.

As accusative: 69 *adehi śramana Caǵuṣenena viṣarjideṣi* 'You sent the monk C. from there'; 86 *adehi Casminena viṣarjideṣi asmaǵena caraǵena* 'You sent C. our spy from there'; 106 *avi ca iśa maṃnuśa Saṃghadham̄ena Ṣaǵanaṣa vaṃti vikrideṣi* 'And here you sold a man S. to Ṣagana'; 272 *cojhbo Soṃjakena aṭh̄ovae ajhate jaṃna suṭha abomata* (= *abhyavamata*) *kareṃdi* 'The serviceable free-born people very much disregard the *cojhbo* S.'; 540 *Kacana uthita Sunaṃtena taḍ̄ita* 'Kacana arose and beat Sunaṃta'.

It is used as the stem-form in quasi-compounds like *ogu Kuṣanaṣenena cojhbo Lṗipeyaṣa ca* 198.

Finally, the confusion goes so far that the genitive termination is added on to the instrumental in 345 *Bugoṣenaṣa prace* 'About *Bu(dha)goṣa*'.

The instrumental plural is rare, but the same confusion is found to occur: 297 *mahatvehi vyochiṃnitaṃti* 'The magistrates made a decision'.

§ 119. The genitive is almost exclusively used for expressing the agent with passives, i.e. the participle in -*taǵa* and gerundives. The instrumental occurs very rarely, e.g. 436 *yatha paṃthami gachamana Maṣḍhigeyena baṃnidaǵa matritaṃti* 'They said that while travelling on the road they were bound by Maṣḍhige'. But this is definitely the exception. Examples of the usual genitive construction are: 45 *Cimikae dhitu Rutrayaṣa uniti giṭae* 'The daughter of Cimikae was taken as foster-child by Rutraya'; 24 *yo edeṣa devaputraṣa padamulade bhumac̄hitra ladhaǵa* 'The land which was received by them from the feet of his majesty'; 157 *se pirovaṃmi goyaṃña na pad̄ichitaǵa devataṣa* 'That sacrifice of a cow at the bridge was not accepted by the deity'; 735 *palayaṃnaga Suǵitaṣa ladhaǵa huati* 'An exile was received by Suǵita'. With gerundive: 83 *Campeyaṣa isa gaṃdavo, tahi Lṗivrasmaṣa pid̄ita osuka avajidavo* 'By you Lṗivrasma zeal is to be shown'; 106 *yo etaṣa maṃnuśaṣa pad̄ivati siyati tusya atra saṃghaṭidavo* 'What information there is about this man is to be put together by you there'; 345 *taha sarva śramana Anaṃdaṣenaṣa viyoṣidavo huda* 'And so everything was to be paid by the monk Anandasena', etc. etc.

§ 120. Beside the genitive there are occasional examples of the nominative used with gerundives, so that the gerundive becomes a kind of active like the past participle passive. The tendency however is not much developed. Examples are: 58 *yo taya arthadana giṭaṃti ṣadha tanu Puǵo Lṗipeya giṃnidavya* 'What property they took from her, along with herself, is to be taken by Puǵo and Lṗipe'; 119 *Supiye Calmataneṣu...agaṃṭavya* 'The Supis are going to come to the Calmatanas'; 322 *eṣa lihitaǵa Khotaṃni maṃnuśa prace Kilṗaǵiya anatha dharidavo* 'This document about a man of Khotan must be carefully preserved by Kilpaǵiya'; 528 *putra dhidara...sama bhaǵa giṃnidavo* 'The sons and daughters must receive an equal portion of the inheritance'; 671 *te valaǵa trina saṃvatsari pac̄avara giṃnidavo* 'Those guards must receive provisions of three years'; 722 *ahuno Svarnabala atra gaṃdavya huati* 'Now Svarnabala is going to come there' (cf. 634).

§ 121. The genitive sometimes appears instead of the nominative accusative: 120 *rajadharaǵa mahatvana Ṣitǵapotǵeyade varidama nivartavidama* 'We stopped and turned back the magistrates in charge of the administration of the kingdom from Ṣitǵapotǵe'; 370 *asmahu goṭhaṃmi Kroraiṃci maṃnuśana asitae huaṃti* 'Men of Krorayina dwelt on our farm'; 655 *teṣa uthavidati* 'They arose'; 450 *rotaṃna avi curam̄aṣa iśa anidavo* '*rotana* and *curam̄a* (two agricultural products) must be brought here'; 422 *Argiceyaṣa bhratarana Kuvayaṣa vaṃte bhuma vikridati* 'The brothers of Argiceya sold land to Kuvaya'; 187 *avi eṣa kaniṭha Cimola Kuvayaṣa taḍita* 'Also this younger (brother) Cimola beat Kuvaya'; 152 *ahuno atra rayaka uṭiyana viṣajidemi* 'Now I have sent royal camels there'. In some of these instances we are certainly dealing with a partitive genitive, e.g. *uṭiyana* 'some camels', *curam̄asa* 'a quantity of *curam̄a*'. In other cases the genitive is erroneously used, e.g. 187 *Kuvayaṣa.*

§ 122. In lists of names followed by *ca* the genitive always appears instead of the nominative, so that for instance *cojhbo Yitaka toṃga Vuktoṣa ca* may mean either 'The *cojhbo* Y. and the *toṃga* V.' or 'of, to the *cojhbo* Y. and the *toṃga* Vukto'. Examples are very frequent, e.g. 9 *yatha edaṣa stri Caḍhi Parsu Alṗaya Raśparaṣa ca aǵasitaṃti* 'That C. P. A. and R. carried off a woman of his'; 69 *Larsu Taṃjakaṣa ca atra viṣajidemi* 'I sent Larsu and Taṃjaka there'; 588 *Kakeya Jeyakasya ca.* The construction is less common in nouns other than proper names, e.g. 71 *eṣa pituṣa ca...gataṃti* 'He and his father went'; 561 *aṃklatsa putǵetsa odarasya ca* (three kinds of camel); 633 *kojava tavastaǵa ghridaṣa ca krinidavo* '*kojava*, *tavastaǵa* and *ghee* are to be bought'. The same construction is used in a similar list in the plural: 544 *Śramaṃna bramana vurcuǵa ṣa ca* 'Monks, brahmans and *vurcuǵas*'.

Descriptive nouns and adjectives in agreement with lists of names like these are put in the genitive plural whether the phrase is to be taken as genitive or nominative, e.g. 157 *bhaṭaraǵana priyadarśanana sunamaparikirtitana priyabhratuana cojhbo Tsmaya tivira Tǵaca caraka Sucaṃmasya ca* 'To the masters, fair to see, renowned with good name, the brothers *cojhbo* Tsmaya, the scribe Tǵaca and the spy Sucaṃma'. On the other hand as nominative: 709 *eda vivada svaya devaputra śruda, oguana Purvayana Rutraya Cinaṣena suveṭhana Aṭhama Ṣpalṗaya Laṣa ...cojhboana Alṗaya...vaśaṃmaṣa ca* 'His Majesty heard this dispute himself, the *ogus* P. R. C. the *suveṭhas* A. Ṣ. L. and the *cojhbos* Alṗaya and...*vaśaṃm̄a*'; 578 *cojhboana Bimbhaṣena Soṃjakaṣa ca pruchitaṃti*; 579 *sac̄hi apsuana Apṣiya Śāṃcāṣa ca* 'witnesses are the *apsus* A. and S.', etc. etc.

§ 123. The locative has taken the place of the accusative in expressing the goal with verbs of going, sending, etc. A similar development is to be observed in Apabhraṃśa (Ludwig Alsdorf, *Kumārapālapratibodha*, p. 65): 1, etc. *hastagata rayadvaraṃmi iśa viṣajidavo* 'He is to be sent here to the king's court under arrest'; 14 *yatha eṣa Khotanaṃmi dutiyaya gada* 'That he went on a mission to Khotan'; 27 *yaṃ kala Deviyae atra Caḋotaṃmi aida* 'When the queen came there to Caḋota'; 506 *Śāṃcaaṣa dajha Sanaca nama tena ṣadha Khemaṃmi palayita* 'Ś.'s slave called Sanaca fled with him to Khema'; 195 *uṭa yaṃñaṃmi... nitaṃti* 'They took a camel to the sacrifice'; 621 *puna iśa sveya viṣeyeṣu aitaṃti* 'Again they came themselves here into (our) territories'. Parallel with this development the locative is used with the preposition *a*, *yava* and *acaṃta* 'up to' (cf. § 92).

This rule has no exceptions except in certain stereotyped phrases like *asaṃna gaṃdavo* 'to take possession of' (*āsanaṃ gantavyam*). It follows that *nac̄ira* in the phrase *nac̄ira gachaṃti* (13, 15) cannot be a place-name or even an ordinary noun indicating the goal. It is probably an Iranian word meaning hunting (*B.S.O.S.* VII, 513).

§ 124. The future may be used as a sort of imperfect to express what used to take place: 182 *Kaṃjaka viṃñaveti yatha eṣa rayaka uṭavala purva rayaka uṭavalana rajade va (ra) c̄havala* *deyiṣyaṃti...purva rayaka uṭa caturtha divaṣa vuḍhiṃ bhaviṣyati* 'Kaṃjaka informs us that he is a keeper of the royal camels, formerly they used to give to the keepers of the royal camels a *vac̄havala*...formerly the royal camels used to be *vuḍhiṃ* on the fourth day'; 309 *yo tahi purva atra rajadhara huaṃti, taṃ kala adehi koyimaṃḍhina aṃna milima* 1 *Sa* 20 20 10 (*iśa*) *aniṣyaṃti* 'Those who were governors before you, at that time they used to bring 150 *milima* of *koyimaṃḍhina* corn'; 376 *caturtha karya, purva māsanumāsa lehare gachiṣyati* 'A fourth matter, formerly letter-carriers used to go every month'; 435 *purva rajadham̄a yasya rayaka dham̄aṃmi maṃnuśa athava stora mariṣyati avaśa rajadham̄ade ciṃtitaġa huati* 'Formerly it was the law of the realm that of whomsoever a man or beast died in state employment, it was reckoned (i.e. paid out) from the administration'; 621 *eṣa Saġamovi ogu Aśoġa ni kilmeci Catoveṣa vaṃti bala simaya asiṣyāti* 'This Saġamovi when young used to dwell on the boundary next to Catove who belonged to the *kilme* of *ogu* Aśoka'. Slightly different is the usage in 634 *tahi isa gaṃtavo asi, ajakra divaṣa iśa na agachiśatu* 'You were to have come here, up till to-day you have not come'.

This usage is interesting because it is exactly what is laid down in Pāṇini 3. 2. 112 *abhijñāvacane lṛṭ* 'The future is used for the past when somebody uses a word recalling something'. The commentary gives us an example: *abhijānāsi Devadatta vayaṃ Kāśmīreṣu vatsyāmaḥ* 'You remember Devadatta, we used to dwell in Kaśmir'. This is obviously the same kind of thing as the examples quoted above. The usage is not found in Sanskrit literature except artificially in imitation of Pāṇini. Pāṇini was a native of the North-West, so this was probably a piece of local syntax, which was not current in the rest of India and so does not appear in literature, but turns up again in the local dialect, where the influence of the grammarians is of course quite out of the question. It is interesting that Paṇini's statement should be confirmed in this most unliterary of dialects.

It is not quite clear how the future should take over this sense. Instances of the future used as a kind of preterite in various Indo-European languages are given by Brugmann (*Grundriss*[2], II,

3.795) and Wackernagel (*Vorl. über Syntax*, I, 217), but there is nothing just like this.

§ 125. As stated above the imperative with the exception of *hotu* has ceased to be used (§ 98). The gerundive in *-tavya* is most frequently used for giving orders. Also both the future and the optative are employed.

Future: 153 *avaśa etaṣa maṣasya* 20 *sasteyaṃmi Kuṃñaǵa iśa agamiṣyati* 'Definitely Kuṃñaǵa shall come here on the 20th day of this month'; 157 *tasuca Lṕimsu cavala viṣajitavya ari Calaṃma ṣaca go aniṣyati* 'The *tasuca* Lṕimsu is quickly to be despatched, along with Calama he will bring the cow'. This is exactly parallel with the English use of the future in giving instructions.

Optative: 152 *avaśa ede kilmeciye tava sarvabhavena jheniǵa siyaṃti* 'Certainly let these people of (my) district be under your care by all means' (cf. 161, 164); 187 *taha ajuvadae kaniṭha bhrata jeṭha bhrata taḓeyati, putra pita taḓeyati* 'So from to-day let the elder brother beat the younger brother, and the father beat the son'. This is the same use of the optative as occurs in the law-books in laying down general rules. 385 *teṣa piḓita anati ditae siyati* 'Let very carefully a command be given to them'; 437 *ajuvadae taya kuḓiyae prace Maṣḓhiǵeyaṣa eśvarya siyati* 'From to-day let there be ownership for Maṣḓhige of that girl'; 696 *yo atra tahi paḓivati bhaveyati emeva mahi lekha viṣarjeyaṣi* 'Anything that may happen to you there, you might send me a letter about it'.

§ 126. Prohibitions.

ma iṃci = *mā kiṃcit* (§ 84) is construed with the present, the future, the optative and the gerundive in expressing prohibitions. The particle *iṃci* is almost always added to the *ma*. (Exceptions, see *Kharoṣṭhi Inscriptions*, Index Verb., *ma*.)

Present: 272 *ede samṛdhae jaṃna varidae hotu, ma iṃci daraṃnaǵena jaṃnasa upeḓeṃdi* 'Let these rich people be stopped, let them not oppress the debtor people'; 288 *ṣe Ṣamaṃnera tehi jheniǵa siyati, ma iṃci abomata kiṃci kareṃdi* 'Let this Ṣamaṃnera be under your care, let them not disregard him' (or 'treat him with disrespect'); 364 *ma iṃci adhaṁena*

Camakaṣa paride niyati 'Let him not be taken from Camaka unlawfully'. (This may be optative = *neya(ṃ)ti*; for *i* = *e* cf. § 1.) 386 *avi Caḍotiye varidavya ma iṃci parvatiyana adhamа karemti* 'Also the Caḍotans must be prevented, let them not be unjust to the mountain people'; 729 *ma iṃci adhamena rajadhama pruchaṃti* 'Let them not administer (lit. "enquire") the law of the realm unjustly'. In most of these examples the *ma*-sentence has practically developed into a subordinate clause so that we can translate 386, for instance, 'The Caḍotans are to be prevented from committing injustice on the mountaineers'.

With Optative: 275 *na vithana kartavo ma omaǵa siyati* 'It is not to be held back, (the amount sent) must not be short' (cf. 306, 307); 519 *ma iṃci vismaridaǵa siyati* 'Let it not be forgotten'.

With Future: 347 *ma iṃci Caule paṃtha chiṃniṣyati* 'Let not Caule cut (= stop) his pathway'; 546 *ma iṃci atra Kolǵeyaṣa vithana kariśati* 'Let him not make a keeping-back (of the camel) from Kolǵeya'; 585 *ma iṃci atra masuṣa viǵa kariṣyati avaśa anavidavo deyaṃnae* 'Let him not make a hindrance about the wine there, certainly he is to be told to give it'. In 310 we have examples of *ma iṃci* with the future (as with the present, see above) used practically as a subordinate clause. *Cima Kaṣikaṣa ca picavidavya ma iṃci para raja nikasiṣyati* 'They are to be put into the hands of Cima and Kaṣika lest they should get away to a foreign kingdom'; and, *teṣa hastaṃmi ede maṃnuśa iśa viṣajidavya ma iṃci puna paṃthade pranaśiṣyati* 'In their hand these men are to be sent here lest they should again escape from the road'.

With Gerundive: 22 *ma iṃci vithana kartavo* 'A holding back is not to be made'; 338 *ma atra maṃtra śrunidavya.*

More common than *ma* with gerundives is *na* (*na iṃci*), which of course originally was the only correct form: 31 *na iṃci tade atikramidavo* 'There must be no transgression from that'; 188 *na nikhalidavo.*

There are only occasional examples of *na* being used in prohibitions otherwise than with gerundives: 399 *bahu varṣa aṃtargata uṭa na preṣeyaṃsi* 'Do not send a camel many years old'.

§ 127. Subordinate clauses. *yo.*

Without verb: 9 *yo garbha, vinaṭha*; 165 *yo iśa vartamana Lṗimsuaṣa paride ñadartha bhavidavo* 'What happenings (there are) here, you must learn from Lṗimsu'.

With Indicative: 31 *yo Lṗimo Puǵoena ṣadha danagrahana hoati* '(That) giving and taking which there is between Lṗimo and Puǵo'.

With Optative. In relative sentences of a general nature the optative is exclusively used. When the future is used it always conveys a definite reference to the future. From this distinction it is possible to assert that the mysterious form *hac̄h̄ati* is properly an optative (cf. § 100). Examples: *yo aṭh̄o-vaǵa palayaṃnaǵa maṃnuśa siyati ṣe...iśa ativatidavo* 'What serviceable fugitive man there is, he is to be sent here'; 187 *yo eka bhitiyaṣa vaṃti ede bhratarana avarajeyaṃti, te varidavo* 'What any of these brothers do wrong one against another, they are to be stopped'; 47 *yeṣa vivada siyati rayadvaraṃmi viṣaji-davya* 'Of whom there is a dispute, they must be sent to the king's court'.

With Future: *yo tava kac̄i puna iśa agamiṣyati emeva ahu teṣa tanu saṃña janiṣyami* 'Who of you shall come here in the future, so I will regard them as my own' (*teṣām tanū-saṃjñāṃ jñāsyāmi*); 272 *yo maṃnuśa cojhbo Soṃjakena abomata kariṣyati ṣe...iśa... viṣajidavo* 'The man who disobeys the *cojhbo* Soṃjaka, is to be sent here'.

§ 128. The usual expression for 'when' is *yaṃ kala* with the indicative: 35 *yaṃ kala Cinasthanade vaniye agamiṣyati, taṃ kala ṛna pruchidavo* 'When the merchants shall come from China, then the debt is to be enquired into'; 272 *yaṃ kala Khotaṃnade yogac̄h̄ema bhaviṣyati, rajya sthiṣyadi taṃ kala śodheṣyaṃdi* 'When there shall be security from Khotan and the kingdom shall be established, they will pay'; 183 *yaṃ kala Supiye Caḓo-taṃmi agataṃti* 'When the Supis came to Caḓota'.

§ 129. *yadi.*

With Optative: *yadi aṃñatha siyati* 'If it is otherwise'; 35 *yadi vivada siyati*; 45 *yati na dṛṭhaǵa na śrudaǵa siyati* 'If they have been neither seen nor heard of'; 144 *yati Soǵanaṣa taḓita-*

ǵena Kacana mṛdaǵa siyati 'If Kacana died through Soǵana's beating'; 189 *yati avasiṭhe nikhalamana siyaṃti* 'If they are removing the remaining ones'.

With Future: 165 *yati tade purima pācima viṣajiṣyatu paṃthaṃmi paraṣa bhaviṣyati, tuo...vyoṣiśaṣi* 'If you despatch it before or after then and it is stolen on the way, you will pay'; 206 *yati Ayamatu vasaṃmi bhuya vithiṣyati* 'If he still keeps it back in Ayamatu *vasa*'; 211 *yati ahuno bhuya eda palṕi na sṕora iśa aniṣyaṃti na cirena tuo...agamiṣyaṣi* 'If now again they do not bring this tax complete, before long you shall come (yourself)'.

yadi is not used with the present indicative.

§ 130. *yatha* with the indicative is regularly used in introducing quoted speech, the text of a complaint, etc.: 7 *Lṕipe viṃñaveti yatha triti varṣa huda Arsinaṣa paride gavi savatsi* 2 *vyochiṃniti* 'Lṕipe announces that the third year has come (since) 2 cows with calf were legally awarded to him from Arsina'; 14 *Ṣameka viṃñaveti yatha eṣa Khotaṃnaṃmi dutiyaya gada* 'Ṣameka announces that he went on a mission to Khotan'.

yatha may be also used meaning 'as', in which case it usually takes the optative: 7 *yatha rayadvaraṃmi vyochiṃnidaǵa siyati tena vidhanena niće kartavo* 'As the award was made at the king's court, according to that ruling a decision is to be made' (cf. § 45).

Rarely with the future (in the sense of *yahi*): 84 *yatha eṣa atra agamiṣyati, tatheva śigra...* 'As (=when) this man shall come there, so quickly...'.

§ 131. *yahi* is used with the future in the sense of 'when, as'. The form is probably to be compared with the Avestan *yezi*: *yahi eda kilamudra atra eśati*; 289 *yahi gaṃnana pravaṃnaǵa...atra aniṣyati* 'when he shall bring there a document containing the reckoning'. It sometimes means 'if', being indistinguishable from *yadi* with the future: 161 *yahi eta karya tuo mahi kariṣyasi* 'If you do this thing for me'; 634 *yahi tatra cita na kariṣyatu* 'If you do not pay attention to that'.

§ 132. *yava* is used with the optative: *yava asti siyati taha sarva iśa prahadavo* 'So much as there is, is all to be sent here'.

yena is used either with the future or the optative, meaning 'in order that': 272 *rajade sama sama parikre dadavo yena raja karyani na iṃci śiśila bhaviṣyaṃti* 'Equal pay to each is to be given from the state, so that the administration of the kingdom shall not become slack'; 320 *avaśa etaṣa Pǩuv̌aṣenaṣa prace ciṃdedavya oḍ̌idavya, yena atra mama kriṣitaǵa vavitaǵa hastaṃmi gṛh̄eyati* 'Certainly thought must be taken about this Pǩuvaṣena, he must be set free so that he can take in hand my ploughing and sowing'.

§ 133. Subordinate clauses without introductory particle.

(*a*) Conditional: *atra na paribujiśatu hastagata iśa viṣajidavo* 'If you do not get clear about it there, they are to be sent here under arrest'; 223 *aṃñatha siyati, yathadham̄ena nic̄e kartavo* 'If it is otherwise, a decision is to be made in accordance with the law'; 266 *puna vivada kiṃci siyati* 'If there is any dispute again'; 546 *yaṃ ca Preyaṣa vivada siyati, iśa agamiṣyati, iśemi ogu vasu Bhimaṣenaṣa vaṃti garahiṣyama* 'And what dispute of Preya there is, if (when) he comes here, we will complain before the *ogu vasu* Bhimaṣena'; 714 *puna ahuno bhuya palp̄i omaǵa viṣajiṣyatu avaśa tanu goṭhade puna vyoṣiśatu* 'If again now you send the tax short, certainly you will pay from your own farm'.

(*b*) Indirect questions: 3 *pruchidavo bhutartha kriti siyati* 'You must enquire whether she has really been bought'; 24 *pruchidavo bhutartha eva hac̄h̄ati*, etc. etc.

With Indicative: 520 *pruchidavo eṣa dui draṃga dhareti puna sp̄aṣavaṃni dham̄a kareti* 'You must ask whether he holds two offices and again (=in addition) is performing the duty of scout'.

§ 134. Reported speech.

As stated above (§ 130) people's words are usually quoted introduced by *yatha*. In addition *ityartha* may be appended to quoted speech, or it may be given without any special indication at all. *iti* is no longer used by itself. Examples of *ityartha* are: 124 *Ṣamasena...Lp̄ipeyaṣa ca garahitaṃti...bhuma praceya 'sac̄h̄i nasti hotamti' ityartha* 'Ṣ. and L. complained about some land... (they said) there were no witnesses'; 272 *avi paruvarṣa uvadae Supiyana paride upaśaṃgidavo huati ityartha* 'Also since last year there is cause of alarm from the Supis so it is said'.

When reported speech is given without any particle at all it is customary to append the verb 'to be' to participles and gerundives, whereas in straightforward statements this is not done. Instances are: 63 *eda prace tu Apǵeyade anati giḍeṣi, Lṕipeyaṣa stri patena stavidavya hoati* 'Concerning this you have received instructions from Apǵeya that the woman is to be restored to Lṕipeya'; 144 *tuo anati giḍeṣi sac̄hiyana śavatha śavidavo hoati, yati Soǵanaṣa taḍitagena Kacana mr̥daǵa siyati aviṃdama maṃnuśa vyochiṃnidavya hoati* 'You received a command that an oath was to be sworn by the witnesses and that if Kacana had died through Soǵana's beating a man was to be awarded as recompense'; 206 *avi ca imade lekha gata tahi putra Apita Sujatena ṣadha masu isa anidavya aṣi* 'Also a letter went from here that your son Apita along with Sujata was to bring the wine here'; 506 *avi samaya kiṭaṃti, ṣe dajha Śraṣḍha goṭhaṃmi na oḍidavya huati tava Śaṃcaena kam̄avidavo huati yava Tatiǵa Bhatraṣa ca agamanaṃmi* 'Also they made an agreement that the slave Śraṣḍha was not to be left on the farm, he was to be made work by Śaṃca until the arrival of Tatiǵa and Bhatra'; 160 *mahaṃte vr̥dhi-jaṃna iṃthu maṃtreṃti cojhbo Lṕipeyaṣa Sacaṃmi goṭha ohara titaǵa uhati, udaǵa bhiśa na titaǵa uhati* 'The very old people speak thus, that the yield (?) of a farm in Saca was given to *cojhbo* Lṕipeya but water and seed were not given'.

NOMINAL COMPOSITION

§ 135. The last member of a dvandva is usually inflected in the singular. A few examples of the old type remain, e.g. *pita-putre* 715 'father and son', *edeṣa pitaputrana* 71, *ede bharya pate* 632.

In 450 *putradhidarehi* is plural because it means 'sons and daughters'. Examples of the usual singular inflection are: *pitumadue* 164, *madupitusya* 109, *hasta padami* 339, *Khema Khotaṃnade* 283, *Calmadana Caḍodade* 246, *śubhaśubhaṣa* 165, *danagrahana.*

This development is further attested inside India in Kharoṣṭhi inscriptions, e.g. *C.I.I.* II, 12, *matapitaram*, whereas the Aśokan texts still always use the plural *matapituṣu.*

§ 136. There has developed in this language a principle of group-inflection, by which the last member only of a nominal group is inflected, e.g. *cojhbo Yitaka toṃga Vuktoṣa ca* 'To the *cojhbo* Yitaka and the *toṃga* Vukto' (on the use of the same form for Nom. and Gen. see § 122). With feminine last 566 *Kupṣuta Tilutamaae ca.* It is not always easy to draw the line as to where ordinary cases of Nominal Composition end and where this loose stringing together of nouns begins. That is noticeably the case in the type quoted in the next paragraph, which corresponds in a way to the Sanskrit Karmadhāraya. In the case of ordinary dvandvas it is doubtful in the light of these facts whether e.g. *Khema Khotaṃnade* should be called a compound, especially when it is considered that in making accumulations of substantives the particle *ca* is not usually employed, e.g. 19 *coḍaga pačevara parikraya dadavo* 'Clothing, food and wages must be given'. Similarly with verbs: 9 *aǵasitaṃti taḍitaṃti* 'They carried off and beat'.

§ 137. Examples of Karmadhāraya are: *cojhbo Taṃjakaṣa*, 43 *stri Suǵisae*, 4 *kori Rutrayaṣa*, 55 *rayaka khulana*, 133 *priya nivasaǵa Svaneyaṣa*, 248 *mahaṃta rajakaryena*, 24 *edaṣa dajha Sarpiǵaṣa vaṃti*, 32 *Peta-avaneṃci Saǵapeyaṣa*, 152 *priyabhratu ṣoṭhaṃga Lp̄ipeyaṣa*, 245 *edaṣa pitu cojhbo Ṣamaṣenaṣa*, 575 *maya rajadivira śramaṃna Dhaṃapriyena.*

In all these cases the words hang very loosely together, and they must be regarded as group-inflection, rather than compounds in the proper sense of the term.

Examples are quite common in the Kharoṣṭhi inscriptions of N.W. India, which shows that the usage was widespread and not a peculiarity of this particular dialect. Cf. *C.I.I.* II, p. cxv, *mahadanapati Patikasa*, *erjhuna Kapasa*, *maharaja rajatitaja Hoveṣkasa.*

§ 138. Genitive Tatpuruṣas are very common: *anati lekha*, *rayadvaraṃmi* 16, *palp̄i uṭa*, *viṃñati lekha*, *padamulade*, *khula* *uṭa*, *parikra aṃna* 25, *goṭhakarya* 31, *Cinasthana* 35, *aṃna nadha* 'pack of corn' 68, *aṃna śeṣa* 140, *ghrita pasu* 141, *go yaṃña* 155, *gaṃnana pravaṃnaǵa* 'document of accounts' 159, *palṕi dhaṁa* 164, *raya sac̄hi* 165, *rajakaryami* 272, *bhuma muli* 624, *maharaya-putra* 622.

Unlike later Sanskrit the Tatpuruṣa compound is practically never made with a personal name as the first member. They say *Lṕipeyaṣa hastaṃmi* (4) *Cimǵeyaṣa śatade* 82, *Catoaṣa goṭhade* 621, etc. etc.

§ 139. Bahuvrihis are rare: *mahanuava*, *ṣovarṣi* '6 years old', *catuvaṛsaǵa* (etc.), *ñadartha*, *maṃnuśa rupa*, 324 *paśuvalana stri Kroae pramuhanaṃ*.

Part II

INDEX

A

a = *ā* rather than *ca* (?), § 92.

akas: (*aǵas*, *aǵajh-*). = **ākāsayati* from *kas* 'to go', i.e. 'to cause to come (to oneself), take away', opposite of *nikas*, *nikhas* = *niṣkāsayati* 'eject, send away', 1 *Lṗipeya garahati yatha edas̱a gavi* 2 *seniye Saciṃciye aǵasitaṃti*, *eka gavi patama oḏitaṃti*, *eka khayitaṃti* 'L. complains that soldiers from Saca took away two of his cows: one cow they let go back, one they ate'. *akasida*, § 16; *aǵajhidati*, §§ 22, 109.

akiṣḍha: (*aǵiṣḍha*, *aǵiṣṭa*). An article of some kind, because it is numbered, not measured, e.g. 431–2 *aǵiṣḍha* 2...*aṃña aǵiṣḍha* 1. Since it is often mentioned in conjunction with *kojava* 'rug' (see s.v.) it will be an article of similar nature.

akri: § 36, where it is derived from *agrya*. But the meaning is uncertain and it may mean 'uncultivated (land)' as suggested by Prof. Thomas, *Acta Or.* XII, 38. There is hardly enough evidence to decide whether *miṣi*-land or *akri*-land was most valuable. In 571 *miṣi*-land of an area requiring 3 *milima* of seed is worth 60 *muli* (see s.v.). In 222 *akri*-land requiring ½ a *milima* (10 *khi*) is worth 10 *muli*, i.e. the same value. On the other hand in 579 *akri*-land requiring 1½ *milima* is only valued at 13 *muli*. But there is not enough evidence to make any generalisations about price. Cf. under *miṣi*.

aṃkr'atsa: i.e. *aṃklatsa* (*agiltsa* in 422 is a variant of this word). An epithet describing camels. It may be = the Toch. B. *aknātsa*, A. *aknats* 'ignorant', meaning an untrained camel. The original form of the Tocharian word was *anknatsa*, which might easily be dissimilated in this dialect into *anklatsa*. *J.R.A.S.* (1935), p. 673.

aǵaṃduv́a: § 16. = *āgantuka-*.

aǵiltsa: Probably = *aṃklatsa* above. Anusvāra is often omitted (§ 47) and the *g* instead of *ǵ* indicates its presence, because simple intervocalic *g* becomes *ǵ* (§ 16).

Aṃkvaka: (*Aṃgoka*, etc. § 7). The name may be Chinese An-chou according to Prof. Thomas, *Acta Or.* XIII, 49, 50.

aǵratu: §§ 12, 92.

aǵaṃtu: § 103.

aǵeta: An official repeatedly mentioned side by side with *yatma* (see s.v.), both of whose functions seem to have been closely connected with the collection and delivery of the tax (*palpi*); cf. 57, where the *aǵeta* and *yatma* are responsible for conveying *palpi*, 714; an investigation is being held into the conditions of collecting the taxes, and the *vasu*, *aǵeta* and *yatma* are commanded to appear. Similar functions appear in 275 and 307. Further, the *aǵeta* possesses judicial functions in connection with legal transactions, e.g. 640 *eṣa likhitaǵa rayakade aǵeta Lṗipatǵaṣa traghade bhuma praceya Lustuaṣa anada dharidavo* 'This document from the royal administration, from the department (office) of the *aǵeta* Lṗipatǵa, concerning land, must be carefully preserved by Lustu'; 715 *taha ko pac̄ima kaṃlaṃmi vasu aǵeta raya dvaraṃmi codeyati*... 'Likewise whoever at a later time makes a complaint before the *vasu*, or the *aǵeta* or at the king's court'; 437 *yo ca koci pac̄ima kalaṃmi tāya kuḍiyae kridena caṃkura Kapǵeya ni bhratare bhratuputro va praputro va ñati, yo aṃña kilmeci vasu aǵetana ṣa ca biti vara maṃtra nikhaleyaṃti* 'And whoever at a later time, (either) the brothers of Kapǵeya or his brother's son, or grandson, or any other relative, brings the matter up a second time concerning this girl before the local (*kilmeci*) *vasus* or *aǵetas*.

aṅǵa: To be read *atǵa*, cf. § 47. Always used in connection with *muli* 'price, payment'. It seems to mean something like 'additional, complementary, subsidiary' payment, e.g. 571 *giḍa muli uṭa* 1 *duvarṣaǵa paṃcaśa muliyena, Koñayena paḍichida aṃña atǵa muli giḍa masu khi* 10 'He received the price, one camel two years' old worth 50 *mūli*. Koñaya received. Further he took a complementary payment of 10 *khi* of wine.'

aco, acovina: The meaning seems to be, as Prof. Thomas points out (*Acta Or.* XIII, 58), a kind of courier or messenger. Not indeed the regular monthly postal service described in 376, but a special courier to report impending attacks from enemies (cf. 133, 139). In that case *aco* might be some kind of outlook post on the frontier.

Against Prof. Thomas' explanation (*ib.*) from Sanskrit *ājava* or *ājūḥ*, internal *j* never becomes *c*. It became regularly *y* and under certain cases *j́* (=*ź*), § 17. *acaṣaṃnaṃna* 415 (=*ajeṣaṃnena*), if not merely to be regarded as an error, represents *jj*, which might possibly have been unvoiced into *cc* according to § 14.

Acokisǵiya: 371. Apparently name of a local god, cf. *Bhatro*.

Acomena: Place-name. Connected with *aco* (?), cf. the article cited above.

achinati: 'encroach on, appropriate', § 101.

ac̄hati: =*hac̄hati*, § 28.

ac̄haniya: 703. Read perhaps *rac̄haniya* 'to be kept'.

ajakra: §§ 36, 91.

Ajiyama: See under *avana*.

ajiṣaṃnae: § 1. *ajeṣaṃnae*, §§ 41, 67=*adhyeṣanayā*.

ajuvadae: § 11.

ajhatu: Only 152. The meaning is quite uncertain, but it seems to have nothing to do with *ajhate*.

ajhate: Probably = Av. *āzāta*, N.Pers. *āzād* 'noble' or 'free', cf. *B.S.O.S.* VII, 509.

ajhateyaṣa: 242. The alternative reading *ajhateyana* is to be preferred, because otherwise it would not be inflected, cf. § 137; = 'of the free men'.

ajhi: 562. Meaning and etymology quite obscure.

ajho: Obscure: but there is no reason to think it is connected with *aco* as Prof. Thomas thinks (*Acta Or.* XIII, 60). The letter deals with the transportation of the state supplies of corn and wine. Apart from that the passage containing *ajho* is far from clear. It runs: *uṭa* 20 20 *tre tre milima nadha kartavo dui vara Piṣaliyaṃmi nihaṃñitavya, masuaṃmi uṭa* 10 4 1 *prathame va ajho tre nikhalidavo* 'Forty camels are to be loaded with 3 *milima* each (of corn), and the two-thirds are to be stored at Piṣali. For the *masu* fifteen camels are to be got out...(?)...'. Certainly *uṭa* is the subject of *nikhalidavo*, but is *ajho* another nominative parallel to it or some kind of adverb? Since we are dealing with wine it might be suggested that *ajho* = S. *āsava* (cf. §§ 7, 22), but that also fails to make the passage clear.

aña: §§ 41, 88. Declension of, § 88.

aṭa: = S. *aṭṭa*, Hindi *āṭā* 'flour'; Prof. Thomas, *Acta Or.* XIII, 67.

aṭha: § 49.

aṭhi: § 49.

aṭhovaǵa: = 'ready, fit (for work), capable, available (for use)', §§ 37, 49. The meaning was first pointed out by Prof. Thomas in *Acta Or.* XII.

aḍini: Some kind of grain or crop. It is grown by seed (579).

adha: § 37.

aṃtaǵi: An epithet of horses and camels. The *ǵ* cannot stand for the suffixal *-ka*, because we never find *aǵi* in these forms. It must be an adjective derived by the suffix *-i* (§ 75) from a noun *antāk*, or *antak*. Probably Iranian, cf. *B.S.O.S.* VII, 779.

ativatidavo: Means 'send, hand over, deliver, dispatch'. Probably = *atipātaya*—rather than *ativartaya*—because *r* is not usually assimilated to *t*, and, in the few instances where it is, a cerebral results, §§ 36, 37.

atvanaṃ: § 44.

adehi: § 91.

adha: § 37.

adhaṁena: § 90.

ana, anati, etc.: § 44.

anata, anada: § 91. Seems to mean 'carefully, well, properly'. It occurs regularly in certain stock phrases, e.g. 1, etc. *eda vivada samuha anada pruchidavo* 'This dispute is to be carefully investigated in person'; 571, etc. *eṣa pravaṃnaǵa Koñaya ni miṣiyaṣa* *praceya divira Ramṣotsasa anada tharitavo* 'This document concerning the *miṣi*-(land) of Koñaya is to be carefully preserved by the scribe Ramṣotsa'. In 569 and 593 *suha* occurs in place of *anada* in the same formula. *suha* seems to mean much the same as *su* 'well' in 419 *sukrida suhavikrida.* Also in the phrase *avi spaṣa jivida paricaǵena anada rac̄hidavya* (cf. under *spasa*). The meaning hardly allows us to equate it with Skt. *ājñaptam* 'ordered'. It is perhaps the same word as Saka *ānata* 'kept preserved' (in the Saka version of the *Suvarṇaprabhāsa Sūtra*, vide Konow, *S.B.P.A.W.* (1935), pp. 428 ff. *ānatu yanda* translates *ārakṣayiṣyatha*). In the Maralbashi dialect the same word appears as *anāḏu*. This identification is strengthened by the fact that in our documents it is most frequently used with verbs like *rakṣ-* and *dhar-*.

anatiyena: § 70.

anavidetu: § 93.

anahetu: either = *ṛṇahetu* or *ana-*, is the extended form of the negative prefix which appears occasionally in Prakrit (Pischel, § 77), the meaning being 'without just cause'. Although the treatment of *ṛ-* is irregular (§ 5), the former interpretation is supported by 719, where Saǵapeya and Pǵo carry off a woman *anahetu*; then the text goes on to say *yo Saǵapeya Pǵoṣa ca dharaṃnaǵa hac̄hati* 'And whatever he (the owner of the woman) shall be owing to S. and P.', etc.

aniyanae: § 103.

aniśati: § 99.

anupurvena: § 90.

anusaṃti: = *anusandhi* or *ānusandhi* 'adjoining' (cf. Prof. Thomas, *Acta Or.* XIII, 79).

apacira: (also written *avacira, apcira*). It appears as a kind of measure in the sale of vineyards (*masu śaḏa*) not of other kinds of cultivated land. Ordinary sown land was measured not by area but by the amount of seed which was sown on it (see *bhijapayati*), and from 655 this seems to have been the case with vineyards. *Budhap̄ham̄aasa vaṃti miṣi vikrida, tatra bhijapayati milima* 1 *khi* 4 1, *masu śaḏa, tatra masu vuta apacira* 10 3 'He sold to B. some *miṣi*-(land), there the capacity for seed was 1 *m.* 5 *kh.*, (also) a vineyard; (and) there vines are planted to the extent of 13 *apacira*'. It is clear that *apacira* is some term indicating the number or quantity of vine-plants, and not the area. According to Stein (*Ruins of Ancient Khotan*, p. 247) vines are trained along low fences running in parallel lines. Perhaps *apacira* means 'row', i.e. a row of standard length in which vines were planted.

apanasya: § 86. = *ātmanah.*

apane: §§ 44, 86. = *ātmanaḥ.*

apyaṃtara: § 14.

aprameǵo: §§ 16, 53.

apru: Only 722. Seems to be some noun of relationship belonging to the native language. Unfortunately no information is available on the actual relationship of the people mentioned.

aprochiti: =*apṛṣṭvā*, § 102.

apsu: Title. There is practically no information as to the nature of their functions. We find them mentioned along with other officials in lists of witnesses, e.g. 571 *cojhbo Kuviñeya sac̄ʹhi, v́asuana Acuñiya Caḍhiya V́apikaṣ̱a ca, apsuana Śāṃcā Pitǵa toṃgha Karaṃtsa ṣ̱aca, sac̄ʹhi Tamcǵo, aǵetana Lṕipatǵa Kuuna Kuviñeya yatma Kuviñeyaṣ̱a ca sac̄ʹhi.* Perhaps *toṃgha* and *apsu* were functions very closely connected, because the most natural translation is '...of the *apsu*'s Śāṃc̄a Pitǵa and the *toṃgha* Karaṃtsa', i.e. subordinating the *toṃgha* Karaṃtsa to the general conception of *apsu*. Otherwise we would have had *ṣ̱a ca* after the name *Pitǵa*. Further, *Karaṃtsa* appears in 579 with the title *apsu*, while Śāṃc̄a appears at the bottom of this same document with the title *toṃgha*.

aṕhiñanu: Cf. *B.S.O.S.* VIII, 432. Konow (*Acta Or.* XIV, 238) equates it with Skt. *abhijñāna*.

ambila: § 45. Possibly the same as *amila* 655, but the meaning of both is quite uncertain.

Ambukaya: Seems to be a title or surname: only 251.

abomata: =*abhyavamata*, §§ 41, 107=used with *kṛ* in the sense of 'disobey', 'disrespect', e.g. 371 *yo eṣa cojhbo Soṃjaka abomata kariṣyati, vacanena na kariṣyati* 'This man who shall disobey the *cojhbo* Soṃjaka and shall not act according to his word'.

abramo: Quite obscure. The *b* suggests that it does not belong to the native language (§ 14).

abhatayutu: 399. One might suggest a reading like *asaṃta *abhuta *yatu tusmaǵa anartha bhavati* '(They say) things which are not, things which have not been, from which you suffer'.

abhiṭhe: 272. There is a variant reading *akista* which might be a proper name. *abhiṭhe* would mean 'desirable, suitable', but it is unusual to find an attributive adjective inflected, § 137 (unless *-e*<*-ae*<*-aǵa*, § 53).

abhirucitaǵena: § 112.

abhisamitaṃti: 'They came to an agreement'.

amaraṃnae: § 103.

amahu: § 78.

ayaǵa: 107. Meaning uncertain.

aya dvara: ='revenue', as pointed out by Prof. Thomas, *Acta Or.* XIII, 71, quoting the *Kāśyapa Parivarta*, where the same phrase is found.

ayaṃnae: § 103.

aya Ridhasena: =*ārya R.*, § 42. The word has a purely religious sense 'reverend', as in Buddhist texts, and does not elsewhere occur. The assimilation of *ry* to *y* is not regular (§ 36, cf. *karya*), but religious terms common to Buddhists in general are naturally liable to irregularities.

ayidana: 676. If the correction *aśitana* be adopted *cam̃a maṃtsa aśidana na nikhalita* might be translated 'By them having eaten the flesh, the skin was not removed'. But there is no other example of the participle in *-ta* being inflected in this dialect.

ayoǵena: Skt. *āyoga.* It is used to denote an additional payment to be made, when an old payment is long overdue, something like interest: e.g. 437, the payment of 3 *muli* has been deferred, consequently a ruling is made *yatha paṭami muli śeṣa vithidae huati taha ahuno se muli eka ayoǵena giṃnitavo huda muli* 4 1 *aṃña varita* 'Just as the rest of the price (mentioned) on the document (*paṭṭa*) has been retained, so now that sum is to be received with one *ayoǵa*, the sum is 5 *muli*, other payment is forbidden'. *eka* is obscure, but it is clear that the *ayoǵa* is the extra 2 *muli* which have been added owing to deferment of payment. 14, an envoy to Khotan had not been provided with a guard (*valaǵa*) at Caḍota at the expense of the state. Now an order is made that the wages of a guard be paid him *ṣadha ayoǵena*, i.e. complete with interest or an extra sum to make up for his own expense and trouble. 68 (two men have eaten a sack of corn belonging to somebody else) *eṣa aṃna ṣa ayoǵena Opǵe Lṕipeṣa ca giṃnidavya* 'This corn plus interest is to be received by O. and L.' There do not seem to be any documents recording a deed of loan on interest, so if usury was practised, which it hardly can have been on a large scale, there is no means of learning what the general word for 'interest' was. *ayoǵa* always occurs where an additional payment has to be made by people who have neglected paying sums due for a long time. *āyoga* in the sense of 'something added on to, an addition, extra' is a quite natural meaning, although it does not appear to be used in Sanskrit exactly in this sense.

ara: § 28. =*hāra* (?).

arabhtidavya: § 116.

ari: =*ārya* (?). *ārya* certainly becomes *aya* in one place (see above), but there is a specifically monkish term. *ari* does not seem to be associated with any particular function, like many of the titles, so that a general meaning something like 'sir', which *ārya* might easily have, is the most likely. On the other hand the term is not applied to very many people.

ariḍi and **ariḍaǵa:** Only 109. Among a list of things sent as a present. According to Prof. Thomas, *Acta Or.* XIII, 78=*ārdrī* and *ārdraka* 'ginger'. The phonetics are irregular, but such a word is likely to exhibit irregularities due to borrowing.

arivaǵa: Probably means 'guide'. The *arivaǵa* is frequently mentioned as conducting envoys to Khotan: 135 *avi arivaǵa maṃnuśa aṭh̃ovaǵa* 1 *dadavo yasya anupurvena gaṃdavo siyati etaṣa arivaǵaṣa tanu storena gaṃdavo* 'Also a capable *arivaǵa*-man is to be given (to the envoys) who shall go in front of them. This *arivaǵa* must go on his own beast.' Similarly 22, 253. The office was hereditary:

438 *Bhimaṣena viṃñaveti, eṣa pitara pita uvadae na arivaǵa asti Khotaṃni mata na anada janati, arivaǵa na kartavo* 'Bh. informs (us): he is not an *arivaǵa* from his father and ancestors, he does not properly know the Khotan *mata*, you make him an *arivaǵa*, he is not to be made an *arivaǵa*'. *mata* unfortunately is obscure. Skt. *mata-* does not seem to give any good sense. Similarly in 10 a man complains that his paternal profession is *klaseṃci* not *arivaǵa*. Etymology uncertain. Prof. Thomas suggests Skt. *arpaka-*, i.e. through **aripaka-* with svarabhakti.

are: 2 *are khi* 1. Apparently the same as *ara* in 176 *ara khi* 1. Perhaps 'half a *khi*'<Ir. *ardaka*. For *r*<*rd*, *r* compare *nokṣari*<*navaka sard-*.

aroǵi: § 9.

areṣa: (and *areṣahi*). Obscure.

aroǵemi: § 97.

arohaǵa: Only 420. Uncertain; perhaps something like the saddle of a camel; =*ārohaka*.

Arǵiyoṅǵiṣavae: § 69. Read *Argiyoṅǵ(=tǵ)iṣaae.*

artav́aśa: 431. Some object.

artha: § 55.

arnavaji: A kind of cloth measured in hands (*hasta*) 83, which may be white (*śpeti* 83, which seems to show that the word is feminine).

aryaǵa: 654. A title, presumably=*āryaka*, cf. *ari* and *aya*.

arṣaǵa(e): Occurs before a few proper names, namely *Apeṃna* (87, 147, 210, 531), *Kolpiṣa* (560), *Uvaṣena* (543). It may be the Iranian proper name *Arṣaka-* (*Arsaces*).

alaṃǵila: Only 109. Some article; *ṣa alaṃǵila* 'along with an *a-*'.

a la va la: 499. Reading uncertain.

alena: Epithet of *kojava* 'rug', 'blanket' 549; =**ālayana-* 'rug for lying down in (?)'.

aloṭa: § 18. =**āloṭṭa* 'plundering'; single *ṭ* would have become *ḍ*.

avaǵajena: §§ 16, 21.

av́ana: Hardly from Skt. *āpaṇa* 'bazaar', because the meaning is rather 'village' or 'parish'. It might first have meant a local market, then market-town including the land round it: 124 *Peta av́aneṃci bhumana prace* 'Concerning the lands belonging to the parish of Peta'. The word is most likely of Iranian origin: O.Pers. *āvahana*, Arm.L.W. *avan*, both meaning 'village'; Saka *vāna*<*(a)vāna*, which shows that the second *a* was long. The meaning is obviously nearer than that of Skt. *āpaṇa*. *nagara* is used as a synonym for *av́ana* in 25, *peta nagaraṃmi*.

The *av́anas*, always mentioned by name (the word *av́ana* does not occur independently), are the following:

(1) *Yave av́ana*; at 497 it appears as *deviyae yav́e av́anaṃmi.*

(2) *Peta av́ana*; in 494 as *deviyae peta av́anaṃmi.*

(3) *Catiṣa devi av́ana*; also *Catiṣa deviae a°* 334, etc., and *devi Catisae a°* at 295.

(4) *Yiruṃḍhina av́ana*, only 297.

(5) *Ajiyama av́ana.*
(6) *Vaṃtu av́ana.*
(7) *Traṣa av́ana.*
(8) *Navaǵa av́ana* 366.
(9) *Toṃgraka maharayaṣa avanaṃmi* 549.
(10) *Deviyae ogu Anuǵaya ni avanaṃmi* 629.
(11) *Paǵina avanaṃmi* 750.

Note also that Armenian *avan* is similarly compounded with proper names, e.g. *Vałarš-avan* (Hübsehmarm, *Arm. Gr.* p. 79).

The *av́anas* frequently appear as administrative units for collecting taxes (cf. 42, 121, 165, 468) or other purposes (e.g. 136, 296, 439). In 16 Peta *av́ana* is put in charge of a *caṃkura.* Individuals mentioned in the documents often have their *av́ana* referred to, showing that it was an important unit of administrative classification.

avamicae: § 55. Perhaps = *apamityaka*, rather than *apamityāya.*

avaliḱa: § 75. Mentioned side by side with *kojava* 'blanket, counterpane', and *namata* 'rough coat' is perhaps an object of somewhat similar nature.

avale: Only 431–2. Unknown.

avaśa: §§ 7, 41. *avaśe*, § 53.

avasama: Not = *āvāsāt*, because the ablative is always in *-ade* never *-ama*, § 56. The meaning seems to be something like 'unsuitable, improper': 69 *mahi iśa avasama Bhoti-nagarade aṃna nikhalaṃnae* 'It was not proper for me here to remove the corn from *Bhoti-nagara*', or 'It was not opportune that the corn should be removed'; 29 *tatra sac̄hi iśa nasti, udiśa avasama hoda iśa nic̄e karaṃnae* 'On that point there are no witnesses here. Therefore it was impossible to make a decision here', or 'It was held that we should...'. Compare Saka *viysama* 'improper' (*B.S.O.S.* VIII, 141) which is opposed to *presama* 'suitable'. The words must be Indian not Iranian. Skt. **apasama* and **prasama.*

avijida: § 17.

aviṃdhama: 'recompense, penalty', e.g. 144 *yati Soǵanaṣa taḍitaǵena Kacana mṛdaǵa siyati aviṃdhama maṃnuśa vyochiṃnidavya hoati* 'If Kacana (a slave) died through Soǵana's beating, a man (i.e. slave) must be adjudged to the owner in recompense'. The term *aviṃd(h)ama* includes both the making good of losses caused to other people by illegal action, e.g. 676 (somebody having stolen a cow) *udiśa triguna aviṃdama chiṃnidama* 'Therefore we have decided on a restitution of three times the amount', and also punishment, retribution in the form of beating, etc. (209, 419, etc.).

avidhameya: The alternative reading *avisaṃmeya* = *abhisamaya* is to be preferred.

aśpa: = *aśva*, § 49. *aśpaṃca*, § 62.

asade: i.e. *ajhade* (*z*). Internal *s* was voiced, so appears written for *z*.

asadhanae: = *āsādanāya* 'to settle' (Act.).

asaṃna: § 123. Only in the phrase *asaṃna gaṃdava*. The meaning seems to be 'take possession of'. Compare *possess* from *sedeo*. Cf. § 123.
asaṃne: 373, is from *āsanna* (opposite to *tura* = *dūra* in the next line).
astama: See under *hastama*.
asmaǵa: § 78.
ahati: § 96.
ahu: §§ 78, 96.
ahuṃneva: = *ahuno eva*.
ahuno: § 91.

Ā

āmečhita: § 50.

I

iṃci: § 84.
ichiyati: §§ 1, 100.
itaṃca: (and *idaṃca*), § 82.
itu: §§ 12, 91.
ityartha: § 134.
iṃthuaṃmi: § 91.
ima-: § 82.
iyo: § 82.
iśa: § 91. *iśemi*, § 91.
istriae: § 10.

U

ukas-: *ut* + √*kas* 'to go', meaning 'depart, go away'. *ukasta*, § 107.
učhivana: Lüders, 'Zur Geschichte des ostasiatischen Tierkreises', *S.P.A.W.* (1933), pp. 6, 7.
ujhmayuǵa: An adjective applied to *manuṣya* (so read instead of *masuṣya*) 283 and *jaṃna* 373. Perhaps an Iranian word meaning 'skilled, experienced', Pahlavi *uzmāyišn* 'experience', *uzmūtak* 'skilled'. Cf. *B.S.O.S.* VII, 780.
uṭa: §§ 25, 37, 49. *uṭavala*, § 20; *uṭi-*, § 68.
uṭha: § 25.
uthaviyadi: 661. Optative, not = *uthāpyate*, § 100.
uthiśa: § 26.
udiśa: §§ 41, 102.
uṃna: § 37.
unidaǵa: (also *uneyaǵa*, *unidi* (Fem.)). The forms are used indiscriminately, compare 538 *stri Ramaśriae unidi giḏae huati* with 542 *sā kuḏi Ramaśriae nama uneyaǵa giḏae*. = 'adopted (child)'. The custom was very prevalent, since numerous documents refer to it. A payment was made by the adopters to the parents which was called *kuṭhačhira* (see s.v.). In 569 it is laid down that they are not to be treated as slaves: *eṣa Ṣaṃmaṃnera unidaǵa na dajha kaḏavo na vikrinidavo...emu kaṭavo yatha uniya maṃnuśa* 'This Ṣ. (is an) adopted (child), he is not to be made a slave, not to be sold, he is

to be treated like an adopted person'. With the permission of their masters, slaves could adopt children in the same way, cf. 39.

From *un-nī* in the sense of 'bring up', 'rear' (39 *unida vardhida*).

upaǵata: § 20.

Upateyu: = *Upadeva*, cf. *Jivateyu* and § 13.

upaṃna: § 107.

upari: § 91. = **uppari*, cf. Panj. *juppar*, Hind. *ūpar*, and J. Bloch, *L'Indo-Aryen*, p. 92.

upaśamǵhidavo: § 46.

uyoǵa: (?). Apparently title of some kind.

uryaǵana: See *vuryaǵa*.

uvadae: §§ 29, 102.

uhati: § 28.

E

eka: § 16. Declension of, § 88.

ekaǵo: § 53.

ekhara: Title or surname. The *kh* shows that it cannot belong to the native language of Kroraina, which was quite devoid of aspirates (or spirants: *kh* may stand for *x*).

eti: § 87.

etriśa: § 5.

ema: § 50. *emaveca*, § 11.

emaṃtara: (and *imaṃtara*). ='in the meanwhile, during this interval'. From *ima-* and *antara*; *emaṃtara* seems to be due to the influence of *ema*.

eśvari: § 9.

O

ogu: One of the commonest of the titles in the documents. The *g* in the middle of the word is striking. Otherwise both in the Prakrit and in native names *ǵ* appears in these positions: *bhaǵa*, *Caǵu*, *Oǵaca*, etc. There is no other word in which *g* appears regularly. In this word it is invariable. This perhaps indicates that it was pronounced **oggu*. Anyway the term cannot have belonged originally to the native language of Kroraina, because it was devoid of voiced consonants (§ 14).

As regards its significance, it appears to have been about the highest title that existed, since in lists of people with their titles the *ogu* comes first, e.g. 732 *astama pruchitaṃti ogu Jeyabhatra caṃkura Cataraǵa cuv́alaina Tiraphara cojhbo Soṃjaka Lpiptaṣa ca*, 574 *tatra sac̄hi hutaṃti ogu Dham̄apala kori Muldeya kitsatsa Lustuaṣa ca*. Similarly 709 (the king—the *ogus*—the *suveṭhas*—*cojhbo*, etc.), 582, etc. The title *guśura* seems to have been connected in some way with *ogu*. A number of people appear both as *ogu* and *guśura*, e.g. Kuṣanaṣena, Cakurata, Aśoǵa; while in the document 584 *eṣa muṃtra guśura Jebhatra caṃkura Caraǵa cojhbo Soṃjakaṣa ca* is the same formula (and the same people) who appear in 582 *eṣa mu(dra) ogu Jeyabhatra caṃkura Ca(taraǵa) (co)jhbo Soṃjakas̱a ceṣa.* About twenty-five *ogus* are mentioned.

oǵana: Some kind of crop measured in *milimas* and *khis* (154). Perhaps connected with Toch. *oko* 'fruit', *okar* 'plant'.

oḏeti: § 99. ='let go', 'send away', 'allow': 211 *edas̱a miṣiyaṃmi khadaṃnarthi Kaǩe Lṗipes̱a ca vaḏaviyani oḏitaṃti* 'K. and L. let mares loose in his cornfield to eat'; 18 *kriṣivatra na oḏeti karaṃnae* 'He will not allow him to do cultivation'. The etymology is not clear. It may be connected with Pali *oḍḍeti* 'throw away, reject' (Pv. A. 256 *oḍḍayāmi=chaḍḍayāmi*) and *oḍḍeti* meaning 'to set or lay a snare' (*pāsa*).

odara: Epithet of the camel. Perhaps=*udāra*, cf. A.M. *orāla* beside *urāla*.

omaǵa: § 7. =*avamaka* 'short' (of measure).

oya: § 17. =*ojas-*.

orovaǵa: =**avaropaka* (?). The meaning is not clear.

osuǵa: §§ 41, 48.

osti: 7. Apparently a mistake for *asti*.

ohara: 160. *goṭha-ohara=avahāra*, perhaps the 'produce of a farm', which can be removed (*ava-hṛ*) annually at harvest time.

K

ka-: § 83. *kači*, §§ 49, 84.

kaśaha vaṃnaǵa: 583. Obscure. Lüders (*Textilien*, p. 21) equates it with *kaṭa thavaṃne* (141), assuming that *ha* is miswritten.

kaṃjhavaliyana: Only 725 *avi(k)aṃjhavaliyana palṗiyas̱a anada pricha ganana kartavo*; the meaning is obviously 'treasury-officials'. *kaṃjha-* = Ir. *ganza-*, another dialectical form of *gañja-*, which also appears in the documents, cf. *gaṃñi*. The last member of the word is obscure.

kañi draṃga: =*gaṃñi draṃga*, cf. § 14.

kaṭa: 607. =*kāṣṭha* (?).

kaṭavo: § 37.

kaṭ̄ha: § 49.

kataṃti: § 5.

katari: 505. Pali *kattari* 'scissors, shears', Skt. *kartari*.

katma: 160. =(?), *katma kriṣivatra kareṃti*.

katvetha: 470. ='you have made'. Read *kaṭetha* (?).

kaṃpo: 43. Apparently something made of gold.

kabhoḍha: Perhaps 'grazing-land, pasture', cf. *B.S.O.S.* VII, 513. Prof. Thomas (*Acta Or.* XIII, 70) thinks that it was communally owned. Cf. s.v. *načira*.

kamita: § 83.

kamuṃta: 207. Lüders (*op. cit.* p. 6) equates it with *kamaṃta* (see s.v. *caṃdrikamaṃta*), but without adequate reason.

kam̄aveti: §§ 29, 104.

kayavatra: 534. (?). It looks Indian. *kācapātra* ('glass vessel') (?). *c* becomes *ś* (*j*) rather than *y*. But the signs are easily confused.

karaṃniya: § 116.
karitu: § 93. *karemana*, § 101; *kariśadi*, § 41.
karoma: 505. Some object.
karsenaṽa: Some kind of official. Closely connected with the *śadavida*. They are mentioned together 482, 590. The *karsenaṽa* is comparatively rarely mentioned, only about six or seven individuals bearing that title.
kala: Title. It may mean 'prince' because *Kala Puṃñabala* is called *maharayaputra* 622, 634. About ten *kalas* are mentioned.
Prof. Thomas has suggested (*Festschrift...H. Jacobi*, p. 51) that it is the same word as appears as *kara* in *Kujula Kara Kadphises* on the coins of that monarch, while *guśura*=*kujula*. The identifications are exceedingly probable, although the phonetics are not easy to explain. On the other hand titles like these are liable to be borrowed from kingdom to kingdom, undergoing phonetic changes *en route*. Cf. s.v. *guśura*.
kālihari: 399, and *kalihari* 709, 'quarrel'. Cf. Saka *kalahāraa-* 'quarreller' and Lüders, *B.S.O.S.* VIII, 641.
kavaji: Perhaps=*kavacikā*, which would give *kavaji* (*kavaśi*) in this dialect (§§ 14, 74 *ikā*>*i*, § 17 *c*>*ś*, *j*). From 505 it is clearly an article of dress.
kaśa: 400. Epithet of *aṃna* 'corn'.
kaśpiya: 534 *kaśpiya* 4 (in a list of objects).
kaṣara: 606: *śramaṃna Ayila viṃñaveti yatha edas̱a stri Cadis̱aae maṃma kaṣara dahita* 'The monk Ayila says that the woman Cadis̱a has burnt his *kaṣara*' (*edas̱a*...*maṃma*, anacoluthon). Compare Toch. A. *kāṣār*=Skt. *kāṣāya* (also B.). The Toch. forms perhaps find their explanation in this dialect. Beyond that the origin of the *r* is mysterious.
kākāni: 399. (?).
kārsenade: 86. Read probably *kārsenaṽa*. The officials *śadavida* and *karsenaṽa* are mentioned together in other places, cf. s.v. *karsenaṽa*.
kāla: Cf. s.v. *kala*.
kikama: § 84.
kica: § 41.
kicamaǵa: 'due, owing' (of tax, etc.). Etymology unknown.
kiḍa: §§ 5, 18, 107.
kiṃtra: A surname. Cf. *kiṃdari*.
kitsaitsa: Title. The *kitsaitsa* was of very high rank, often being mentioned along with *kālas* (581, 606, 640, etc.), also with *tasuca* (495, 648). The functions of the *kitsaitsa* were of a judicial nature (e.g. 495, 581, 606, 719, 730). Connected possibly with Toch. B. *ktsaitsañe* 'age'. The meaning 'elder', i.e. member of a sort of council of elders, would be quite appropriate. Cf. *J.R.A.S.* (1935), p. 673.
kiṃna: §§ 1, 83.
kirsos̱a: Epithet of *uṭi* 'female-camel', 570.

kilamudra: 'wedge-seal', i.e. wedge-shaped wood on tablet with the royal seal on. Stein, *Ruins of Ancient Khotan*, p. 368.

kilme: ='estate'; *kilme(ṃ)ci* 'tenant' according to Prof. Thomas (*Acta Or.* XIII, 63).

It is not easy to be quite sure about the precise meaning of the word. It seems to be the same as the Toch. A. *kälyme* 'direction, district' and often a general meaning like that is suitable: *Yav̆e av̆anaṃmi kilme-ci* 'belonging to the district of Yav̆e *av̆ana*'. But there are certain indications that it has a more specified meaning. Notably 374 *samvatsari palp̄i ciṃditaǵa yo kilmeciyana paride yaṃ ca rajade* 'The year's tax was assessed, both that from the *kilmecis* and that from the *rājya*'. That may mean that the *rājya* was the land directly owned by the king, while the *kilmes* were fiefs or estates granted to the nobility of the realm. The titles of people who have *kilmes* under them are those which for other reasons are known to have been the most exalted. Most frequently *ogu* (209, 254, 393, 621, 639, 734). Also *caṃkura* (437 and 16, where Peta *av̆ana* is handed over to the *caṃkura* Arjuna), *kala* (256, 367) and possibly *cojhbo* (152). No one without a high title is mentioned as having a *kilme*, so that it is not just a case of ordinary landed-proprietorship and tenancy but something more approaching feudalism. Cf. also *J.R.A.S.* (1935), p. 674. A connection may be suggested with the 'Lord's land' of the Tibetan documents (Prof. Thomas, *J.R.A.S.* (1934), p. 96).

kiṣaṃnae: § 5. *kiṣivaṃnae*, § 104.

kukuḍa: § 18.

kuṭh̄ach̄ira: § 49. Technical term indicating the payment made by people adopting a child to the parents (cf. s.v. *uneyaǵa*). This usually consisted of a horse (45, etc.) or camel (569). Except in 741, the word always occurs in the genitive, e.g. 569 *kuṭh̄ach̄iraṣa uṭa aklatsa ditaǵa* 'An *aṃklatsa* camel was given (as a return for) *kuṭh̄ach̄ira*', i.e. as a return for having nourished the child in its earliest infancy, a payment was due to the parents from the people who adopted the child. *kuṭh̄a-* is obviously the participle of *kuṣ-* 'extract' (connected with *cūṣ-* (?)), meaning the milk which had been sucked by the child. The *ṭh̄* instead of *ṭh* is unexplained (§ 49). The genitive is difficult unless we understand something like *kuṭhach̄iraṣa pratikara*.

kuḍa: 358=*kuḍaǵa*.

kuḍaǵa: Fem. *kuḍi* (*i*=*ikā*) 'boy' and 'girl'. The word is common in a number of the modern Indo-Aryan languages, e.g. Panjabi *kuṛī* fem., Lahnda *kuṛā* masc., *kuṛī* fem., etc., chiefly in the languages of the North-West. A connection with N.Pers. *kūdak* 'child' is not out of the question.

kuthala: Both meaning and etymology are difficult. It might appear from 327 *Kolaṣiyaṣa vaṃti miṣiyaṃmi kuthala* 10 3 *vikrida* 'In *miṣi*-land he sold 13 *kuthala* to K.' that it was a unit of land-measurement. On the other hand land is not usually measured by area, but by the amount of seed it takes (see s.v. *payati*, *bījapay°*), and the fact that *kuthala* is placed before *bhuma*, qualifying it (e.g. 419, 582), indicates that it was a particular form or kind of land. Since undoubtedly the *kuthala*s are numbered (see above) a meaning something like a 'strip of land' would be most adequate, and *kuthala bhuma* would mean land divided up in such a fashion. Such systems of land-tenure are of course common. The word cannot belong to the native language because of the aspirate *th*. Nor can it be Iranian because internal *th* would appear as *h* at this time (both in Saka and Pahlavi). As a rule (§27) *th* would become *h* in Indian words too, so that the word may represent **kutthala*.

kurora: Epithet of land, *bhuma kurora*. Perhaps = N.Pers. *kurār* = 'a plot of land with a raised border prepared for sowing'; *B.S.O.S.* VII, 780.

kulola: § 28.

kuv́ana: *kvav́ana* 430. (1) Epithet of corn (*aṃna*), collected as tax. There are three technical terms applied in this sense: *kuv́ana*, *koyimaṃḍhina*, *tsaṃghina* (e.g. 272), but their precise signification is not clear. (2) in 318 *kuv́ana prahuni*; compare Saka *kuhaṃ thau* = Skt. *cailapaṭṭa*.

kuśava: § 2.

kusaṃta: Surname or title.

kuhani: (and *khvani*, *khuv́aneṃci*). = 'The Capital' or 'Citadel'; cf. Prof. Thomas, *Acta Or.* XII, 61. 530 *mahanuava maharaya lihati...yatha...iśa kuhaniyaṃmi* '...here in the *kuhani*', i.e. Krorayina, the capital from which the great king is writing. In 489 the *Khuv́aneṃci Bhic̄hu-saṃgha* lays down the ecclesiastical rules for the provincial *saṃgha* at Caḍota.

keti: § 87.

ko: § 83.

kojalya: § 21.

kojava: = Pali *kojava* 'a rug or cover with long hair, a fleecy counterpane'. Both words may be connected with *kaucapaka*, which is enumerated among the different kinds of rugs (*kambala*) at *Arth. Śāstra*, II, 11. 100.

kotareyana: 414. Obscure.

kopi: 198. Read *ko pivaraǵa* 'whichever is fat' instead of *kopi varaǵa* in the text.

kobala: Surname. = *koṃpala* (?).

koyimaṃḍhi: (and *koyimaṃḍhina*; in *koyimaṃ* 38, -*ḍhi* has perhaps been omitted by mistake). The term is applied to a particular class of officials in charge of collecting grain, e.g. 38 *Apeṃnaṣa pitu Opǵeya Koyimaṃ* (*ḍhi* (?)) *hoati*; 309 *taṃ kala adehi koyimaṃḍhina aṃna milima iśa* 1 *sa* 20 20 10 (*iśa*) *aniṣ*...(*ti*) 'At that time the *k*.s used to bring from there 170 *m*. of corn'. Cf. *tsaṃghina*.

korara: Surname or title. Applied to Suḡita (73, 181, 577), Rutraya (147, 180, 382) and Cakrala (334).

kori: An official whose functions seem to have been most closely connected with the royal herds. Thus in 4 *kori* Rutraya is given instructions about the dispatch of camels. Further orders about camels are given to *kori*s in 40, 64, 228, about horses in 213, 223, 228. They occasionally however appear in other functions, namely legal disputes, e.g. 32 (instructions to *kori* Rutraya about a marriage dispute), 49 (Rutraya: along with *cojhbo* Yitaka and *toṃga* Yukto: dispute about property).

koro: 383. Apparently a kind of camel.

korno: 46 *striya na korno dhidare* 2 (? *striyana korno*... or *striya nakorno*). Quite obscure.

koltarṣa: Surname or title. Applied to Kuunǵe (66), Salv́eta (210, 281) and Tsuǵenaṃma (266).

kośalǵa: § 16.

kośava: Cf. *kojava*.

krataǵa: 534 *krataǵa* 2 (in a list of objects).

kriṭha: 580 *dhaṃḍa deyaṃti aśpa tre na kri ṭha prahara satati* (*nakriṭha* or *na kriṭha* (?); epithet of horse (?)).

krita: § 5.

kriśaǵa: § 74.

kriṣati: § 5.

kriṣivatra: § 76.

krisivaṃnae: § 103.

kremeru: 318, 660. Some object which has to do with cloth or clothing, as appears from 660.

krona: 163. Epithet of *uṭa* 'camel' (or *nikrona*).

klaseṃci: Officials whose duties were concerned with looking after horses and camels connected with the army: 562 *ede Kuunǵe Oǵana s̱aca caura seni klaseṃciye, tusya puna rayaka uṭavala karetu, yo paṃca seniyade as̱i siyaṃti eda aṃña rajadhaña kareṃti, taha suṭha na laṃcaǵa karetu, mahi maharayas̱a anatiyade aṃñatha karetu, yahi eda kilamudra atra eśati praṭha yo atra aṭhove jaṃna siyaṃti teṣa Kuunǵeyas̱a paride (uṭa) uṭi picavidavo, uṭavale kartavo ede Kuunǵe Oǵanas̱a ca piṃḍa klaseṃna dhaña kartavo* 'These (people) Kuunǵe and Oǵana are *klaseṃci*s for four armies (divisions of the army), but you are making them keepers of the royal camels. They are performing another state duty which on the top of their army-(work) (*seniyade as̱i*: *as̱i* = *ajhi* which occurs below *tade ajhi*. It = *adhi*, cf. *as̱imatra*) makes five (jobs). In this you are certainly not acting rightly, you are acting differently from the command of me, the great king. When this wedge and seal shall come there, such people as are available there, the camels must be handed over from Kuunǵe to them, and they must be made keepers of camels, (while) these people Kuunǵe and Oǵana perform their fundamental *klaseṃna*-duty.' It is clear from this passage that the duties of the *klaseṃci* were sufficiently near those of the *uṭavala* for them to be confused by the authorities. In 10 a man complains that he is *klaseṃci* at Peta *av́ana* and is being made an *arivaǵa* ('guide', see s.v.).

Ḱ

Ḱema: § 83.

KH

khakhorna: An attempt is made in *B.S.O.S.* VII, 780 to show that this word should be read *khakhorda* and is = Av. *kax*^{v}*arda* 'wizard', Arm.L.W. *kaxard* 'magician', Skt. *kākhorda, kharkoṭa*, etc., meaning the same. *khakhorna stri* would then mean 'a witch', a meaning which fits the passages well.

khaja: § 41.

khaṃje: § 60.

khatva: § 107.

khadaṃnarthi: § 55.

khaṃnavaṭaǵes̱i: Cf. s.v. *vaṭaǵa*.

khara: = (1) 'ass' 598, 628; (2) a surname or title, e.g. *kha° Kunǵeyas̱a* 456. Connected with *ekhara* (?).

kharaǵi: 292. Perhaps means 'asses'.

kharav́arna: 318. Some object.

khi: Measure of capacity: 20 *khi* = 1 *milima*. Since *milima* has been shown to be = Gk. μέδιμνος, *khi* is probably = χοῦς. As regards the change from *ū* to *ī* Konow says (*Saka Studies*, p. 20) that in Saka a dental or guttural fricative effects the change *ū* > *ī* (*ttīma* 'seed' = **tauxma* through **tūxma*, although here the *x* comes last).

khula: = *kula* 'herd (of camels, etc.)'. On *kh*- for *k*- in Prakrit, cf. Pischel, § 206. But the change does not occur elsewhere in this word. Both Pali and Prakrit have *kula*.

khuv́aneṃci: Cf. *kuhani*.

kheni: = *khani* 'a pit'.

khema: Has hitherto been taken as = Skt. *kṣema*. But *kṣ* becomes *c̄h̄* not *kh* in this dialect. *khoritaǵa* 'shaven' is an exception. But this word in the compounds *śvastic̄h̄ema* and *yogac̄h̄ema* exhibits the regular form.

Further, it suits the sense of the passages better to take it as a place-name. In 214 *yava khemaṃmi* means obviously 'as far as Khema', because we are dealing with the stages of the journey of an ambassador to Khotan, and the provisions to be made for them. Khema appears from this document to have been a town between Caḍota and Khotan. In 506 and 709 we hear of slaves fleeing to Khema. Apart from this *khema* only occurs in the stock phrase *yahi Khema Khotaṃnade vartamana hac̄h̄ati iṃthu ami mahi maharayasa padamulaṃmi viṃñadi lekha prahadavya* 272, etc. 'When there is news (*vartamana* = *pravṛti*) from Khema and Khotan you must send a letter of information to the feet of me the great king'. For the construction *Khema Khotaṃnade* compare *Caḍota Calmadanade*, etc. and § 135.

Khotaṃna: =Khotan. *Kh* no doubt stands for *x* to judge from Saka *Hvatäna*, N.Pers. *xutanī*, etc.

khoritaǵa: § 48. (=*kṣor-*.)

khoṣa: Name of a man. Probably a Khotanese. *B.S.O.S.* VII, 516.

khvani: Cf. *kuhani*.

Khvarnarse: n.pr. *B.S.O.S.* VII, 515 and 789.

G

ǵachamana: § 101.

ǵachiṣyāti: § 99.

ǵaṃñavara: 'treasurer', § 45, and *B.S.O.S.* VII, 509.

ǵaṃḍa piṭaka: 511. ='boils and eruptions'.

ǵatosmi: § 106.

ǵademi: § 105.

ǵaṃdavo: § 46.

ǵanasaǵa: A surname applied to Śakha, who was a Khotani (335). *kanasaka*, which is obviously the same, appears alone in 30 *Khotani Kanasaka*.

ǵamaṃ: =*gamana*, § 13.

ǵamiyana: Cf. Pali *gamika*=*gamiya* 'courier'.

ǵameṣati: § 50.

ǵameṣiśa: § 99.

ǵarahati: § 10.

ǵarbheni: § 3.

ǵalṕiti: 162. Lüders (*B.S.O.S.* VIII, 641) suggests plausibly that it is a mistake for *saṃgalṕiti* 'having collected', with *lṕ* (i.e. *lý*) for *l* according to § 31.

ǵiḍa: §§ 28, 107.

ǵiḍya: § 41.

ǵiṃta: or *gita*; 225 *aṃña giḍa giṃta khi* 1, something measured in *khis*.

Girakaṣa: § 15.

ǵilanaǵa: § 10.

ǵuṭa: =*gūḍha*, § 18.

ǵumoca: 534. Some object.

ǵuśura: Title. It is among the highest titles like *kāla* and *ogu*. With the latter it seems to have rather close connections, because a number of people appear with both titles (see s.v. *ogu*). Their functions were judicial (216, 295, etc.). There were *guśuras* in Khotan as well as in Shan-Shan (413).

Prof. Thomas (*Festschrift...H. Jacobi*, p. 51 and *Acta Or.* XIV, p. 66) proposes to equate *guśura* with the title *kujula*, *kuyula*, *kozoulo*, which occurs on the coins of the Kuṣan kings.

Leaving aside this problem for a moment I propose to equate *guśura* with N.Pers. *vazīr*, Av. *vičira*. The N.Pers. is reborrowed from Ar. (Horn, *Neupersische Etymologie*, s.v.), the correct N.Pers. form would be **guzīr*. The change from *vi-* to *gu-* which is characteristic of N.Pers. was also at work among the Iranians who appeared in North India in the first century A.D.

Gudap̄hara = *Vindafarnā*. Further, *c* is regularly changed to *ś* in this dialect (§ 17), so that the form we would expect corresponding to *vazīr* if borrowed into a North-West Prakrit would be *guśira*, and the assimilation of the vowels produced the form we have, *guśura*.

If this is true *kujula* of the Kuṣana inscriptions, if connected with this word, will have to be a corruption of *guśura* in the mouths of non-Iranians of some kind.

In support of this hypothesis it may be further pointed out that *guśura* cannot belong to the native language of Kroraina on account of the initial *g* (§ 14), and if *kujula* were the original form it is incredible that a people possessing no voiced stops would substitute *guśura* for it. *gauśura* appears as an official title in a Sanskrit document from Kuci (Lüders, 'Zur Geschichte u. Geographie Ostturkestans', *S.P.A.W.* 1922).

ĝoduma: § 24.

ĝoni: S. *goṇī* 'sack', 214 *goniyaṃmi*.

ĝoma: =*godhūma* 'wheat'; *gohomi* 83 represents an intermediate stage. In 72 (*ja*²) *huma* (²*ga*-) read *gohuma* probably. Cf. § 27 and § 28.

ĝośato: 157. Read certainly *go vito* (cf. s.v. *vito*).

ĝramiye: § 60.

ĝrahito: § 53.

ĝrihasta: § 5.

GH

ĝhrida: § 5.

Ṅ

ṅĝaca: Read *Tĝaca* as in the notes. A variant is *Taĝaca*, cf. § 13 and § 47.

C

caura: 'four', § 19.

caṃkura: An official title. Peta *av̄ana* is put in charge of a *caṃkura*, 16. They appear from time to time as judges along with *ogus*, *cojhbos*, *tasucas*, *cuv̄alayinas* (318, 506, 583, etc.). *Caṃkura* Kapĝeya has *kilmecis* (see s.v.) under him. Other administrative duties are entrusted to them (64, camels, 532). Prof. Thomas compares *caṅ-khyir*, *caṅkhyur* of the Tibetan documents (*J.R.A.S.* (1927), pp. 75 n., 79; (1933), p. 550; (1934), pp. 97, 252). He has further shown that its meaning in Tibetan is 'protector' (*Acta Or.* XIII, 73), and proposes to equate it with the Skt. *nagara-rakṣaka*, i.e. guardian of the city or chief of police. The Tibetan word is presumably borrowed from some Central Asian language.

cakhorade: 320 *ogu je ya śa ni ro cakhorade.* Read *ogu Jeyaśa ni rocakhorade*, but the expression is quite obscure.

caǵali: § 75.

caṃñatrena: =*jaṃñatrena*, § 14.

Caḍota: It is noteworthy that there are surprisingly few native names containing cerebrals, so that the language was probably devoid of them. *Caḍota* is definitely exceptional. *J.R.A.S.* (1935), p. 669.

Caḍotiye: § 60.

Caḍodemci: § 77.

Cataroyaeṣa: § 69.

catu: § 89.

catuvarṣaǵa: § 139.

caṃdrikamaṃta: 372. *cāṃdrik°* 714. According to Prof. Thomas 'moonlight-workings'='jade' (*Acta Or.* XII, 46), only in that case we ought to have had -*kam̄aṃta*, § 36. In 714 the word should perhaps be read *cāṃdrikamaṃtana*, because the *na* which is printed separately seems inappropriate. It is not clear whether we are dealing with a compound expression or with two separate words (*caṃdri* and *kamaṃta*) which happen to be mentioned together. *caṃdri* might be connected with Skt. *cāndrakam* 'ginger'. *kamaṃta* has been compared with N.P. *kamand* 'noose' which is uncertain as long as its meaning is unsettled, and also with *kamuṃta* (see s.v.). A further connection with Saka *kāṃmadi* is suggested by H. W. Bailey, *Z.D.M.G.* 1936, p. 576.

capariśa: ='46', §§ 43, 47.

camari: 585: *camari vavala* 1. Probably a mistake for *camari vala*, i.e. the tail of the *camara* or chowrie.

carapuruṣa: 'Spy' or 'intelligence agent' as in Sanskrit.

caru: Surname or title applied to Kutǵeya (103), Mutreya (277), Lustu (327), Jimoya (385), Pratǵa (576).

Calmadana Caḍodade: § 135.

cavala: ='quickly', § 90.

caṣaǵa: =Skt. *caṣaka*- 'cup', used of a small measure of capacity, less than a *khi*.

ciṭughi: Cf. *jiṭughi* and § 14.

cita: =*citta*; *cita kartavya* 'attention is to be paid'.

ciṃd: =*cint*-, § 46. It is used in the sense of 'reckoning' or 'assessing' the amount of tax, e.g. 468 *yahi purvika adehi Yav́e av́anaṃmi kilmeciyana paride saṃvatsari palṗi aṃna nadha piṃḍa milima* 10. 4. 1. *ciṃditaǵa* 'Formerly from there at Yav́e *av́ana* the yearly tax from the *kilmecis* (see s.v.) was assessed altogether at 15 *milima* of corn'.

citiśati: 667. Perhaps =*cintiṣyati.* On the omission of anusvāra see § 47.

citranae: 703. Read *civ́anae*=*jivanae* 'to live', which makes good sense. The akṣaras *tra* and *v́* are quite easily confused.

Cina: Skt. *Cīna*='Chinese'.

Cinapħara: *B.S.O.S.* VII, 515. Probably *cina-* = Chinese and Iranian *pħara* = *farnā*, just as *Cinaṣena* is formed with the Indian *-sena*.

cina veḍa: 353. Pali *veṭha*, *veṭhana* according to Prof. Rapson and *cina* = 'Chinese'.

cinika: § 32.

ciṃnita-da: §§ 24, 45.

cimara: = *cīvara* (Prof. Rapson), cf. § 50.

ciraiṃta: 587. Epithet of *bhuma* 'land'. *cirāyita* (?) (i.e. land that has grown poor by being used for a long time). Quite doubtful.

cilaṃḍhina: 'common, shared': 21 *yatha edaṣa Lṕipamena ṣadha uṭa cilaṃḍhina hoati* 'That of him there is a camel owned in common with L.'; 256 (they have divided property...) *sudha Patraya cilaṃḍhina hoda* 'Only Patraya was (remained) common property'. On the suffix *-ina*, cf. § 77.

Civamitra: § 14.

ciśa: § 11.

cuḍaso: 206. Obscure.

cudiyadi: §§ 1, 2.

cuṃpita: 585: *śastrena cuṃpita taravacena cuṃpita*. Apparently means something like 'cut, chopped'. Dhātu P. *cumb-* 'to hurt' (?).

curom̄a: (*crom̄a*, *cirom̄a*). Some kind of agricultural commodity, sent as tax (*palṕi*). From 264 *curom̄a paśu* 2 '*curom̄a* sheep 2' it would seem to be something that is got from sheep or goats (cheese?).

culaǵe: § 53.

culo: 304. Apparently a surname.

cuv́alayina: An official title. *cuv́alayina*s act as judges (582, 709, 732). In 135 *cuv́alayina* Pħurmaṣeva goes on an embassy to Khotan. His name has a definitely foreign appearance (possibly Iranian, see s.v.). Judging by the position they occupy in lists of titled people, the *cuv́alayina*s were inferior in rank to *ogu*s, *guśura*s and *caṃkura*s, possibly superior to *cojhbo*s (cf. 582, 584, 709, 732).

Only a few *cuv́alayina*s are mentioned, namely: Malbhuta, Onuǵi, Pħum̄aṣeva, Pumñavaṃta and Tirapħara. In certain cases *cu°* seems to be a proper name, cf. 278, 573, 702.

Coka: Surname of Pǵita, 103.

cokto: Surname of Soṃcǵeya and Arkaṃtǵa (558).

cokho: (*cokaṃ*). Surname of Suǵita (72).

coc̄ha: (*coc̄haǵa*). = Skt. *cokṣa*, Ardh.M. *cokkha* 'clean'.

cojhbo: The commonest of all the local titles. About forty people are referred to with the title *cojhbo*. Judging from the position he regularly occupied in lists the *cojhbo* was inferior in rank to *ogu*, *guśura*, *kāla* and *caṃkura* (478, 709, 732, etc.). On the other hand *cojhbo* Soṃjaka was certainly governor of the province of which Caḍota was the capital (272 *ekisya etaṣa raja picavidemi*), so that he at least must have been superior in power to all the *ogu*s, etc. residing there. But again the large number of *cojhbo*s mentioned, much larger than that of *ogu* or *guśura* or *caṃkura*, shows that they cannot as a rule have held such high positions as Soṃjaka.

Their functions were both judicial and administrative (tax-collecting, etc.). Also national defence in the case of Soṃjaka (cf. especially 272). How closely they were connected with the army it is impossible to say, because most of the documents are dealing with civil life. In 713 *cojhbo* Taǵira reports a victory over an unspecified enemy, where it looks as if he had been commanding. In 478 apparently *guśura*, *speṭha*, *cuvalayina* and *cojhbo* are all said to be military men: *Iśa c̄hunaṃmi khvaniyade seniye ayitaṃti guśura Kuṣanasena, caruveta spetha Vidhura, cvalayiṃna Puṃña-vaṃta, cojhbo Naṃtipala Palaǵeyaṣa ca.*

The bulk of the wedge tablets (*kilamudra*) and leather documents (*anadi-lekha*) from the court are addressed to *cojhbos*, so that while their rank was not so high as *ogu*, etc., they certainly played the most active part in the administration of the kingdom.

Since the native language of Kroraina had no voiced stops the group *jhb* (=*zb*) indicates that the title must have come from outside.

cojhbo is no doubt identical with the *cazba* mentioned in the Maralbashi documents edited by Konow ('Ein neuer Saka-Dialekt', *S.B.P.A.W.* (1935), pp. 772 ff.). Dr W. Henning points out in a communication that it is derived from Av. *čazdahvant-* (Nom. Sing. *čazdahvå*) which is translated by Pehl. *vičārtār*.

coṭaǵa: 'clothing', § 18. =*coḍaǵa*.

coḍina: 489. Obscure.

cotaṃ: =*cotaṃna*, § 13.

codeyati: § 100.

cori: § 60.

coritaǵa prace: § 112.

corko: 641. Surname of Suǵita.

CH

chataǵa: 505. =*chadaka-* or *chādaka-* 'clothing'. Cf. *B.S.O.S.* VII, 783 and Lüders, *Textilien im Alten Turkistan*, p. 34.

chaṃni: 231: *chaṃni syati*. Not a future of course, because it would be *ṣy* not *sy*.

chaṃlpita: § 14.

chiṃnati: § 45.

chotaǵa: 161. =(?).

choreti: *chorayati*, which occurs in Buddhist Sanskrit, ='throw away, abandon': 134 *ma iṃci edeṣa ajhia dhaṃena raja dhaṃa choretu* 'Do not abandon the law of the kingdom for a law (emanating) from the mouths of these people'. It may perhaps sometimes mean 'to send' (265); *jhorita* seems to be a variant, cf. § 15.

choretu: § 93.

C̄H́

c̄h́itra: § 1.
c̄h́iraṣa: 415, 434. Both times in the technical sense of *kuṭh́ac̄h́ira* (see s.v.).
c̄h́una: = 'time, date', occurring in the formula *iśa c̄h́unaṃmi*, which comes after the year, month and day of the king's reign.
= Saka *kṣuna* with the same meaning. It is also borrowed into Kuchean as *kṣuṃ*. In the Maralbashi Saka it appears as *χšana*.
c̄h́ema: § 48. Cf. s.v. *khema*.

J

jaṃñatriyena: Cf. § 76.
jaṃdunaṃca: 565 'worms'. Cf. Lüders, 'Zur Geschichte des ostasiatischen Tierkreises' (*S.P.A.W.* (1933), pp. 15–19). He prints a text from Šorcuq in debased Sanskrit, where *jantuna* is used parallel to *ahi* in the animal cycle. For the plural, cf. § 62. This renders it unnecessary to assume that *sarpa* or *bhujaga* has been omitted.
janaṃta: § 101.
janati: § 96.
jaṃñiyae: 506. *tanuv́aǵa goṭhadare paṃca jaṃniyae ṣadha śata* (= *śapta*) 'Collection of five people' (?).
janemi: § 97.
jaṃnma: § 44.
jamata: § 72.
jayaṃta-: §§ 6, 101.
jalpita: § 40.
jalma: = *jālma*, § 40.
jāna: = *dhyāna*, § 41.
Jiṭugha: A title of the kings of Shan-Shan, which appears first in the seventeenth year of the reign of Aṃgoka. Its meaning and origin are unknown but it must certainly be foreign, because the native language possessed no *j* (§ 14), with the result that the title often appears as *ciṭugha*, and almost certainly no *ṭ* either.
jinida: § 15.
Jimoya: § 15. = *Cimoya*.
jivaṃtaǵa: § 101.
jivaṃtiyae: § 69.
jivaṃto: § 53.
Jivadeyu: = *Jivadeva*, cf. *Upateyu* and § 13.
Jivaśaṃma: § 36.
jivo: § 53.
juṭhi: (*cuṭhiye*, *jhuṭhi*). An obscure term connected with sowing and agriculture. It is not an adjective because it is placed after *bhija* 'seed' in 703: *bhija juṭhi*. The form *cuṭhiye* 422 looks like a plural (cf. § 60). It cannot belong to the native language (§ 14, and cf. under *Jiṭugha*).

Jeṭuǵha: =*Jiṭugha*, § 3.
jeṭha: =*jyeṣṭha*, §§ 41, 49.
Jepriya: =*Jayapriya*, cf. § 6.
Jeyanaṃta: =*Jayānanda*.
jeyaṃtasa: § 6.
Jiryaśyaṣa (?): Read as in the note *Jeyaśa* or *Jayaśa*. It is obviously the same *ogu* Jayaśa who is mentioned elsewhere.

JH

=*jh* or *z*. Cf. *Khar. Inscr.* III, 303. They are distinguished in the originals but not in the transliteration.
Jhaǵimoya: *B.S.O.S.* VII, 789.
jheniǵa: ='under the care of'; Saka *ysīnīya*, Sogd. *zynyh*. Konow, *Acta Or.* x, 80. The *i* must have been long to judge from the Saka, i.e. **zenīǵa*. Compare also N.Pers. *zīn-hār* 'protection' and *zindān* 'prison'.
jheniya: § 16.
jhorita: =*chorita*, § 26.

Ñ

ñatiyo: § 53. Perhaps to be read *ñati yo*, e.g. 437 . . .*putro va praputro va ñati yo amña kilmeci* 'Son or grandson (or) relation (or) any other *kilmeci*'.
ñadartha: § 139.
ñadarthemi: § 108.

Ṭ

ṭera: =*sthavira*.

ḌH

=(1) *ḍha*, (2) an akṣara of quite uncertain value. Cf. *Khar. Inscr.* p. 305 and plate XIV.
ḍhipu: 722. Some part of a bow (*dhanu*) or something connected with it.
ḍhyaĉhiyaṣa: 685. =*dryaĉhiyaṣa*, which occurs in the following document, i.e. *tryakṣi* 'three-eyed'. Some god (?), Śiva (?). Also which of the two forms of *ḍha* (see above) is it?

T

ta-: Demonstr. pron. § 80 (declension and syntax).
taǵaḍo: Surname of Suǵita 137.
taǵastehi: Uncertain, since it only occurs twice, 12, 43. In *taǵastehi varidavo* 12 it might be either instrumental or ablative plural, 'They are to be kept away from *taǵastas* or by *taǵastas*'. Or is it possibly an adverb?
taṃcaṃ: 117 *sarva piṃḍaiṃ taṃ caṃ gavi*. Read perhaps *sarva piṃḍaiṃtaṃcaṃ gavi*, i.e. °*itaṃca* (§ 82) (*piṇḍāyita*='collected together'). Or perhaps *sarva piṃḍa iṃtaṃca gavi* (cf. § 82 for *itaṃca*).

tac̄ham̱na: § 72.
taṃḍa: § 14.
taḏitaǵena: (and *taḏitaǵade*), § 112.
tati: 570 *uṭi tati varṣi* 'A female camel so many years old'. Cf. § 87.
tatiyemi: 58. Adverb derived from *tati* (above). Cf. § 91.
tatremi: § 91.
tade: § 12.
tanana: § 24.
tanu, tanuv́aǵa: § 86.
tanutri: Read no doubt *tanuv́i* as suggested in the notes, i.e. fem. of *tanuv́aǵa* (§ 74). *tr* and *v́* are easily confused, cf. *jaṃñatrena* and *jaṃñav́ena*; also *citranae* (above) = *civ́anae*.
tapadaya: = 'thereupon, straightaway'. Etymology obscure.
Tamasṕa: Iranian name = **Taxmāspa*, *B.S.O.S.* VII, 515. On the *sṕ*, cf. § 49.
tam̄ena: Title or surname of Suǵita (118, 384) and Kuleya (174).
taravacena: Some instrument for cutting or chopping, 585. (It is used parallel with *śastrena*.)
tarvardha (?): 479. Obscure.
tavanaǵa: See *thavaṃnaǵa*.
tāvastaǵa: = 'carpet' (Prof. Thomas comparing Gk. τάπης, a loan-word from Persian, and N.Pers. *tāftan*, *tābam*). From the same base is *thavaṃnaǵa* (see s.v.). Arm.L.W. *tapast* and *tapastak* 'mat', N.Pers. *tabastah* = 'fringed carpet'.
taśavita: = *daśavita*, § 14.
tasuca: An official title. Nothing very definite is to be learned about their functions. Prof. Thomas (*Acta Or.* XIII, 78) suggests that it means interpreter, but does not quote any evidence from the documents. To judge by their position in official lists the *tasuca* were not amongst the highest titles (*ogu*, *guśura*, *kāla*) but on a lower level with *cojhbo*, *v́asu*, *ṣoṭhaṃga*, e.g. 709, 588, 422.
In 580 *sac̄hi divira Apǵeya*, *sac̄hi sotira tasuca Catata*, *sac̄hi kāla Karaṃtaṣa putra Kaṃjiya*, Catata has a double title *sotira tasuca*. Is *sotira* the Greek σωτήρ used as an honorific title and is *tasuca* an equivalent of that?
taṣemi: § 80.
tasmartha: § 80.
taha: § 27.
tahi: § 79.
tik̄e: 147 *tik̄e giḏaṃti*. Read *pak̄e* (?).
tiṭhi: Cf. *diṭhi*.
tita (etc.): § 14.
tina: § 1.
tiṃpura: § 50.
timitavya: Only in the phrase *prahuḏarthaya na timitavya*. The

meaning is clear from comparing a variant of the same phrase: 320 *prahuḍarthaya na manyu kartavya*, i.e. 'You must not be angry or worried, upset about a present'. (It was customary always to send a present with a letter, and this phrase is used when an excuse is given for not doing so.) *dimidavo* also occurs, and it is difficult (cf. §§ 14, 15) to be sure which is the correct form. *timi°-* occurs oftenest, which is in its favour. Possibly connected with *tāmyati*, although the phonetics are difficult. We may have a special treatment of original **tm̥myeti*. Has N.Pers. *tīmār* 'sorrow' anything to do with it?

Tiraph̄ara: Iranian name. *B.S.O.S.* vii, 515. The deity *Tīra* appears on the Kuṣan coins (Stein, *Ind. Ant.* (1888), p. 95) as TEIPO.

tirṣa: (and *tirsa*, *torṣa* 39 is apparently a mistake). Epithet of horse or mare. It is only used in the existing documents about those horses or mares which are given as a payment when children are adopted (see s.v. *kuṭhach̄ira*). The meaning is obscure but it is interesting to note that the form *tirṣa* is always masculine (used with *aśpa*) while *tirsa* is feminine (used with *vaḍavi* 39. 771), thus giving a glimpse of the morphology of the native language.

tivajhe: § 22.

tivas̱ehi: § 58.

tiṣu: § 1.

tu (*tuo*): § 53.

tuǵuja: Title of Cimola (306, 360), Sudarśana (374). In 187 read probably *tuǵuja* for *vuǵaja* (as in the notes).

tuṃbhich̄a: §§ 37, 47.

tumahu: §§ 27, 79.

te: =*tasmin*, § 80.

teyaṃgadhi: 271 (or *teyaṃgami*). Read perhaps *te yaṃgami nidavya*.

toṃga: An official. He comes among the list of officials who are qualified as *ajhade* 'noble' or 'free' (436). His functions were closely connected with those of the *cojhbo*. The *cojhbo* Yitaka and the *toṃga* Vukto repeatedly have letters addressed to them in common (11, 23, 28, 37, 42). These functions seem to have been most closely connected with camels and horses, and the conveying of things from one part of the kingdom to another (see, for instance, 387, 622). No. 96 consists of a list of *toṃgas* and a statement of the number of people belonging to each of them. These are perhaps the *vaṭh̄ayaǵa* (=*upasthāyaka*), who are referred to in 387, 622, i.e. the staff of subordinates employed by the *toṃgas*. From that document it appears that *toṃgas* were pretty numerous. Perhaps it was a military rank, 'captain'.

Prof. Thomas, *Acta Or.* xiii, 53; *J.R.A.S.* (1934), p. 255, suggests a connection with ***stom-gyaṅ*** and ***stoṅ-dpon*** of the Tibetan documents. The latter seems, however, to have been a much more important official (*J.R.A.S.* (1934), pp. 96–7). Possibly = an Iranian **tuvānaka-*.

tomi: = *tvayā* according to Prof. Thomas, *Acta Or.* XIII, 52. The form can be explained as *to* = *tava* and *mi*, which is frequently appended to pronominal forms (§ 91). On the genitive as agent see § 119. It seems to mean *tasmin* at 123.

toṃmihi: 165 *toṃmihi ṣadha iśa viṣajidavo* 'Is to be sent here along with the *toṃmis* (?); if *toṃmi* here is instrumental plural, it is the only one of its kind. We expect *-iyehi* (§ 70). Also a noun *toṃmi* appears nowhere else. No doubt it is written for *tomi*, for which see s.v.

toṣu: § 53.

trakhma: §§ 14, 44.

traǵhade: §§ 14, 47.

Traṣa Avanaṃmi: See s.v. *aʋana*.

tricha: § 50. Perhaps = **tirikṣa* dissimilated out of *titikṣā* (cf. *dilicha*): 565 *nāga nachatrami tricha, sarva karya sahidavya* 'In the *nāga-nakṣatra* forbearance: everything is to be endured'.

triti: §§ 5, 89.

trina: § 89.

triśa: §§ 47, 89.

trubhicha: § 39.

truṣǵa: 581 *truṣǵa kalaṃmi* 'in a time of drought'. Cf. *B.S.O.S.* VII, 511 (= *dur* and *huška*). Alternatively we might read *ʋuṣǵa*. The akṣaras *tra* and *ʋa* are very much alike, cf. s.v. *citranae, tanutri aṃñaʋena* and *Khar. Inscr.* Plate XIV. The *h-* might easily be omitted leaving *uṣka*, § 28. On *ṣk* becoming *ṣǵ*, cf. § 49. On initial *ʋu-* (*vu-*) out of *u-*, § 30.

truso: 631. Title or surname of Kunaṣena.

trepe: Surname of Jivamitra (5 times).

tvaca: 702. In a list of spices. Skt. *tvac* and *tvaca* = 'cinnamon' and 'cassia-bark'.

tsaṃg(h)ina: or *tsaṃghinaʋa* (for the *-ʋa* as a suffix cf. *karsenaʋa*). A particular class of official engaged in providing corn to the state, usually mentioned side by side with the *koyimaṃḍhina*. Possibly *tsaṃg(h)ina* is an epithet describing a particular class of grain collected as tax, and *tsaṃg(h)inaʋa* the official connected with it, in which case *koyimaṃḍhina* would have to have both senses, e.g. 164 *yo puna adehi rajade tsaṃghina kvemaṃḍhina palpi dhama iśa mama pruchaṃti*, either 'What arrangement about tax from that kingdom (province) the *ts*.s and *k*.s ask me' or 'What arrangement about *tsaṃghina* and *koyimaṃḍhina* tax they ask'. The first seems most probable.

TH

thamavaṃte: § 60.

tharitavo: § 14.

thavaṃnaǵa: (*thavaṃnae, thavaṃna-mae*, also *tavanaǵa*). = Saka *thauna* 'cloth' (*B.S.O.S.* VII, 512). Cf. also for the form N.Pers. *tafnah* 'web'.

thavitaǵa: 416: *tha°* 1. Participial form from the same base as *thavaṃnaǵa* (?).

thaviti: § 112.

thiyaṃti: § 96.

thiyanae: § 103.

thubada: 378: *thu ba da u na.* Obscure.

D

dajavita: Cf. *daśavita.* Only we would have expected *daǰavita.*

Daǰapala: n.pr. =*Dhvajapāla*; cf. *daśa* in Saka (loan-word)=*dhvaja.*

dajha: § 22. *dajhaṃca,* § 62.

daṃḍa praptaṃ ca: Possibly plural in *-aṃca,* § 62.

dadavo: (and *dadavya*), §§ 9, 116.

daditva: § 102.

danaǵrahana: (*dvandva*), § 135; *danagrana,* § 28.

darśaveti: § 20. ='show'. Used when somebody tries to prove that some property belongs to him: 734 *yo atra ogu Bhimasenaṣa tanu kilmeciyana bhumac̄hetra Rutraya Paṃcama ṣa ca tanu darśaveti* 'The land that there belongs to *ogu* Bh.'s own *kilmecis.* R. and P. are attempting to prove it is their own property'.

darṣ-: 'to pack', =Av. *darəz. B.S.O.S.* VII, 510.

daśaṃmi: § 89.

daśavita: Occurs associated with lists of names beside which are placed amounts of grain, etc. which they have either paid or received. Construed with the name of the official in charge of the transaction, e.g. 627 *daśavita Caneya ima* 10. 2. It is not quite clear whether the people receive or give the things mentioned, since the object of *daśavita* is always the people mentioned in the list. On the first alternative we might regard *daśavita* as a denominative from *daśa* '10', i.e. 'He collected the tithe from'. Or secondly, if the meaning is to 'distribute' (i.e. wages in the form of corn, animals, etc. to people employed in the royal service), it may be causative from √*dāś,* Skt. *dāśayati* 'give, grant, bestow'. For the latter alternative speaks the fact that people with official titles (*apsu, vasu, toṃgha,* etc.) are frequently mentioned in the lists. On the other hand, lists of names are frequently headed by *śadade* (an administrative unit, see s.v.), where the ablative would seem to imply that something was taken from *śada.* Alternatively the word might be taken as a title parallel to *śadavida* (O. Stein, *B.S.O.S.* VIII, 770).

daśutara: § 89.

dasya: § 15 (and *daha, dahi,* etc.).

dasyāti: § 99.

dahita: =*dagdha* (passage explained under *kaṣara*).

dāsyatu: =*dāsyasi,* § 93.

diṭhi: Measure of length. Skt. *diṣṭi*. There is no need to compare directly Av. *dištay-* (see *Khar. Inscr.* Index Verb.).

dita: May be either **dita* or **ditta*. The first would correspond with Indo-Eur. *dətó-*, Skt. *-dita* (in compounds). Torwali *dit* 'gave', preserving the *t* speaks for original **ditta*; *dita* would give *dī* in Torwali. Cf. further, *B.S.O.S.* VIII, 431, where it is shown that the form *dhitu* in 661 must represent **dittam*.

ditae: (and *ditaǵa*), §§ 8, 16, 53.

Dirpara: Native corruption of the Iranian name *Tirap̄hara*. On elision of vowels, § 13. The *d-* is curious but of no significance for pronunciation in this language, cf. §§ 14, 15.

dilic̄ha: § 50.

divira: 'scribe, writer'. Iranian loan-word. M.Pers. *dipīr*, N.Pers. *dabīr*. The Iranian forms show a long *ī*, so that we may have **divīra*. On the other hand, the word is borrowed into Sanskrit with a short *i*, *divira*.

diśita: 295. Read probably *yaśita* as in note 6 (i.e. *yācita*, which goes well with the ablative *goṭhade*).

du: § 89 (*dui*, *due*).

dutaǵa: 722. =*dutaka-* 'burnt' (not *dūta*).

dutiyae: § 67.

dura: § 90.

durbhale: § 53.

durlāpa: § 14.

dṛṭhati: 3rd plural, *dṛṭhati*=*dṛṭhaṃti* 'they saw'.

denati: § 96.

denuǵa: Title, 418. Cf. *B.S.O.S.* VII, 5. Possibly from Av. *daēnā* 'religion'.

deyaṃnae: § 103.

deyāṃti: § 100.

devaputra: A title introduced into India by the Kuṣan kings, and by them adopted from the Chinese 'son of heaven'. That it is used by the kings of Kroraina indicates some connection between the two dynasties.

draṃga: Cf. *B.S.O.S.* VII, 510. The question is put there as to whether the meaning is not 'office, department' in general rather than 'Frontier-watch station' as Stein suggested, or even 'toll-house', and this seems to be rendered quite clear by 520 *Suǵiya garahati yatha eṣa ṣoṭhaṃga, avi rajaṃmi divira eṣa puna sp̄asa̱vaṃni dham̄a Salveyena s̱adha saṃma kareti Salve aṃña draṃga na dhareti...pruchidavo eṣa dui draṃga dhareti, puna sp̄asa̱vaṃni dham̄a kareti* 'Suǵiya complains that he is *ṣothaṃga*, also scribe in the royal administration, and that again he is performing the duty of *sp̄asa̱vaṃna* along with Salve. Salve does not hold any other offices...you must ask whether he (Suǵi) holds two offices and on top of that is performing the duty of *sp̄asa̱vaṃna*'. It is quite clear that the office of *divira*, etc. is here referred to as a *draṃga*.
Similarly *draṃgadhare* (*tr°*, etc.) means people employed in the

government administration. Cf., for instance, 554 *sarva tramghadhare goṭha bhaṭara jaṃna śramaṃna bramaṃna vurcuǵa ṣa ca*. List of the different classes of subjects: Officials—householders—*śramaṃnas* and *brahmanas*—*vurcuǵas* (= ?).

It must be the same word as *draṅga* of the *Rājataraṅgiṇī*, but the development of meaning is not quite clear. The same word appears as *udraṅga* in *Kuṭṭanīmatam* 936. For the etymology, cf. (rather than *drang-*, *B.S.O.S.* VII, 510) Av. *θraxta* 'zusammengedrängt', N.Pers. *tarañjīdan* 'to be compressed', *turang* 'a prison'. This suits well if the original meaning was 'a fortified place'. The initial *dr-* would be the Saka development of *θr-*. If we take *udranga* as the original form we might explain the word out of Skt., i.e. *ud*+*raṅga* 'an elevated structure'.

driju: 661. =*triṃśat* (?). The passage is not clear. Read probably *aṃghi tadriju* and cf. Konow, *Acta Or.* XIV (1936), 238.

driṃpura: § 50.

dvadaśa: § 43.

dvaraṃmi: § 43.

dvi: §§ 43, 89.

DH

dhaṃnuena: § 72.

dhane: A small weight, 702. It cannot be *dhānya*, because that would give **dhaña*. It is no doubt a loan-word along with *trakhma*. N.Pers. *dāng* 'fourth part of a dram' (Steingass, *Pers. Engl. Dict.*). The earlier forms, quoted by Horn (*Neupersische Etymologie*, s.v. *dāng*), are: δανακή (O.Pers. Heracleides in *Et. Magn.*), Arabian loan-word *dānaq*, Pehl. *dāng* as in N.Pers. Originally therefore **dānaka-*. For *-e* in the Kharoṣṭhi corresponding to *-aka*, cf. *ajhade*= **āzātaka*, N.Pers. *āzādah*, and *saste*= **sastaka-* 'day'.

Dhameca: § 15.

dhama̅: § 36. Note the idiomatic sense of 'employment in the royal administration', e.g. 567 *eṣa Suǵiya ṣoṭhaṃga dhama̅de nikhalidavya* 'This S. is to be removed from the post of *ṣoṭhaṃga*'; 10 *arivaǵa dhama̅na*, etc.

dharaṃnaǵa: =*dhāraṇaka* 'owing (a debt)'.

dharmiaṣa: § 36.

dhalavaǵu: 661. Perhaps means 'document': *maya dhalavaǵu Bahudhivä likhidu Khvarnarsasya ajiṣanayi* 'By me Bahudhiva this document was written at the request of Khvarnarse'.

dhitu: Declension of, § 68.

dheśati: § 99.

N

na iṃci: § 126.

naǵara: § 16.

naǵa: § 64.

nac̄ira: *B.S.O.S.* VII, 513. 'hunting'=N.Pers. *naxčīr*, Pehl. *naxčīr*, T.Phl. *naxčihr*, Arm.L.W. *naxčir-k'*, Sogd. *n'γšyr*= **naxšīr*.

nadi: 368. Fragmentary. Probably (*a*)*nadi*.

nadha: =Skt. *naddha-*. Used as a substantive='parcel', e.g. 59 *sā aṃna teṣa jaṃnaṣa tana tanu nadha iśa anidavo* 'That corn of those people is to be brought here in separate parcels for each of them'; 291 *tre tre milima nadha kartavo* 'The parcels are to be made each of 3 *milima*'. Much the same as *darṣa*.

namakero: § 53.

namatae: (and *namataǵa*), § 53. =N.Pers. *namad* 'felt: a garment of coarse cloth' (Steingass), Pahl. *namat* 'rug' (Tavadia, *Šāyast-nē-Šāyast*, Index, s.v.), Anglo-Indian *numdah* (Stein, *Ruins of Ancient Khotan*, I, 367).

Borrowed probably from Iranian, also Pali *namataka*, and *nantaka*= **namtaka*=some kind of coarse garment.

namaṃniya: (also *namanaǵa*). Only in the phrase *namaṃniya deyaṃnae* 'to exchange' (?). Four methods of disposing of property are mentioned in deeds of sale (cf. 571, 580, 581, 587, etc.): (1) 'sell' (*vikrinanae*), (2) 'give as a present' (*prahuḍa deyaṃnae*), (3) 'mortgage' (*baṃdho(ṽa) thavaṃnae*), (4) 'exchange' (?) (*namaniya deyaṃnae*). Both forms must be derived from a word *namana*. This may be < an Iranian *nimāna* (for *na*<*ni*, cf. *namata*<*nimata*), cf. Arm.L.W. *nman* 'instar', 'similis', N.Pers. *namūnah* 'similar, like', 'pattern', etc. The meaning 'exchange', i.e. give something for something like it, might easily develop from this.

Namarajhma: Iranian name (*nāma* 'fame' as first member of names, Justi, *Iranisches Namenbuch*, p. 220, and *razma*, *ib.* p. 507).

namena: § 72.

Narasaka: 500 n.pr. Iranian, adopted from Narsēs (M.Pers. *nerseh*) with the suffix *-ka* (?).

naśati: § 41.

nasti: § 95.

ni: § 17. =*nija* 'own': used as a suffix in place of the genitive after proper names, e.g. 593 *Śarsena ni putra Balaṣena*; 437 *Kapǵeya ni kilmeci Koṃpala*; 582 *Yipiya ni bhuma praceya* 'Concerning Y.'s land'.

Often a word like *putra* or *dajha* is omitted without it being possible to tell the exact relationship of the people, e.g. 129 *Kunǵeya ni Lamǵa*, 210 *Jeyaka ni Taṃjakaṣa*, etc. In 318 *Saṃgila ni Kacanoaṣa coridaǵa* 'A theft by Kacano of Saṃgila' it appears from the document that Kacano was slave of Saṃgila.

Compare the similar use of *hīvī* 'own' in Saka, just to strengthen a genitive, without any particular force of its own; cf. *B.S.O.S.* VII, 790.

nikaliṣyati: § 24.

nikasati: (and *nikhasati*). =*niṣ*+*kas* 'go' (cf. *a-kas*, *ukas*) 'depart, go away'. Sanskrit only causative *niṣkāsayati* 'to expel': 436 *Maṣḍhiǵe taṣa prace śavatha śata, tade coc̄ha nikasta* 'M. swore on oath concerning him, then went away cleared'. 'To come out' of witnesses: 326 *avi tatra bahu Caḍotiye vṛdhe nikastaṃti* 'And there, many old men of Caḍota came forth as witnesses'. 'To be expended, used up' of corn, etc.: 140 *yo tade aṃnade nikhastaǵa amñeṣa ditaya* 'So much of that corn as has been expended, given to others'. The prevalence of the form without the aspirate (*nikas-* more frequently than *nikhas-*) is noticeable compared with *nikhal-*, where it is usually preserved; cf. § 24.

nikraṃta: =*niṣkrāntā*; absence of aspiration as in *nikas*.

nikrona: 146. Epithet of *uṭa* 'camel'. Perhaps *krona* (see s.v.).

nikhaleti: =S. *niṣkālayati* 'expel, remove, eject, take out, bring out': 69 *na nagarade jaṃna nikhalidavo* 'The people is not to be removed from the city'. With *ṛna* to 'lend' on, 'have out' on loan: 495 *Močhapriyaṣa vaṃti suv̇arna ṛna nikhaleti* 'He lends or has on loan gold with Močhapriya'. (More likely than 'recovers a debt', because then we would expect the preposition *paride* 'from' rather than *vaṃti* 'with'.) Without *ṛna*: 160 *yaṃ kala Sarpiǵa iśa asitaǵa uhati bhuma ṣe nikhaleti, udaǵa bhija Saciṃciye nikhaleṃti katma kriṣivatra kareṃti* 'When S. was living here, he used to let the land, the people of Saca lent, (provided) water and seed and *katma*s (= ?) did the cultivation'.

nikhalyati: § 94.

niǵata: An adverb twice used with verbs of going somewhere: 83 *yaṃ kala tuo nigata rayadvaraṃmi ukasidavo ačhati* 'When you are going to travel away to the king's court'; 119 *iśa śruyati Supiye Calma-taneṣu ima caturtha masaṃmi nigata agaṃtavya* 'Here it is heard, the Supiyas are going to come to Calmadana on the fourth month of this year'. 'Down to', adverbial use of *nigatam* 'gone down'.

nigraha: 'punishment'.

ničiri: 677. Epithet of *harga* 'tax'. Prof. Thomas takes it as an adjective from *nacira* (*B.S.O.S.* VIII, 792).

ničhatra: =*nakṣatra*. *ni°* also appears in Toch. loan-word *nikṣāṃträ*. The first part was taken as the prefix *ni-*.

nitya: Never **nica*, § 41.

niyati: § 94.

niravaśiṣo: § 1.

niryoǵa: 'relaxation', § 42.

nivasaǵa: 'neighbour'.

nivarakaya: 320. Read probably as in note 4 *nirāvakāśa*.

nisaǵa: Epithet of *aṃna* 'corn', which is paid to people in the king's service. The meaning seems to be something like the corn required for their current subsistence.

nisaṃǵana: 8. *nisaṃǵa aṃna* is intended. The *aṃ* perhaps indicates *ā* (*Khar. Inscr.* III, 300).

nihañ: § 27. =*nikhan*, also *nihañanae*. The *-ñ-* perhaps due to native phonetic tendencies mentioned in § 32.

nuava: Apparently short for *mahanuava*=*mahānubhāva* (royal title). Less likely an independent (non-Indian) title.

nokṣari: The month of the new year. Arm. *navasard*. Konow, *Acta Or.* II, 121; cf. also *B.S.O.S.* VII, 512.

noñi: Epithet of *uṭa* 'camel'.
novati: § 89.

P

paḱe: ='package, parcel' (of rations, allowance paid to state employees), =Tibetan *pha-tsa* in documents from the same region. See Prof. Thomas, *Acta Or.* XIII, 54 ff. Compare perhaps Kuchean *pāke* 'portion'.
paḱeyu: § 62.
paṃcara: (and *paṃcarayina aṃna*). Perhaps='fodder' and 'grain for feeding': 146 *aṃña mṛga uṭas̱a paṃcaraina aṃna huda milima* 4 *khi* 10 'Also for a *mṛga*-camel the corn for fodder (?) was *m.* 4, *kh.* 10'. But the sense cannot be established with certainty. It might be something more definite, such as the food to be consumed on a journey, etc.
paceya: 79. =(?).
pac̄a: §§ 49, 91, 92.
pac̄adara: Comparative of *pac̄a* 'later'.
pac̄evara: ='food, provisions', as is clear especially from 505 *Tsuǵenaṃma satu milima* 2 *khi* 10 4 1 *maḱa khi* 4 1, *kavaśi* 1; *pac̄evara piṃḍa milima* 3 *chataǵa* 1, *tena Tsuǵenaṃma giḍa* 'Tsuǵenaṃma-meal, 2 *milima*, 15 *khi*, maḱa *khi* 5; one tunic: the sum of provisions 3 *milima*, clothing—1 (article), that Tsuǵenaṃma received'. Here clearly *pac̄evara* is the general term 'food' in opposition to the particular kinds of food enumerated, just as *chataǵa* (=*chādaka*) 'clothing' is in opposition to the particular garment mentioned. Cf. also 19 *coḍaǵa pac̄evara parikraya dadavo* 'Clothing, food, wages must be given'.

Etymology uncertain, but a connection may be suggested with the Sogd. *pš''βr* 'food, provisions'. Original *paθya°-*='food for a journey', cf. Skt. *pātheya-*.
pachaṃgayina: 65. Read *paṃcarayina* probably.
pajeka: 349. Read probably *paḍeka*, which is the regular form in this dialect corresponding to *pratyeka*.
paṭa: =*paṭṭa* 'roll of silk'. The word is discussed at length by Lüders, *Textilien*, p. 24 ff.
paṭaṃca: § 62.
paṭanaǵa: 223, 383. Read probably *paḍuvaǵa* (see s.v.).
paṭami: 437. Probably locative of *paṭa* in the sense of 'tablet'.
paṭayas̱a: Read *Patrayas̱a*, which is the same name. Since the akṣaras *ṭa* and *tra* are very much alike, cases like this are obviously a question of confusion of writing, not of a phonetic *ṭ*=*tra* (cf. § 36). Similarly *paḍaya*.
paṭi: 437 *eṣa paṭi.* =Skt. *paṭṭikā* in the sense of 'tablet' (*ikā*=*i*, §§ 74, 75).
paḍiǵa: 140. =*paḍeǵa* (*pratyeka*).
paḍiciṃtati: § 109.
paḍuvaǵa: Skt. *pratibhū-* and the suffix *-aka* 'security, surety', §§ 28, 41: 446 *Katiyas̱a paḱe, Cama Sumati paḍuvaǵa* 'Kati's

parcel. Cama Sumati is security'; 703 *śarira huḍiyama osuǵa avajidavo civanae, ko jivitasya paḍuvaǵa amaraṃnae* 'Care is to be taken in the maintenance of your body to live, (and) as far as there is a security for life, not to die'. Read *paḍuvaǵa* in 546 for *patruvaǵa* and in 223, 762 for *paṭanaǵa*. In 223 *hasta paḍuvaǵa* the *hasta* is reminiscent of Iranian idiom. Cf. forms like N.Pers. *dast yār*.

paḍeǵa: § 41.

patama: Adverb. ='back', § 91. Cf. Torwali *pat* out of **patta-*: 64 *imade aṃtaǵi uṭa* 4 *Samarsade patama nikhalidavo, Samarsade uṭa* 4 *dadavo, S̄unade patama nikhalidavo, S̄unade uṭa* 4 *dadavo, Pis̱aliyade patama nikhalidavo* '4 *aṃtaǵi* camels from here are to be turned back from Samarsa, from Samarsa 4 camels are to be given; they are to be turned back from Snuna and 4 (fresh) camels are to be provided from Snuna; these are to be sent back from Pis̱ali'; 1 *eka gavi patama oḍitaṃti, eka khayitaṃti* 'They let one cow go back, one they ate'.

patena: § 91.

pateyo: § 66.

paṃthaci: § 77.

patsa poña: 303. =(?).

padebhyaṃ: § 66.

payati: Cf. *bhija payati*.

payita: 703 *bhuma payita*. Causative from *pī* 'drink'. 'The ground has been watered.'

paraṃpulaṃmi: 586. No doubt the same as is written *parabulade* (415). Obscure, but not a place-name because it is used immediately after *Caḍota* in 586 *iśa Caḍota paraṃpulaṃmi*. Prof. Thomas thinks it is the Gk. παρεμβόλη 'camp'.

paras̱a: In the phrases (1) *paras̱a bhav-*: 165 *yati...paṃthaṃmi paras̱a bhaviṣyati, tuo ṣoṭhaṃga Lṗipeya tanu goṭhade vyoṣiśas̱i* 'If it disappears (is plundered) on the route, you, *ṣoṭhaṃga* Lṗipeya, shall pay from your own farm'; (2) *paras̱a kar-*: 324 *se kuḍaǵa Lṗimiṃnas̱a goṭhade Khotaniye paras̱a kritaṃti* 'The Khotanese carried off (kidnapped) that boy from Lṗimiṃna's farm'.

From *paras̱a* there further occurs a denominative verb *paras̱ita, paras̱itaṃti* 'plundered': 324 *Supiya Calmadanaṃmi aǵataṃti, raja paras̱itaṃti, maṃnuśa rupa paras̱a kiḍaṃti* 'The Supis came to Calmadana, plundered the kingdom and carried off the inhabitants'. Perhaps Iranian *parā* + *āza*.

paric̄hinavitaṃti: § 104.

paride: § 92.

pariniyaṃti: § 94.

paribujiśatu: 2nd Sing. (§ 93) Fut. of *pari-budhya-te* 'understand'.

paribhuchanae: §§ 2, 26.

parimargiṣya: § 99.

pariyaṭitaṃti: 130 (text *pariviṭitaṃti*). Read perhaps *parivaṭitaṃti* 'they exchanged'.

pariyanaṃti: 373. =(?).
parivaṭida: § 37. Skt. *parivartayati* 'exchange'.
parivanae: 214. =The stock of provisions carried by a horse. Skt. *paribhāṇḍaka* §§ 20, 45; or **paribandhaka-* (?).
pariśamiśati: 130. =(?).
pariharṣa: Obscure. Only in the phrase *pariharṣa ajhati* 216=*paridharṣa* 'assault' (?).
parihaṣa: (and verb *parihaṣati*). Skt. *paribhāṣā* and *paribhāṣate* (='revile, abuse'). The meaning is obviously something like 'complains'. It is construed with *vaṃti* and the genitive: 212 *ede vaḍavi praceya edaṣa vaṃti parihaṣaṃti* 'Concerning these mares he makes complaint against him' (or perhaps more specifically as in Skt. 'abuses').
paru: Perhaps *paraḥ* (rather than *param*) with *-u* for *-aḥ* as in *itu, yatu*, § 12.
paruvarṣa: =*parudvarṣa-* 'last year'.
paropiṃtsamānā: §§ 28, 48.
parosp̄ara: §§ 49, 88.
Parvata: 'The Mountain'. Name of a mountainous district near Caḍota, presumably the hills to the south. Whence *Parvatiye* 'the people of the mountains'.
palaǵa varna: 660. Some object. It appears in a list of kinds of cloth or cloth articles.
palayanaǵa: 'fugitive'.
palayaṃne: § 53.
palayiti: § 102.
paliyarnaǵa: 318. =(?).
palp̄i: 'tax'. =Skt. *bali*, modified by the phonetic system of the native language of Shan-Shan. Cf. § 31, and *J.R.A.S.* (1935), p. 675. Lüders (*B.S.O.S.* VIII, 647) has come to the same conclusion.
pavanaǵa: 234. =*pravaṃnaǵa* (?).
paśaṃnae: 721 (and *paśidavo* 159). Probably from *paśyati*, although in Sanskrit it is not used outside the present tense.
paśu: Declension of, § 71.
paṣḍha: 345. =(?).
pasaṃnaṃno: or *pasaṃnaṃta*. Something made of cloth (*thavaṃnamae*), 534.
pasāṃnakara: 627. *p°* *Suǵita* 'A maker of *pasāṃnas* (=?)'. Alternatively the reading may be *patsaṃna* or *pachana*.
pāǵanātsa: 320 *eta puna pāǵanātsa lihitavya.* =(?).
pādayo: § 66.
pādemi: 320. =(?).
piṃga: 416 *p°* 4=Skt. *piṅga* (?) (something yellow-coloured); *piṃgha* 264.
picara: =*pratyarha* according to Prof. Thomas, *Acta Or.* XII, 66, and *B.S.O.S.* VIII, 792. 288 *lekha prahuḍa preṣiśama yo tehi*

picara syati 'We will send a letter and present which will be worthy of you'; 107, etc. *picaradivyavarṣaśatayupramanas̱a* 'Whose span of life is a hundred divine years worthy of him'.

There are considerable phonetic difficulties in the way of this etymology. *prati-* in this dialect is represented by *paḏi-* or *prati-* but never by *pati-*. Nor is there any reason why the *a* of the first syllable should be changed to *i*. *picavaṃnae* may be a parallel (see below, s.v.).

picav-: (*picavaṃnae, picavita*). The same difficulties are against identifying it with *pratyarp-* as in the case of *picara-*, *pratyarha*. Further, *rp* would probably be preserved in this dialect (§ 36) and even if assimilated *pp* would not become *v*.

The meaning, too, does not correspond exactly. Skt. *pratyarp-* always means 'give back, restore' not simply 'hand over to', which is *arpayati*.

picavaṃnae means 'to hand over to, entrust': 16 *maya maharayena Peta-avana caṃkura Arjunas̱a picavida* 'By me the great king, Peta *aṽana*, has been put in charge of *caṃkura* Arjuna'; 439 *ahuno rayaka gavi picavetu* 'Now you are putting the royal cows into his hands'.

If *picav-* is really = *pratyarp-* its irregularity may be due to its being a loan-word from another dialect. Likewise *picara*. Alternatively it might be referred to an original **pi-cyāvayati* 'to cause to go to, send, hand over'.

piḏita: = *pīḍita-*. Used as an adverb, § 90, 'expressly'.

piḍhiyāva: 532: *Yaṽe aṽanaṃmi kilmeciya Vusmeka nama madu dhaṁena yaṽe aṽanaṃmi nikastaǵa, se Caḏotaṃmi piḍhiyāva huati, sa Caḏodade palayida atra kaṁaveṃti, Yaṽe aṽaneṃci piḍhiyāva Yaṽe aṽanaṃmi kaṁavidavya.* From the general sense of the passage, it seems that *piḍhiyāva* must have something to do with *pitṛ* 'father'. 'A (man) called Vusmeka who is *kilmeci* in Yaṽe *aṽana* has gone out to Yaṽe *aṽana* by mother right (because his mother was native there). On his father's side he is of Caḏota. He fled from Caḏota (and) they have him working there (i.e. in Yaṽe *aṽana*). People who belong to Yaṽe *aṽana* on their father's side are to be made to work in Yaṽe *aṽana*.' Then instructions are given for him to be sent back. It appears that labourers or serfs were more or less tied to the soil and not allowed to migrate from place to place. The actual form, *piḍhiyāva*, is quite obscure.

pita(-u): § 72 (declension).

pitupitamaǵa: = *pitṛpaitāmaha* with the suffix *-ǵa* substituted for *-ha*, and loss of vṛddhi as commonly.

Pitoe: § 69.

pidarana: 648. = (?).

piro: (and *pirova, pirovala* 'keeper of the *piro*'). Probably = 'bridge', since it is something closely connected with roads which can be seized to prevent people passing: 639 *yaṃ kala imade anati lekha* *atra eśati paṃtha varidavya piro ṣayidavya siyati tam kalammi varidavya, avi piro ṣayidavya* 'When there comes a letter from here (saying that) the road is to be stopped and the bridge to be seized, then it is to be stopped and the bridge is to be seized'; 120 *pirova ṣarva jaṃna kam̃akare aitaṃti...prapaṃna bahu kha...ṣa utaǵa* 'All the workmen went to the bridge...the water was very disturbed (reading *kha(lu)ṣa = kaluṣa*)'. The passage has not been fully read, but the sense is clear. The work on the bridge had caused the water in some drinking place (*prapaṃna*) to become impure. Further corroboration can be drawn from 310, where it is feared some men will escape from the country—*praṭha ede maṃnuśa anada parimargidavya, piroṽa Cima Kaṣikaṣa ca picavidavya* 'Forthwith these men are to be carefully sought for, the bridge is to be put in charge of Cima and Kaṣika' (if this is a proper name) —and 333, where we hear of fugitives from Khotan getting on to the bridge. In 122 a large cow is destroyed on the Parcona bridge (i.e. by falling over): *Parcona pirovaṃmi go mahaṃta* 1 *naṭha.*

As to the etymology it may be connected with N.Pers. *pul*, Pahl. *puhl*, Av. *pərətu* and *pəšu.* The original form would be *pr̥θwaka*, giving **pirhvaka*, **piroǵa*, *piroṽa* and *piro*. For the final *ǵ* disappearing compare *aganduṽa* and § 16. For *va*, *o*, cf. *ṣvaṭhaṃga* and *ṣoṭhaṃga*, etc., § 7.

pivaṃnaṃnae: § 20. = **pi-bandhanāya* 'to bind on'.

pivarae: *pīvaraka-* 'fat'. In 198 read *ko pivaraǵa* for *kopi varaǵa.*

Piṣalṕiyaṃmi: § 31.

Puǵohaṣa: § 28.

puṅǵebha: Read *putǵetsa*, § 47. Epithet of *uṭa* 'camel'. For the suffix *-tsa*, cf. *aṃklatsa*. Exact meaning uncertain.

puc̄h̄ama: 534. Some object.

puñ̄a-: § 41.

puṃñ̄arthi: § 55.

putradhīdarehi: § 62.

Puṃniyade: § 14. Cf. *Buṃni.*

punu: §§ 12, 91.

puraṭha: § 92. = *purastāt* 'in the presence of'.

puraṭhida: = *puraṭha* (*puraḥsthita-*).

purata: = *purataḥ*. Same meaning as *puraṭha.*

puradu: 661. = *purataḥ* in the dialect of Khotan.

purta: 78. The variant reading *pursa* is to be preferred (cf. s.v.).

pursa: Epithet of *uṭa* 74, *paśu* 157. The n.pr. *Pursavara* will mean a person who rides on a *pursa* (horse or camel). Perhaps a castrated animal from *pursa* (*purta*) *biṃnita* (*bhind-*) 78, though of course *biṃnita* may just as well refer to some other operation, such as making a hole in the nose or ear, etc.

pursaka: 383. = *pursa.*

Pulaya: Surname of Sunaṃta (8), Suǵiya (384), Kuuta (613).

puṣǵa: 383. = (?).

Puṣǵariyade: § 49.
puṣpa: § 49.
Pusṁavika: n.pr. 472. =*Bujhimoyika*, cf. § 14.
peḍa: 207. Skt. *peṭa*, *peṭaka* 'basket', Pali *peṭa*, Buddh. S. *peḍā* '*id.*'
Peta aváaṃna: See *avána*.
peta vaṃnidaǵa: 318. =(?).
petri: 399. =*paitrika*.
poǵa: § 14.
potǵa: 225. The same as *potǵoñe(na)*. Perhaps the latter part of the word has been accidentally omitted.
potǵe: (*poṅǵe*). Connected with water (347, 397). 397 is fragmentary, but the subject seems to be that soldiers had been going into a *potǵe* for water. In 347 a *potǵe* is said to be without water, and a letter is sent about the affairs of the *potǵe* (*potǵeci karyani praceya*): 120 *ṣitǵa-potǵe* (*ṣitǵa* may be a proper name). With regard to this *potǵe* water is said to have become turbid because workmen went to mend a bridge (cf. s.v. *piro*). No. 701 is a list of people sent to keep guard over a *potǵe* (*potǵe rac̄haṃna jaṃna*). The meaning 'tank, reservoir' seems most suitable.
potǵoña: 207. Usually *potǵoñena*; always used in conjunction with *masu*, e.g. 637 *masu prahuḏa preṣidavya khi* 3 *potǵoñena*. Apparently some particular form of wine: distinguished from *ṣamiyena* (cf. s.v.). The suffix, as Lüders (*B.S.O.S.* VIII, 641 n.) remarks, would seem to be connected with Saka *-auña* and Toch. *-oñe*. [Read in 207 *potǵoñena* instead of *potǵaña* 1.]
potaǵe: § 60.
pothi: 17 (*cam̄a pothi*), 534. Compare N.Pers. *pōst* 'skin' (?).
Pośarsa: § 14. Same as *Bośarsa*.
posara: 382. Some object.
praǵaṭa: § 5. *praǵaṭa nikhalitaṃti* 17 'They fetched out into the open'.
pracukamaṃ: 392 *pracukamaṃ nagara*. =(?).
prace: 'concerning', §§ 6, 92. Borrowed into Saka as *pracai*, Skt. *pratyaya-*.
praṭha: § 91. 'forthwith', from *pra* and √*sthā*.
pratu: § 12.
prathade: 152 *prathade eda lekha atra prahidemi* 'from a journey, from on a journey'. Skt. *pra-sthā-*.
pramuha: § 27.
pravaṃnaǵa: =*prapannaka* 'deed, document'. The rectangular double tablets are headed *yiyo pravaṃnaǵa*.
praśura: =*pracura*, § 17.
praṣavita: (and *praṣavitaǵa*). ='granted, allowed', and as a noun, 'a grant'. It differs from the ordinary word for 'present', *prahuḏa*, by being used chiefly of royal grants to individuals, especially of fugitives (*palayaṃnaǵa*). The idea is relinquishing one's claim to something and letting somebody else have it: 403 *iśa Jeyakaṣa*

palayamṃnaǵa praṣavitaǵa asi 'Here a fugitive was given as a special grant to Jeyaka', cf. 161, 355. Also of corn: 637 *aṃna Yitayaṣa milima* 1 *kala praṣavida* 'Another (thing), the *kala* made Yitaya a grant of 1 *mi*'; of a farm: 375 *suveṭha Cinaṣena ni goṭha maya maharayena edaṣa Dmusvaṃtaṣa praṣavita dita* 'The farm of the *suveṭha* was given as a special grant by me the great king to *Dmusvaṃta*'; 504 *prasavidavo*='They are to have a grant made them' (*ahuno ede prasavidavo*, the subject of the (passive) verb being the people to whom the grant is made, instead of (as usually) the thing granted).

Skt. *pra* + $\sqrt{\textit{sū}}$='to allow, give up, to deliver'.

prasta: 721. Skt. *prastha* (a measure).

prastami: 225. Locative of *prasta*=Skt. *prastha-*, in the sense of elevated land.

prahatavo: =*pradhātavya* 'to be sent' from *prahita* 'sent', § 116.

prahita: 'sent' might be either *prahita* from *prahiṇoti* or *prahita* from *pradadhāti*. The gerundive *prahatavo* points to the latter, the meaning to the former. The two verbs have probably become confused.

prahuḍa: §§ 5, 27.

prahuḍartha: § 55.

prahuni: 318. =Saka *prahona* 'garment' (?). *B.S.O.S.* VII, 514. It might also be read *prahoni*, cf. § 4.

prigha: 316, 318. Lüders (*Textilien*, p. 30) identifies it with *pṛṅga* of the *Mahāvyutpatti*, which means a kind of silk material.

pricha: § 5.

pritiyena: §§ 67, 70.

priyaśpasuae: § 50.

prihitosmi: § 28.

pruch-: § 5.

preṣi: S. *preṣya-* 'servant'.

preṣeyati: § 97.

preṣeyiṣyasi: § 99.

PH

phaḍitaǵa: 760. =(?).

phalitaǵa: 214. Some kind of horse's food.

phalophala: 524. Cf. Pali *phalāphala* 'all kinds of fruit'.

PH́

Ph́um̃aṣeva: Probably an Iranian name. The latter half of the word seems to be=O.Iran. *zaiba-*, N.Pers. *zēb* (cf. *Aurangzebe*) 'beautiful, or beautifying'. The first half is not clear.

Ph́uvasena: Not a native name on account of the initial *ph́*.

B

badaśa: § 43.

badho: (also *baṃdhava, baṃdh(o)va* and *baṃthova*). In 331 *na ba vo thavidavo* is miswritten for this. It occurs always in a list of phrases stating the various ways of disposing of property, e.g. 591 *eśvarya huda vikrinanae badho thavaṃnae, namani deyaṃnae, aṃñeṣa prahuḍa deyaṃnae.* In distinction to the other phrases the verb used is *thavaṃnae* 'to place' not *deyaṃnae* 'to give'. The meaning may be 'pledge, mortgage' like the Skt. *bandhakaṃ dā-* (Kullūka on *Manu* 8. 143, explaining *ādhau* by *bhūmigodhanādau bhogārthaṃ bandhake datte*). The form is difficult to explain. From the various spellings it might seem that *baṃdhova* is the best form, and this would correspond to Skt. *bāndhavaka-*. But against this Skt. *bandhu-* and its derivatives never had any meaning except that of 'relation, kinsmen'. If we take *baddho* as the original form =*baddha-* the meaning would be all right, but a final *-o* corresponding to the nominative or accusative is irregular. However, there are examples, § 53. In that case the *ṃ* may have been inserted from other derivatives of *bandh-*. As for the alternation of final *-o* and *-ova*, compare *piro, pirova*.

baṃnanae: § 45.
Baladeyu: =*Baladeva*, cf. *Upateyu, Jivateyu.*
bahi: § 91.
bahiyade: § 91.
bahu: Declension of, § 71.
bahudhivä: 661. =*bahudipi-*; ? name or title of a scribe.
biti: § 43.
biṃnaṃti: § 45.
buo: § 91.
Bujhimoyika: Iranian name. *B.S.O.S.* VII, 789.
Butsena: § 13.
Budhaphar̄ma: 655. Written thus for Budhavar̄ma (?).
Buṃni: Place-name (?). Cf. *Puṃniyade* and § 14.
bedhana: 288. Miswritten for *vedana* or *vidhāna* (Prof. Thomas) (?).
boyaṃna: § 17.
Bośarsa: Cf. *Pośarsa* and § 14.
bramaṃna: 554 *śramaṃna braṃmana.* Perhaps taken as an indefinite phrase out of Buddhist literary usage, rather than indicating the presence of Brahmins in Central Asia.
brahmacariṭa: §§ 36, 76.

BH

bhaǵena: ='on behalf of, in place of', § 92. For the development of meaning compare N.Pers. *zi-bahr-i* 'on behalf of'. The idiom may be due to Iranian influence.
bhaja: 566. =(?).
bhaṭaraǵa: § 37.
bhaṭariae: § 68.
bhaṭare: § 63.
Bhatro: 157. Name of a deity.
bhana: 149. =*bhāṇḍa* (?), cf. § 45.

bharya pate: § 135.
bhaviṣya: § 99.
bhiǵi: or *kiǵi* 318. Some article described as blue and red.
bhiǵhu: § 48.
bhija: =*bīja* 'seed', § 17.
bhija payati: =Skt. *bīja-paryāpti-* 'capacity for seed'. Land is not measured by area but by the amount of seed it will take to cultivate it, e.g. 549 *Saṃghabudhiyaṣa vaṃti buma vikrida bhija payati milima* 1 *khi* 10 'He sold to Saṃghabudhi land (of which) the capacity for seed was *mi.* 1 *khi* 10'. The treatment of *ry* is not usual (§§ 36–7) as compared with *niryoǵa karya*. But another example is *aya* 409, which certainly=*ārya-*.
bhiṃnita: § 47.
bhiyo: 579. =Skt. *bhūyaḥ*, Pali *bhiyyo*.
bhudva: § 102.
bhumaṃca: § 62.
bhrata: Declension of, § 72.

M

maimci: § 126.
Mairi: § 28.
maḱa: A commodity appearing among a list of items sent as tax (*palpi*) 714–15, and taken along with *satu* 'meal' as a man's provisions 505. One might think of a connection with Toch. *malke* 'milk', except that in 715 it seems to be sent a long distance (to the capital as tax). The value of the sign *ḱ* is uncertain.
maǵhalartaya: § 55.
Maṅǵeya: § 13.
maṭavo: 278. The meaning required is 'should be measured'. Perhaps it is miswritten for *matavo*.
mata: =*mṛta* (?), § 5.
matu: Declension of, § 68.
maṃtsa: § 48.
madu pitusya: § 135.
madhya: § 41.
manasikaro: § 53.
maṃnasiyaṃmi: § 72.
maṃnuśa: § 41. *maṃnuśe*, § 60.
mama: § 78.
maravara: *B.S.O.S.* VII, 510 and 785.
marǵanae: § 103.
maṣu: (=*śmaśrū-*), §§ 38, 49.
maṣa: § 22.
maṣe: § 58.
masu: §§ 22, 50, 71. ='wine', Lüders, 'Zur Geschichte des ostasiatischen Tierkreises', *S.P.A.W.* (1933), p. 3. For the treatment of *dh*, cf. *aṣimatra*=*adhimatra*. A similar change appears in Palestinian Gypsy (*gesū*=*godhuma*), though since it occurs in only

one dialect it must have taken place after they left India and can have no direct connection with this. *masu* (i.e. *mazu*), § 22, itself might be an attempt to pronounce an Iranian *maδu*, but that leaves *a̱simatra* unexplained. Cf. further under *śuka masu*.

masuv́i: § 75.

masu śaḍa: 'vineyard'. = Skt. *śāla* 'enclosure, fence' (Lüders, *loc. cit.*).

masuṣya: 283. Read *manuṣya*.

mahatva: §§ 44, 72.

mahatveya: § 60.

mahanuava: § 28. Cf. *nuava*.

mahaṃta: § 72.

mahi: § 78.

mahuraǵa: 355. Something measured in *khi*s. In Skt. *mahoraga* is given by the dictionaries as the root of a certain plant.

mahuli: Lüders (*B.S.O.S.* VIII, 640) denies that this = Skt. *mahilā*. It may mean 'grandmother', because Ramotiae, who is said to be the *mahuli* of Sunaṃda (528), is mother of Suǵnuta (538) and a Suǵnuta is father of a Sunaṃda in the same series of documents (524). More likely however it = 'aunt' (< *mātulī*) with *t*, as very rarely, omitted and *h* as hiatus-filler (§ 28).

milima: = μέδιμνος (Prof. Thomas). Cf. *khi*. There is a confusion between *l* and *d* (δ) in Sogdian (Gauthiot, *Grammaire Sogdienne*, vol. I, 12–13), but the evidence seems to be against Sogdian influence in these documents. Cf. also *B.S.O.S.* VII, 785.

miṣi: § 38, where it is explained as *miśrya*, but that is uncertain, cf. under *akri*. Prof. Thomas (*Acta Or.* XII, 38), quoting 582 (*pura-naǵa*) *miṣiya bhuma huati, tade paru eṣa bhuma akri patida* 'Formerly it was *miṣi*-land, after that it fell *akri*', regards *miṣi* as = 'cultivated' and *akri* as uncultivated. In that case one might suggest a connection with Saka *ttumäṣä* 'seed-field' (as representing **tauxmamiṣi*-).

mukeṣi: See under *lote*.

muǵeṣa: Can hardly be the same as *mukeṣi* because the sibilants are never confused, § 33. It is some legal expression, probably with the same meaning as *aviṃdama* (cf. s.v.): 591 *ko...aṃñatha icheyati karaṃnae muǵeṣa giḍaṃti śaṃḍa aśpa* 1 *prahara* 20 20 10 'Whoever tries to make it different they have taken upon themselves a penalty (fine) of one *śaṃḍa* horse and 50 blows'.

mutaṃti: 63. = *mukt-* 'they released', § 107.

muti lata: Skt. *muktā latā*: *mukti* for *muktā* in *Suv. pr. S.* IV, 84.

muli: § 9. = *mulya*. It is used to mean both 'price' in general and also a particular unit of value: (1) 422 *niyida muli Kuv́ayaṣa paride uṭa agiltsa* 1 'The price was taken from Kuv́aya, 1 untrained (?) camel'; (2) 345 *taha sarva piṃḍa gaṃnanena muli huda* 1 *Sa* 'So the whole sum being reckoned comes to 100 *muli*'. The locative or instrumental of *muli* is used alongside the name of the object serving as payment to indicate how many *muli* it is worth, e.g. 437 *Koṃpala Suǵiyaśa ca du capariśa muliyami viyala uṭa* 1 *paḓichitaṃti* 'Koṃpala and Suǵiya received 1 wild camel worth 42 *muli*'. The following table, collected from the documents, illustrates the value of various articles in *muli*:

571	1 *uṭa duvarṣaǵa*	= 50 *muli*
571	*masu khi* 10	= 10 *muli*
579	*tavastaǵa hasta* 13	= 12 *muli*
580	*aśpa* 1 *catuvarṣaga*	= 40 *muli*
589	*uṭa* 1 *ekavarṣaǵa*	= 40 *muli*
590	*eka uṭa viyala*	= 40 *muli*
590	*uṭa aṃklatsa*	= 30 *muli*
592	*uṭa aṃklatsa*	= 30 *muli*
598	*khara*	= 15 *muli*
327	1 *go*	= 10 *muli*
327	1 *kojava*	= 5 *muli*
222	1 *kojava*	= 10 *muli*

From 431 it appears that 13 *hasta* of tapestry (*tavastaǵa*) is worth one golden stater. The same is said in 579 to be worth 12 *muli*. So provisionally we may regard the *muli* as being equal in value to $\frac{1}{12}$ of the golden stater (*suv́arna ṣadera*).

muṣaya: An adverb used with 'give, sell, present', meaning 'without reservation', i.e. so that the previous owner has no further claims: 621 *yo puna edaṣa Saǵamovi bharya putra dhidara yaṃ ca daṣi sarva edaṣa Saǵamovi muṣaya praṣavita* 'Again what wife, sons and daughters and what slave-girl of him Saǵamovi (had) Saǵamovi presented all to him without reservation'; 39 *uniti teṣemi muṣaya tanuv́i hotu* 'The adopted girl belongs to them without reservation'. The etymology is obscure.

muṣka: = *mūṣika*, § 13.

muṣǵeṣu: § 49.

mṛga: § 5.

mṛda: § 5.

mṛdhena: 385 *uparyaṃ mṛdhena pratiċhami* = 'I await with the greatest impatience (?)', i.e. *aṃmṛdhena* = *a* + Pali *middha* (Vedic *mṛdh-*, *mṛdhra*). But *upari* is not usually used to make a kind of superlative.

meta: Only 179 *meta paḓichitaṃti* 'They received *meta*'. Quite obscure.

mepoǵa: 721. Something sent as a present.

Moṅǵeya: Read *Motǵeya*, § 47. Obviously the same as *Motaǵe* (§ 13).

Y

ya-: §§ 85, 127.

yaṃ kala: § 128.

yajita: § 17.

yaṃña: § 44.
yaṭita: 376. Read *yajita*.
yatu: § 12.
yatma: An official connected with the collection and conveyance of taxes, especially of corn. His functions are to some extent connected with those of the *aǵeta* (cf. s.v.). In 305 the *yatma* has to pack parcels of corn (*nadha*). In 374 the *yatma* Aco, along with the *tuǵuja* Sudarśana, assesses the annual tax at Masina. *yatma* is construed with the genitive of *aṃna* 'corn', e.g. 349 *eda aṃnaṣa aṃña pajeka* (read *paḏeka*) *yatmi kartavo* 'Of this corn other *yatmas* are to be made severally'; 430 *kvaǘana aṃnaṣa yatma* '*yatma* of the *kvaǘana* corn'. We also hear of them in connection with conducting camels, 23, 546.
yatha: § 130.
yadi: § 129.
yala: 431 *aṃña yala*. Cf. § 16.
yava: § 92.
Yaǘe aǘana: Cf. *aǘana*.
yahi: § 131.
yitavya: 164 *aṃnapana suṭha dhaṃnayitavya*. A sort of causative from *dāna-* (?) ('food and drink are to be given them well').
yima: §§ 32, 82.
yiyo: §§ 32, 82.
Yiruṃḍhina: Cf. *aǘana*.
yirka: or *śirka*. According to Sir Aurel Stein (quoted *Khar. Inscr.* p. 308)='silk'. Uncertain.
yena: § 132.

R

racana: 225. =(?).
raja: § 41.
rajakaryani: § 61.
rajiye: § 60.
raju: Skt. *rajju-* 'rope'.
raṭhi: 574. Some part of the equipment of a vineyard *raṭhi vṛcha paṃni giṃnidavo*, possibly an epithet of *vṛcha*.
raḍi: or *saḍi*; 431–2. =(?).
ratu: *B.S.O.S.* VII, 514. =Av. *ratu*. Pahl. *rat* 'authority, judge', used of the elders in an order of the *bhikṣus*. If it is really the Iranian word it is noteworthy that the final *-u* is preserved at so late a date.
ratriae: § 67.
Ramṣoṅka: Read *Ramṣotsa* and compare *Ramaṣtso*, which is apparently a different form from the same base.
raya: § 17.
rayadvari: § 58.
rayana: See *śamuḍa rayana*.

rasaṃna: 345 *rasaṃna* 2. If = Skt. *raśanā* it should have had the palatal *ś*: perhaps Iranian N.Pers. *rasan* 'rope', cf. *B.S.O.S.* VII, 786.

rasvata: 80. *rasoṃta* 137, 211; *rāsuvaṃta* 209. Surname or title.

rucate: §§ 2, 94.

rutriyāṃna: 600. Epithet of *vaḍaḿi* 'mare' (?).

rupya: Skt. *rūpya* 'silver'.

rete: 690 *rete uṭaṃ ca*. Obscure.

rotaṃna: (*rotaṃ*). Some commodity which had to be sent as tax, 295, 385, etc. *curoma*, another commodity equally obscure, is often mentioned beside it, 272, 357, 430. In 272 *caṃdrikamaṃta* is mentioned along with it.

There is an Iranian **raudana* which means 'madder' (N.Pers. *rōyan*, *rōyang*, North Balōčī *rōdin*). It might possibly be that, but unless the meaning in the Kharoṣṭhi documents can be fixed, it naturally remains uncertain. Cf. *B.S.O.S.* VII, 787.

L

lautǵaiṃci: 272 *lautǵaiṃci jaṃna*. Quite obscure. May or may not be a proper name.

laǵeśati: Only 166, which is fragmentary. Skt. *lag-* 'follow' (?).

laṃgho: § 53.

laṃcaǵa: Seems to mean 'rightly, properly, adequately'. Cf. 562 *taha suṭha na laṃcaǵa karetu, mahi maharayaṣa anatiyade aṃñatha karetu* '(In behaving) thus, you certainly do not act rightly, you act differently from the command of me the great king', where the second clause more or less paraphrases the first (cf. 272, 399); 283 *khajabhojena laṃcaǵa paripalitavya* 'They are to be adequately looked after (nourished) with food'. (Very frequent in this phrase, cf. 358, 362, 475; *parival-* has the sense of N.Pers. *parvarīdan*, i.e. 'nourish, feed up, fatten'.) When used in connection with paying taxes, etc. it means 'the full amount due': 622 *avi ciromaṣa laṃce iśa anidavo* 'Also the amount of *ciroma* due is to be brought here' (*laṃce* here may be the noun from which *laṃcaǵa* is derived, or it may = *laṃcaǵa* by § 53); 586 *loteya na laṃcaǵa tita* 'He has not given an adequate ransom'.

Prof. Thomas (*Acta Or.* XIII, 66) regards the word as derived from Skt. *lañcā* 'gift', and that it means as an adverb 'gratis', and sometimes just a gift. But the meaning does not seem so suitable in a survey of all the passages in which it occurs.

laṭhanami: 392. Obscure, but probably not a proper name. Rather (like *kabhoḍhami*) some particular kind of land. A connection with Pers. *dašt* 'plain, desert' is suggested in *B.S.O.S.* VII, 786.

laṭhaya: 298. Epithet of *kriṣivatra* 'cultivation', opposed to *apyaṃtara* (= *abhy°*). So apparently land lying outside a particular boundary round the village. Read *laṭhani*, taking it as an adjective from *laṭhana* (?).

laṣ̱i: i.e. **laṣni*, § 44, means 'a gift', as is shown by 678 *eśvarya bhaveyati...baṃdhova thavaṃnae vikrinanae aṃñeṣa laṣ̱i deyaṃnae.* In this formula, which occurs frequently (cf. 582, 591, etc.), *aṃñeṣa prahuḏa deyaṃnae* is usually used in place of *aṃñesa laṣ̱i d°* here. Cf. N.Pers. *dāšan* 'gift', and for the change *d*>*l* *B.S.O.S.* VII, 786.

lasta: 358 *na ba lasta bhaviṣyati.* It may be one word *balasta.* In the Index Verb. *ba* is taken as = *vā*, but that does not occur elsewhere. In 331 (which is given) *na ba vothavidavo* there is certainly a miswriting, *na baṃdhova th°* is intended. Anyway the meaning is obscure.

lastana: 'quarrel, dispute'. = Saka *lāstana*, as Konow points out.

lastuǵa: Some article of dress because it is made of cloth: 566 *citra paṭa mae lastuǵa* 'a *l°* made of many coloured cloth'. It is frequently sent as a present. It was not of great value (184 *lahu manasiǵara matra*). Cf. *B.S.O.S.* VII, 786.

lahaṃti: § 27.

laho: §§ 4, 27.

livaṣa: Only 109. Some object sent as a present.

liṣita: Cf. *leṣita* and § 1.

lihati: § 27.

leṅga: i.e. *letǵa.* Only 419. Epithet of *bhuma* 'land'; *aṃña letǵa kuthala bhuma.*

levistarena: § 3.

leśpa: Some object sent as a present (140).

leṣ-: Means something like 'to conduct': 376 *edas̱a Sacade uṭa 2 valaǵaṃ ca dadavya, simaṃmi leśiṣaṃti tade Caḏodade stora aṭh́ova valaǵaṃca dadavya* 'To him from Saca 2 horses and a guard are to be given, they will conduct him as far as the boundary: then from Caḏota a horse fit for its work and a guard must be given'. Skt. *śleṣayati* 'bring near to, in contact with', § 49. (Cf. Prof. Thomas, *Acta Or.* XII, 51.)

lote: In 585 *lote* is the ransom paid by a slave for his freedom: *tanu pranas̱a lote tita maṃnuśa Ciṃǵeya nama paśavi* 4. 2. 'He gave as a ransom for his own person a man called Ciṃǵeya and 6 sheep'. In all other passages *lote* is used in connection with wedding contracts. No. 32 illustrates what happened: *yatha Opav́e Peta-av́aneṃci Saǵapeyas̱a dhitu Ciṅǵa Opav́e Peta-av́ana kilmeyaṃmi anida taya lode śvasu Ciṅǵa Saǵapeyasa ichida deyaṃnae eda śvasu aṃñeṣa dita, na kiṃci Saǵapeyas̱a dita* 'That Ciṅǵa took as his wife in the district of Opav́a Peta *av́ana* the daughter of Saǵapeya (a native) of Opav́e Peta *av́ana.* As her *lode* Ciṅǵa was going to give his sister to Saǵapeya; this sister he gave to others: he gave nothing to Saǵapeya'. The *lote* is something given in exchange for a wife. Here Ciṅǵa gives his own sister in exchange. Usually it is not mentioned what the *lote* was. It may always have been a question of exchange of women, or there may have been payments for a wife in cattle, etc. (such are actually never mentioned). The custom of exchanging women is illustrated also by 279 *Yav́e av́anaṃmi kilmeci kala Acuñiyas̱a śvasu Cakuv́aae nama Ajiyama av́anaṃmi kilmeci Pǵenasa bharya aniti huati. taya striyae Yav́e avanaṃmi (lo)te—ṣina nidaya, tatra taya putra dhidara jataṃti, Yav́e avanaṃmi kilmeciye Caṃcā Pǵenas̱a dhitu bharya anida tade avaśiṭhe sarvi Ajiyama av́anaṃmi tanuv́ae hutaṃti, matuae bhaǵena Yav́e av́anaṃmi Caṃcāas̱a bharya Sarpina huda* 'Cakuv́aae sister of *kala* Acuñiya a native of Yav́e *av́ana* was taken to wife by Pǵena of the *kilme* of Ajiyama *av́ana*. Of that woman *lote* (and *muke*)*ṣi* were not taken to Yav́e *av́ana*. There (*in Aj° a°*) sons and daughters were born to her. Caṃcā *kilmeci* of Yav́e *av́ana*, took to wife the daughter of Pǵena. All the rest (of Pǵena's children by Cakuv́aae) have remained belonging to Ajiyama *av́ana*. On behalf of her mother Sarpina is in Yav́e *av́ana* as wife of Caṃcā'. Here it is clear that no *lote* (and *mukeṣi*) having been given for Cakuv́aae, her daughter Sarpina, when grown up, is married by a man in Yav́e *av́ana*, and this serves instead of a *lote*. The interesting thing is that, as far as one can judge, the dealings are not between families but between *av́anas* (parishes or townships). It was necessary that one woman having gone from Yav́e *av́ana* to Ajiyama *av́ana* in marriage, another should come from Aj° to Ya° in exchange. Further information on the regulations prevailing between *av́anas* is supplied by 481 *Yapǵu viṃñaveti yatha edas̱a śvasu Suǵnumae nama Dham̃apri Sumadatas̱a ca matu, na loti mukeṣi diti...pruchidavo yo Suǵnumae veǵa kilme dham̃a hoati taha Suǵnumae putranaṃ eda palṕi Yav́e Av́anaṃmi kartavo* 'Yapǵu informs us that his sister called Suǵnumae is mother of Dham̃apri and Sumadata; *lote* and *mukeṣi* has not been given.... You must enquire, and whatever Suǵnumae's *veǵa kilme dham̃a* was, according to this, tax is to be provided by her sons in Yav́e *av́ana*'. It appears from 474 that Suǵnumae had been married by the monk Saṃgapala, who belonged to *Catis̱a deva av́ana*. The meaning of *veǵa kilme* (usually applied to *stri*) is unfortunately obscure, but it emerges from this document that until the *lote* (and *mukeṣi*) had been paid by the husband for her, or by his children on his behalf, they were under liability to pay the tax in the *av́ana* from which the wife came, which was assessed on her head. *lote* usually occurs side by side with *mukeṣi* (474, 481, 585) without it being possible to distinguish exactly between the two terms. Occasionally they occur by themselves: *lode* 32, *mukeṣi* 338, 555. It may indicate different ways in which a substitute for a wife taken was made, e.g. if *lote* as suggested by 32 (see above) meant providing a wife for the people from among whom a wife was taken, *mukeṣi* might mean making some kind of payment. But this is uncertain. Another term which seems to have some connection with this custom is *muṣḍhaṣi* in 573 *Aral-*

piyasa matu Ajiyama avana de aniti huati, taha matuae muṣḍhaṣi ta kuḍiya atra nidati 'Aralpi's mother was taken as wife from Ajiyama *avana*, and so they took that girl there as *muṣḍhaṣi* (something like 'as a return for') her mother'. It appears that the girl was adopted by Cateya and Catarağa (presumably of Ajiyama *avana*) as a kind of return because her mother came from there. All the same the usual payment for an adopted child was made for her.

Prof. Thomas (*B.S.O.S.* VI, 522 ff.) wants to regard the *mukeṣi* as some individual by whom *lote* was paid, but it necessitates forcing the grammar and syntax of certain passages, e.g. by regarding *mukeṣina* as instrumental of *mukeṣi* (instead of *mukeṣi na*), although the instrumental of nouns in *-i* is invariably *-iyena*, § 70.

lomaṭi: 17. ='foxes'. Skt. *lomaṭaka-*.

V

vaka: (at 574 *vağa*). ='rent' paid for the use of land: 498 *mahi atra bhumac̄hetra na kasya ditağa kriṣaṃnae, tasmartha ahuno iśa Lpipeyasa paride vaka giḍemi, taha bhumac̄hetra edasa Lpipeyasa kriṣaṃnaye, tasya kriṣidavo* 'I have a field there, which has not been given to anyone to plough. Therefore I have here received rent from Lpipeya, so (I have given) the field to this Lpipeya to plough, it is to be ploughed by him'. Similarly in 496 the *vaka* paid by Lpipeya for a piece of land is two *khi* of ghee. In 559, 574 *vaka aṃna* '*vaka* corn' is that part of the produce which is paid to the owner of the land.

vakuṭha: =*apakruṣṭha* (?). If so it is irregular, § 37. It is the participle of *vakośaṃti* (see below).

vakośaṃti: Meaning and etymology uncertain. It occurs only rarely: 298 *Caku Moği Aṣena saca lastana kritaṃti, Caku vakośida goṭhi kam̄a karaṃnae Aṣena Moğiya saca rayadvaraṃmi vakośaṃti garahaṃnae* 'Caku, Moği and Aṣena made a law-suit. Caku was assigned the duty of doing the work at home while Aṣena and Moği take upon themselves the part of presenting the complaint at the king's court'. Such is obviously the general meaning of the sentence. Similarly 750 *na cojhbo Lpipeyasa vivataṃmi vakuṭha nevi garahida* may mean something like 'He did not take part in Lpipeya's law-suit and did not present a complaint'; 107 *puna śruyati suḍe draṃghadare atra punar eva* (*tu le*) *ṣena vakośaṃti ayağa karyeṣu* 'Further it is heard that the *suḍe* (=?) officials are again interfering in the affairs of your worship ((*tu le*)*ṣena*=?)'.

vaghu: Only 383 *uṭa vaghu*. A kind of camel.

vacari: Some kind of vessel used for holding ghee (159), corn (266), meal (*satu* 214), pomegranates (*dhaḍima, taḍima* 617, 295). They were of various sizes. A *vacari* of 1 *khi* is mentioned (295) and one of 4 *khi*. There is no indication as to what they were made of, whether wood, earthenware, etc.

vacarina: 345. Apparently the same as *vacari*.

vacitu: § 102.

vac̄havala: 182. Another reading is *ra°*, which is perhaps to be preferred: *eṣa rayaka uṭavala purva rayaka uṭavalana rajade rac̄havala deyiṣyaṃti* 'He is a keeper of the royal camels; formerly they would give to the royal camel-keepers a guard (*or* guards) from the realm (administration)', i.e. in case of attacks by bandits, etc.

vac̄hu: 630 *vac̄hu jaṃna* and 338 *nave avaśa vac̄hu prasavetu* 'You are certainly sending new *vac̄hus*'. They were supplied by the *uryaǵas*. There is no clue to the nature of their functions.

vajo. (1) A mistake for *vara*: 419 *bhiti vajo. bhiti vara* 'a second time' regularly occurs in this phrase. (2) *bhija vajo* appears in 580 and 587 as a substitute for the usual *bhija payati*. An attempt to explain *payati* is made under *bhijapayati*. The etymology of *vajo* is quite obscure.

vajita: § 102.

vaṭaǵa: (1) 357. Written by mistake for *vaṭayaǵa* (see below) unless it is another form of the word = Pali *upaṭṭhāka-*. (2) *khaṃnavaṭagesi* = 'you are a procrastinator' from **kṣaṇavartaka-* according to Prof. Thomas (*Acta Or.* XIII, 67). The treatment of the *kṣ* (usually = *c̄h*, § 48) is irregular.

vaṭayaǵa: (and *vaṭ̄hayaǵa*). = Skt. *upasthāyaka* 'attendant'. The same form is borrowed into Khotanese *vaṭhāyaa-* (Konow, *Saka Studies*, Vocab.), e.g. 579 *kori Ṣṕalṕayaṣa vaṭayaǵa Śirāsa sac̄hi*, 'Śirāsa, servant of the *kori* Ṣṕalṕaya is a witness'; 622 *ede uṭehi toṃgha vaṭ̄hayaǵana ṣadha tahi puraṭhita iśa anidavo* 'These camels are to be brought here along with the *toṃghas* and their assistants, under your supervision'.

vaṭ̄hayaǵa: (see above), § 49.

vaḋavi: 'mare', § 68.

vaḋaviyani: § 61.

vaṃtaḋe: § 94.

vaṃti: = *upāṃte* 'in the presence of, near, with'. Khotanese *bendi*. Illustrations of its use are 546 *ogu Bhimaṣenaṣa vaṃti garahiṣyama* 'We will make a complaint before the *ogu* Bhimaṣena'; 579 *tivira Ramṣotsaṣa vaṃti bhuma vikrida* 'He sold land to the scribe Ramṣotsa'; 24 *yatha edaṣa dajha Sarpiǵaṣa vaṃti Caule aśpa ṛna nikhalati* 'That Caule has a horse out on loan with his slave Sarpiǵa'. Cf. § 92.

vatu: 140. Something sent as a present to a woman.

vaṃnaṃte: 517. Surname or title of Balasena.

vaniye: 'merchants', § 17.

vayaṃ: § 78.

vara: For *pac̄e vara*, see s.v. *pac̄evara*.

varaǵa: (1) 198 *kopi varaǵa*. Read *ko pivaraǵa* 'which(ever) is fat'. (2) 667 *udhisa varaǵa na oḍita*. Obscure because the text is fragmentary.

varaya: (1) 291. ='part'; cf. *B.S.O.S.* VII, 787. (2) 371 *eka varaya bhuya iśa gameṣiśama* 'Once again we will examine them here'= *vāra* 'time' (and *-ka*>*ya*).

varayaṃ: 206 *ma iṃci varayaṃ bhaviṣyati, ma mahi toṣa kariṣyutu* 'Don't blame me in case there is nothing to stop it' (taking it as =*vāraka-*, but the construction is exceedingly difficult and obscure).

vartaḍe: =*vartaṭaka*. (*Lokaprakāśa*, ed. Weber, p. 98, quoted by Prof. Rapson, *Khar. Inscr.* Index Verb.) There ought not to be an intervocalic *ḍ*. It becomes *ḍ̄*. The reading is doubtful. *varaṃḍe* is a possible alternative.

vartamana: Is used as a substantive meaning 'what is happening, events, news' in the phrase e.g. 272 *yahi Khema Khotaṃnade vartamana hac̄hati iṃthu ami mahi maharayaṣa padamulaṃmi viṃñadi lekha prahadavya* 'If there is any news from Khema and Khotan verily a letter of information should be sent to the feet of me the great king'. Cf. also 165 *yo iśa vartamana Lṕimsuv́aṣa paride ñadartha bhavidavo* 'What the news is here, you must learn from Lṕimsu'.

vartamano: § 53.

vardhi: 565. =*vṛddhi-* 'growth' with *guṇa* taken from the verb *vardha-*.

varmi: or *sarmi*; 163. Something to do with a camel, but the reading of the whole passage is uncertain.

varṣaǵa: 311 *hastavarṣaǵa*, something sent as a present; 318 *varṣaǵa* 1, among a list of objects stolen; 243 *hastavarṣe* 3.

varṣaǵana: 530 *uṭa varṣaǵana ciṃtidavo*; *°grana* possibly to be read (i.e. *varṣagra(ha)na*, cf. *danagrana*). Possibly also *varṣaǵana(na)*, the meaning in any case being 'The age of the camel is to be reckoned'.

valaǵa: =*pālaka-*. The *v-* is due to compounds like *paśuvala, uṭavala*, etc.

valac̄hidavo: 569 *emu kaṭavo yatha uṃniya mamnuśa valac̄hidavo* 'He is to be done to as an adopted person...(?)...'. Obscure. Read perhaps *yatha uṃniya maṃnuśa va lac̄hidavo* (=*manuṣya iva*) 'He is to be characterised as an adopted person'.

vala matra: 573 *Yimila laṣiya pruchama vala matra na kiṃci* 'We do not ask of Yimila any gift, not even a hair (*vāla-*)'.

valiyana: 725 *avi kaṃjha valiyana palṕiyaṣa anada ganana pricha kartavo* 'Also a careful inquiry into the accounts of the tax is to be made by the (*k*)*aṃjha vali*'. The first member seems to be a variant of *gaṃña, kaṃña* (=Ir. *gañja*), i.e. Ir. *ganza-* (?).

vavala: 585 *camari vavala* 1. Probably dittography for *camari vala* 'chowrie'.

vaśidemi: 'I read', § 17.

vaṣe: 534 *vaṣe* 4, in a list of objects deposited.

vaṣḍhiǵa: Obscure. 622 *eṣa masu parvataṃmi giṃnidavo vaṣḍhiǵa kartavo* 'This wine must be taken to the mountain, and a *vaṣḍhiǵa* must be made'; 634 *tuo masu milima* 4 2 *nikhalidavo, Cǵito Cakuv́ala tahi ṣadha parvataṃmi gaṃtavo vaṣḍhiǵa karaṃnae* 'By you 6 *milima* of wine is to be brought out (provided) and Cǵito Cakuv́ala has to go with you to the mountain to make a *vaṣḍhiǵa*'; 637 *kala Kirteya iśa agata Caḍotaṃmi parvataṃmi vaṣḍhiǵa kṛta* '*kala* Kirteya came here to Caḍota and made a *vaṣḍhiǵa* on the mountain'. It may have been some kind of regular festival held on the mountain, at which wine was consumed.

vasaṃmi: In the phrase *ima varṣavasaṃmi*='Rainy season'. Compare Saka *varṣavāysa* (*B.S.O.S.* VIII, 932).

vasu: An official title. The *vasu* is mentioned in close connection with the *aǵeta* in the formula (571, 715, etc.) *ko pačima kalaṃmi vasu aǵeta rayadvaraṃmi codeyati vedeyati*... 'Whoever at a later time shall find fault or bring the matter up either before the *vasu*s and *aǵeta*s (i.e. the local judicial authorities) or at the king's court...'. In 714 the *vasus*, *aǵeta*s and *yatma*s are summoned to the king's court, on account of an inquiry into the conditions of taxation. *Vasu*s were common; about twenty-five are mentioned.

vastarna: Is perhaps = *upastaraṇa* rather than *avastaraṇa*. It is doubtful if *ava-* could ever appear as *va-*. Either it remains as *ava-* or it is contracted into *o-*.

vastaraṃnena: Only in the obscure phrase 431–2 *eṣa masu ṣarva astarana vastaranena vikrinidavo*. It is also possible to read *astaranena* (432, note 1).

vastava: (and *vastavya*). = *vāstavya* 'residing in, an inhabitant of'.

vikranaṃnae: § 103. = *vikrinanae* (which also occurs). Since it occurs a number of times (586–7, 590, 592) it must be a genuine form and not simply a mistake for *vikrinanae*.

vikrinita: 'sold', § 107.

vikriśaṃtu: 'you will sell', § 93. For **vikriśatu*; on the insertion of anusvāra where it does not belong, cf. § 47.

vijitaǵena: § 112.

(viciṃnanae): 654. Probably to be read (*vikriṃnanae*).

viṃñavatu: § 93.

viṃñavayaṃmi: § 104.

viṃñav́eti: (and other forms with *v́*). § 29.

vito: An epithet connected with *aśpa* 'horse' (209, 415, 574, 648), *paśu* 'sheep' (609) and *go* 'cow' (157, so read instead of *śato*). It may be placed either before or after the noun with which it is used, e.g. 609 *vito paśu* 1; 648 *aśpa* 1 *vito*. The meaning is quite uncertain.

vithida: (*vithiṣyati*, causative *vithavideṣi*, etc., verbal noun *vithana*). = Skt. *vi-ṣthā-*. It is remarkable that the dental *th* always appears. It must have been reintroduced from the simple verb *thiyati*. The meaning is always active in the sense of 'keep away from, hold back from', not only in the causative *vithav-*, but also regularly in the simple verb *vithi-*, e.g. 165 *ma iṃci toṃgana paride uṭa vithiṣyatu* 'Do not keep the camel back from the *toṃgas*'. The assumption of an active sense on the part of this verb was probably associated with the change of the past participle passive to an active past tense (see § 105), so that *vithita* meaning 'stood aside, set aside, kept back' developed in a manner parallel to the ordinary transitive verb the meaning of 'he put aside, kept back'. Similarly the verbal noun *vithana* has the active sense of 'keeping back', 57 *ma vithana kartavo* 'There must be no keeping back, putting aside', with reference to the tax that is demanded in the letter.

vidapana?: or *vidapa* 1; 318. Separation of words uncertain. Some object among a list of things stolen.

vinaṭiṣyaṃti: The sense of the passage seems to demand that it is =*vinaśiṣyaṃti*: 368 *athava kala...atikramiśaṃti, yo Sacaṃmi karyani vinaṭiṣyaṃti s̱arva ahu maharaya tahi paride parimargiṣya* 'On the other hand if they...overstep their time, whatever affairs in Saca are ruined, I the great king will seek everything from you'. Read probably *vinajiṣyaṃti* with *j* for *ś* (§ 21). The akṣaras representing *j* and *ṭ* are not very different (*Khar. Inscr.* Plate XIV).

vinila: 292 *avi bhija dadavya yena kṛṣivadra vi ni la vistirna kariṣyati*. No doubt a mistake for *vipula*, compare 216 *vistirna vipula ciṃtidavo*. That is obviously what the sense demands: 'And also seed is to be given so that they can make full and extensive cultivation'.

vibhaśita-: =**vibhajita-* for *vibhakta* (which also occurs), § 17. The alternative reading *vibhayita* is probably to be preferred because *j* seems always to have become *y* (while *c* becomes *ś*, *j* (*ź*)). The meaning is 'made a legal decision'.

viyala: =*vyāla-*. Epithet of *uṭa* 'camel' meaning 'wild, bad to manage'. Lüders (*B.S.O.S.* VIII, 647 ff.) wants to separate it from this and regards it as a native word. But the group *vy* is unfamiliar in the native language.

viyalitavo: (*viyalidavo*, *vyalidavo*). Always in the formula addressing letters, e.g. 140 *bhaṭaraǵanāṃ ṣothaṃga Lṕipeya Sarpinae ca padamulaṃmi viyalidavo*. According to Prof. Thomas (*Acta Or.* XII, 15)=**vijālitavya-* 'to be untied'.

viyoṣita: (*viyoṣidavo*, etc., also *vyoṣ-*), §§ 37, 42. ='hand over (a payment that is due)': 434 *eda Kutreyas̱a viyoṣidavo, Budhasenas̱a niyidavo* 'This (horse) is to be delivered by Kutre and taken by Budhasena'; 142 *Lṕipeya pačevara avamicae dita milima* 1 *khi* 1 *yahi purvika iśa giṃnaṃti atra diguna viyoṣeṃti tena vidhanena atra ṣoṭhaṃga Lṕipeyas̱a pācevara viyoṣitavo* 'Lṕipeya gave some food as a loan, *mi* 1, *khi* 1; the traditional rule is that people pay back twice as much as they receive; according to that rule the food is to be repaid to the *ṣoṭhaṃga* Lṕipeya'.

The verb is no doubt = Pkt. *vosiraï*, which the grammarians derive from *vy- ava- sṛj-*. That would not account for this form, which seems to represent **vy- ava- śrayati*. This is further supported by the forms which occur (without *vi-*) in the *Mahāvastu*, cf. Senart's note on I. 13. 6. There are three forms: *osarati*, *osirati* and *ośirati*. The difference of the vowel (*a* and *i*) would be understandable, if it were a svarabhakti vowel out of an original group *śr*, and the *ś* in the third form may be original.

viraǵa: § 16.

viloṭa: 'plundering', usually in conjunction with *aloṭa*, e.g. 494 *Khotaṃniyana aloṭa viloṭade purva* 'Before the ravaging and plundering by the Khotanese'. The *ṭ* (not *ḍ̄*) indicates a double consonant *-ṭṭ-*. The corresponding Sanskrit word appears as *luṇṭh-* or *luṇṭ-*, with a nasal inserted.

vilomaya: 510. Probably to be read *vilomani*.

vivatha: = *vivāda-*, § 26.

viśati: '20', § 46.

viṃśpade: Only 82 *Suǵutaṣa viṃśpade Cimǵeyaṣa śatade* 'From Suǵuta's *viṃśpa* and Cimǵe's *śata*'. *śata*, literally 'hundred', is an administrative division: *viṃśpa* being used parallel to it must be something the same, but the form is obscure. Phonetically it must represent *viśva-*, which does not fit the sense.

viṣaj-: 'to send'. The two forms *viṣaj-* and *viṣarj-* are used indiscriminately, § 37.

viṣalavita: = *visaṃlap-*, § 47.

vismaridaǵa: 'forgotten'. The group *sm* is preserved in this word though usually *s* is omitted. Cf. § 49.

viheṭa: § 18. Usually *viheḍ̄-*.

viheḍ̄eti: = *viheṭhayati* 'trouble, molest, harass': 164 *avi ca ahono iśa Peta aǵaneṃciye palṕi dhama̅ prace suṭha viheḍ̄eṃti* 'And now here the people of Peta *aǵana* are causing trouble about the conditions of taxation'; 206 *Sujata iśa suṭha viheḍ̄itaṃti* 'They harassed Sujata a great deal here'.

vucati: § 94.

vuta: 655. = *upta* 'sown'.

vurcuǵa: Denotes a particular class of people: 554 *sarva traṃghadhare goṭha bhaṭara jaṃna śramaṃna bramaṃna vurcuǵa ṣaca ede jaṃna ...iśa anitavo* 'All the state officials, the people who are heads of houses, monks, brahmins and *vurcuǵas*...' *vurcuǵa* is a title of Luṭhu in 277; *vurcuǵa luṭhuaṣa pradeǰade* 'From the district of the *vurcuǵa* Luṭhu'. We also have the phrase *vurcuǵana pradeǰade* 'From the district of the *vurcuǵas*' twice (277, 304), both times heading lists of camels and the individuals connected with the transaction.

vuryaǵa: Some kind of official. Four or five people are given this title: Opǵeya (290, 384), Vuru (569), Ratǵe (586, 715), Pǵita (579). In 215 *vuryaǵa* is given as a possible alternative reading to the one given in the text. The *vuryaǵa* Opǵeya is head of a *pradeja* 'district': 762 *aṃna muli vuryaǵa Opǵeyas̱a pratejade lihitaǵa* 'The price of the corn from the district of Opǵe was written'. A variant of the word is *uryaǵa* (cf. § 30) in 630 *treya uryaǵana paride jaṃna* 10 4 1 *kala Puṃñabalas̱a dadavo* 'From the three *uryaǵa* 15 people are to be given to *kala* Puṃñabala'.

vṛtaǵa: = *vṛddhaka-*, § 24.

vṛdhe: Plural, § 60.

veǵa: (also *v́eǵa*). In the phrase *veǵa kilme striyana* the term indicates some class of women: 211 *veǵa* (so read instead of *draǵa*) *kilme striyana palpi na aniṣyaṃti* 'They will not bring the tax of the *veǵa kilme* women'; 714 *avi v́eǵa kilme striyana palpi spura pruchidavo* 'Also the tax of the *veǵa kilme* women is to be demanded (or enquired into) in full'. After general instructions about *palpi* 'tax', the *palpi* of the *veǵa kilme* women is mentioned by itself as a special class. 165 *veǵa kilme striyana palpi bhuma na va ka aṃna spora vis̱ajitavo* admits of two readings, either *bhuma navaka aṃna* as in the text or *bhumana vaka aṃna*. Translated according to the latter reading it runs: 'The tax of the *veǵa kilme* women (and) the corn paid as rent (see under *vaka*) for the lands is to be sent in full.' 481 *Yapǵu viṃñaveti yatha edas̱a śvasu Suǵnumae nama Dham̃apri Sumadatas̱a ca matu, na loti mukeṣi diti*. . .*pruchidavo, yo Suǵnumae veǵa kilme dham̃a hoati taha Suǵnumae putranaṃ eda palpi Yav́e avanaṃmi kartavo* 'Yapǵu says that his sister called Suǵnumae is the mother of Dham̃apri and Sumadata *loti* and *mukeṣi* have not been given. . .you must enquire into it, what obligations Suǵnumae has concerning *veǵa kilme*, this tax is to be paid by the sons of Suǵnumae in Yav́e *av́ana*'. There is obviously not enough material here for deciding the meaning of the word, but it is possible that it represents **vēka* out of Iranian *vidavak* (Pahl. *vēvak*, N.Pers. *bēvah*), meaning 'widow'. Certainly Suǵnumae in 481 was a widow, because the dealings are with her sons, not her husband. Even then the phrase *v́eǵa kilme* is difficult; *kilme* usually means something like 'district'. The *veǵa kilme* might mean something like the 'widows' department', 'widows' state'.

veda: (or *reda*). A particular object (655).

veya: 'we', §§ 6, 78.

vera saṃśaya: 283 *yo teṣa vamti purimaǵa vera-saṃśaya taṃ vismaritavya* 'They must forget their old hatred and suspicion'.

velaṃmi: § 67.

vela velaya: § 67.

vevatuǵa: § 75.

vothavidavo: 331. It is not equal to *vyavasthāpayitavya-*. Initial *vy-* is not assimilated to *v* (§ 42). The passage runs: *na vikrinidavo* *na ba vo thavidavo nevi goṭhade dura nikhalidavo.* By comparison with similar formulas (see s.v. *baṃdhova*) there is little doubt that *ba vo* has been miswritten for *badho* or *baṃdhova.*

vyaǵa: =*vyaya* 'expense', § 16.

vyalidavo: See *viyalitavo.*

vyarivala: *vihāra pāla-*, cf. § 28.

vyalṕi: Fem. of *vyāla* 'wild', § 31.

vyavasthavidaǵa: 229 'arranged, settled'.

vyochiṃna: 506. =*vyavachinna-* used as an active past tense (§ 107). The form *vyochiṃnida-* is the usual one; 'decided'.

vyoṣeti: See *viyoṣeti.*

vrac̄hi: 586 *vrac̄hi chiṃnaṃnae* obviously represents *vṛkṣa* 'to cut down the trees'. Probably miswritten for *vric̄ha* (i.e. the vowel stroke attached to the wrong akṣara). That would regularly = Skt. *vṛkṣa*, § 5.

V́

V́eṣ̱i: 719. Cannot = *veśyā* on account of the *ṣ̱*. The palatal *ś* is always kept distinct.

Ś

śakara: 'sugar', § 37.

śakoma: § 95.

śagri: Epithet of *masu* 'wine' (or 'grapes') 349, opposed to *śuki masu* (see s.v. *śuka*). It seems to be equivalent to *śaḏi*, which occurs twice (169 and 221), and perhaps should be read so. *śaḏi* would mean 'wine or grapes fresh from the vineyard' (*śaḏa*).

śac̄hami: (*śac̄he, śac̄hyami*), §§ 41, 99.

śaṃḍa: Epithet of *aśpa* 'horse'. No doubt = Skt. *ṣaṇḏha*, meaning 'a castrated horse'. The confusion of sibilants is noticeable, but the writing wavers in Sanskrit between *śaṇḍa* and *ṣaṇḏha* (Monier-Williams, *Skt. Dict.*). We find initial *ś-* for instance in the *Bower MS.* (see the Index, s.v. *śāṃḍya*).

śaḏa tammi: § 18.

śata: An administrative division meaning something like 'a hundred (households)'. Frequently at the head of lists containing accounts of taxes, etc., e.g. 168 *Svayaṣ̱a śadaṃmi masu śeṣa khi* 10 4 'In the *śada* of Svaya, arrears of wine 14 *khi*'.

śata racana: Something among a list of objects stolen (225).

śato ǵo: Read *vito*, as suggested alternatively.

śadani: Plural, § 61.

śadavida: An official title. They were closely connected with the *karsenav́as*. They are mentioned together, e.g. 482 *edaṣ̱a kilmeyaṃmi Molṕina bhuma ladhaye, śadavida karsenav́a achiṃnaṃti, na oḏeṃti kriṣaṃnae* 'In his *kilme* Molṕina has received some land, the *śadavidas* and *karsenav́as* take it from him and will not let him plough'. Also in 86. They are mentioned as transporting the commodities paid as tax to the king (159, 247); Ricikǵa is called a *śadavida* at 715, a *karsenaǒa* at 590.

One might regard it as a denominative from *śada* meaning 'a person put in charge of a *śada*' (see above s.v.). Of the people given the title of *śadavida*, most are mentioned as being in charge of *śada*'s, namely Suǵita (76; 247), Yapǵu (76; 656), Maṣḍhiǵe (41; 436), Kapǵeya (41; 569). The title is comparatively not very frequent, about nine being mentioned by name.

śamuḍa raya(na): Occurs twice: 252 *śamuḍa rayana khayana māṃtsa dadavo* '*śamuḍa rayana* and meat to eat shall be given'; 387 *ahuno śamu(ḍa) rayana iṃci viṣajidavo sudha namata* 2 *viṣajidavo*. In the latter passage it is obvious that *°raya na iṃci* should be read, because *iṃci* does not occur by itself but only with the negatives *na* and *ma*. Translate: 'Now the *śamuḍa raya* are (*or* is) not to be sent, only (*sudha*) the two felt garments are to be sent.'

The significance of the term is quite obscure. In 387 *śamuṃta* is given as a more probable reading in the corrections (*Khar. Inscr.* p. 292). If so it may be the same as *śamuta* in 15, which is equally obscure.

śamuta: 15. Possibly the same as *śamuṃta* (*śamuḍa*) (see above).

Śamṣena: § 13.

śarataṃmi: § 72.

śavāvitavya: Causative of *śap*-, § 104.

śaśana: =*śāsana*, § 33.

śiṃgavera: 'ginger', § 5.

śigra: 'quickly', § 90.

śiṭha: *śiṣṭa*- (*śās*) 'punishment, chastising': 248 *śiṭha nigraha kartavya* 'Chastising and punishment is to be made'; 248 *ahuno Cimolaṣa śiṭha kiḍa prahara dita* 'Now chastisement was performed on Cimola, blows were given'. Similarly 371, 517.

śiṭhidavya: 482 *go aviṃdama śiṭhidavya* 'They are to be punished by paying a cow as damages'. On double formations like this see § 116.

śiṭhe: 'remaining, left over', 305, 519. =*śiṣṭaka* (*śiṣ*-). On -*e*<*aka*, see § 53.

śitiyaṃmi: Seems obviously from 678 to mean 'side': *Kroraiṃnaṃmi mahaṃta nagaraṣa dačhina śitiyaṃmi bhuma* 'Land in Kroraina on the right-hand side of the great city'. The only other passage where it occurs is 604 *yaṃ kālaṃ Ramakaṣa śitiyaṃmi Caṣǵeya soṃgha anita* 'At the time when Caṣǵeya brought *soṃgha* (=?) to the side of Ramaka'. The reading *yiti*- is also possible (*Khar. Inscr.* p. 308).

Śilaprava: § 20.

śilpiǵa: 'artisan', § 40.

śiśila: =*śithila*- 'slack', § 50.

śuka: Epithet of *masu* 'wine' or 'grapes' (see s.v.). Not=*śulka* 'tax' as Lüders ('Zur Geschichte des ostasiatischen Tierkreises',

S.P.A.W. (1933), p. 6) takes it, because it is used exclusively of *masu* and never of other commodities, while the usual word for 'tax' is *palpi*.

masu undoubtedly means wine, because it is referred to as a liquid (cf. s.v. *masu* and 633, 175). Possibly however it may have had the meaning of 'grapes'. At any rate *śuka* is easiest to explain on that supposition, i.e. *śuṣka-* 'dried grapes'. The aspirated form *śukha* occurs once (387). On the omission of aspiration see § 24. More difficult is the fact that the regular treatment of *ṣk* is *ṣǵ* (see § 49).

Dried grapes also figure in Tibetan documents from the same region. Prof. Thomas, *J.R.A.S.* (1934), p. 475.

If *masu* means wine, *śuka* might be regarded as connected with the Skt. *śukta-* meaning 'fermented'. The relationship of the two forms would be something like that between Pkt. *mukka-* and Skt. *mukta-*. A further possibility is *śukla*, referring to the colour of the wine.

śuǵa bhava: (°*Bava*) 252. Quite obscure.

śudha: 'cleared off; clearing off' (of payments, debts, obligations). Usually in the phrase *śudha upagata*. Cf. *śodheti* in the sense of 'pays off'.

śune lomaṭi: 'dogs and foxes' (see s.v. *lomaṭi*).

śeṣa: 'arrears' of tax.

śodhitavo: (*śodheyiṣyasi*, etc.). ='pays off' of *śudha*.

śpeta: =*śveta*, § 49.

śramaṃ: =*śramana*, § 13.

śrutaǵena: § 112.

śruniti: Indecl. part., § 102.

śruyati: 'it is heard', § 94.

śvasu: 'sister', §§ 22, 49, (decl.) 68.

śvasti: § 49.

Ṣ

ṣada: See *B.S.O.S.* VII, 514. There are two alternatives: (1) that it =N.Pers. *šād*, etc. 'pleased'. If so it is interesting, because the Khotanese Saka is excluded as the dialect from which it was borrowed. They have *tsāta-*; (2) that it is Indian Pali *sāta* 'pleasant', *assāta-* 'unpleasant', out of *śrāta-*, 'cooked', hence 'sweet'. In view of the prevalence of Iranian influence in the language, the first alternative is probably to be preferred, as being less complicated.

ṣaṃdedavo: § 116.

ṣadosmi: § 106.

ṣaṃna: 'hemp', Skt. *śāṇa*, with palatal. Cf. N.Pers. *šan* (*š*=*ṣ*).

ṣamana: =*śramana*, § 68.

ṣamiṃna: 318. Some article.

ṣamiyena: A completely obscure term used in connection with *masu* 'wine' (637) and *aṃna* 'corn' (103). Also *ṣamiyo* (225), e.g. 703 *s̱e amna saṃgalidavya Saṃgos̱asya picavidavya milima* 4 1 *du khi ṣamiyena* 'That corn is to be collected and delivered to Saṃgas̱a, five *milima* and 2 *khi, ṣamiyena*'; 637 *Cikiṃto, vasu Saǵamoya Tuṃpala Cakola s̱aca masu parvateṣu ṣamiyena milima* 4 2 *giḍ̄ati* 'Cikiṃto, the *vasu* Saǵamoya Tuṃpala and Cakola took wine into the hills *ṣamiyena* 6 *milima*'.

ṣayati: 'seizes'. =*śrayati -te* §§ 6, 38: 324 *vasu Yonuas̱a dajha maṃnuśa Saṃrpina nama Supiya ṣayitaṃti, Cinaṣǵaṣiyasa prahuḍ̄a prahitaṃti* 'The Supis seized a slave man of the *vasu* Yonu called Saṃrpina and sent him as a present to Cinaṣǵaṣi'; 713 *yaṃ ca yudhaṃmi maritaṃti, yaṃ ca jivaṃtaǵa ṣayitaṃti* 'Both those which they slew in battle and those they took alive'.

ṣiṅga poṅǵe: i.e. *ṣitǵa potǵe*, cf. § 47. See s.v. *potǵe*.

ṣilṕoǵa: 'document' or 'tablet'. Some of the documents refer to themselves as *eda ṣilṕoǵa* (470). They are regularly mentioned as being written *ṣilṕoǵa lihitaǵa* (312, 470). Lüders (*B.S.O.S.* VIII, 652) compares Toch. A. *ṣlyok*=Skt. *śloka*. It is there perhaps a native Tocharian word identified with the Sanskrit rather than a borrowing. Otherwise such irregularity would be difficult to explain. Perhaps too with an originally more general meaning as seen here.

ṣulǵa: 582 *eta ṣulǵa lihitaǵa*. Obviously the same as *ṣilṕoǵa*. A phonetic variant (*ṣilṕoǵa*=*ṣilyoǵa*, § 31), or merely an error of spelling (?).

ṣulṕaǵaṃdha: Some article that has to be sent.

ṣeyita: § 6.

ṣeraka: 289 and 431–2. A proper name (?).

ṣo: '6', § 89.

ṣoṭhaṃga (and *ṣoṭhaṃgha*): An official in the royal administration charged with keeping the accounts of taxation and royal property (camels, etc.), 'tax-collector'. Such in general seems to have been the nature of their functions to judge from the allusions which occur. We find individual *ṣoṭhaṃgha*s charged with peculation: 272 *eda masu masuv́i ṣoṭhaṃga draṃghadhare s̱arve parič̄hinavitaṃti* 'This wine the *ṣoṭhaṃga*s belonging to the wine department and the officials have consumed entirely'; 567 *suǧiya viṃñaveti yatha edas̱a caturtha varṣa huda ṣoṭhaṃgha huda, goṭhaṃmi suṭha vinaṭhaǵa, iśa masuvi dramgaṃmi gaṃnana kiḍ̄ae huda, Suǧiya Pǵis̱a s̱aca dharanaǵa hutaṃti masu śada paṃcaśa milima pramana. . . .yati eṣa Suǧiya goṭhami vinaṭhaǵa siyati, eṣa Suǧiya ṣoṭhaṃga dham̄ade nikhalidavya, aṃña ṣoṭhaṃga kartavya, yo masu rayaka masu masuvi draṃgami dharanaǵa hutaṃti, taha se masu Suǧiya Pǵis̱a s̱aca viyoṣidavya, puranaǵa masu saṃgalidavo, yo navaǵa masuvaṃmi Suǧiyas̱a nasti karya, aṃñeṣa ṣoṭhaṃgana saṃgalidavya* 'Suǧiya says that this is the fourth year that he has been a *ṣoṭhaṃga*; he has lost a lot on the farm. Here in the wine office a reckoning has been made. Suǵiya and Pǵisa owe 150 *milima* of wine.... If this Suǵiya has lost it on the farm, he must be removed from the duty of *ṣoṭhaṃga*. Another person must be made *ṣoṭhaṃga*. The wine, royal wine that they owe to the wine department, this wine Suǵiya and Pǵisa must pay: the old wine is to be collected, as regards the new wine Suǵiya has nothing to do with it, it is to be collected by the other *ṣoṭhaṃgas*.' From this it is quite clear that the *ṣoṭhaṃghas* were engaged in collecting commodities, wine, etc., paid as tax: also that they were appointed by the local *cojhbo*, the letter being addressed to *cojhbo* Somjaka.

The office was nearly related to that of *divira* 'scribe'. The *divira* Ramṣotsa is also referred to as *ṣoṭhaṃgha* Ramṣotsa. In 520 Suǵiya is said to hold two offices, that of *ṣoṭhaṃgha*, and that of scribe. The *divira* Moǵiya (598) is son of the *ṣoṭhaṃgha* Moteǵa. The *divira* Vuǵaca (507) is son of the *ṣoṭhaṃgha* Luṭhu. The *ṣoṭhaṃgha* Kaṃjaka (182) is said to be in charge of the royal camels. *ṣoṭhaṃghas* are charged with conducting camels to the king (341). They were charged with making payments from the royal treasury. Letters are addressed to the *ṣoṭhaṃgha* Lṕipeya to make provision for envoys to Khotan (14, 135), to pay a woman's wages (19), in connection with the appointing of officials (435), etc. The word occurs in Toch. A. as *ṣoṣtäṅkāñ* 'tax-collectors' (cf. H. W. Bailey, *B.S.O.S.* VIII, 905).

ṣodhama: 'sixth', § 89.

ṣǵabhanae: *skabh-*, § 49.

ṣvaṭhamga: § 7.

S

sa: § 90.

saṃgalitaǵa: (*saṃgalitavo, samgh-*, etc.). ='collect'; Skt. *saṃkalayati*, § 46.

saǵaji: § 1.

sa ca: (1) § 122. Meaning 'and'. Possibly=Vedic *sacā* 'with', although the writers seem to have regarded it as the genitive termination with *-ca*. At any rate they occasionally wrote *-asya ca* instead: 561 *aṃklatsa putǵetsa odarasya ca* (three different kinds of camel: subject of the sentence).

(2) An introductory particle appearing at the head of messages in letters, e.g. 1 (and *passim*) *mahanuava maharaya lihati, cojhbo Taṃjakasa matra deti, saca*... 'The great king writes, he gives instruction to the *cojhbo* Taṃjaka, namely...'. In private letters after the introductory formulas the contents of the message are introduced by *evaṃ ca viñati, saca*... (288) 'And thus is the message, namely...' or more often *evaṃ ca, saca*....

sacadhaṃastidasa: Title of king Aṃgoka. =*satyadharmasthita* 'abiding in the true law'.

saṃcaya: =*saṃśaya* 'doubt', § 48.

Sacyami: Miswritten for *Sacaṃmi*, § 41.

sac̄hi: 'witness'; declension of, §§ 60, 70.
saṃc̄hitena: =*saṃkṣiptena* 'in brief'.
sajavanae: 'to make ready', § 103.
sajeyati: Optative, § 100. Only used in the phrase *ko pac̄ima kalaṃmi vedeyati codeyati sajeyati*, a formula referring to bringing a question before the law and finding fault with an agreement already made. In its place we find in 661 *yo pacema kali...cudiyadi vidiyadi vivadu uthaviyadi*. It is not clear how the meaning can be connected with Skt. *sajyati* 'cling'.
saṃña: =*sañjña-*, § 44. Usually in the phrase *tanu saṃña janidavo*, e.g. 585 *asmabhi kilmeci avaśa jheniǵa hotu tanu saṃña janidavo* 'The people belonging to our *kilme* must certainly be under your care, they are to be recognised as your own'. Either the phrase is to be regarded as a Bv. compound *tanusañjña-*, something like 'characterised as one's own', or more probably *tatpuruṣa* = *tanusañjñā jñātavyā* 'an idea that they are your own is to be recognised', because in 331 *tanu* and *saṃña* are separated: *yatha tanu dita saṃña janidavo*.
saṃta: § 101.
satriśa: 209, may be *sadṛśa* 'a penalty equal for both parties'.
saṃdena: 475 *sarva saṃdena aroǵemi* 'I am well with all that belongs to me'.
sadha: 'with', §§ 22, 37, 92.
saṃdhiṣec̄hyama: 702. Quite obscure; probably something has been miswritten.
sapiṃḍa: 71. = 'owned in common'.
saṃprajaya: 399 *saṃprajaya kartavya kujala kartavya brahmacariṭa*. The letter closes with formulas from the Buddhist religion, naturally in a different style and language from that of the ordinary documents. Obviously *saṃprajānya-* is meant, Pali *sampajañña* 'care, attention, circumspection'. The treatment of *ny* is unexpected.
saṃpreṣeyati: § 6.
saṃbaṃdhamma: *mitra saṃbaṃdhaṃma*. Written for *saṃbadhama* 'We have formed a friendship'. On the insertion of anusvāra where it does not belong, cf. § 47.
samao: 'with', §§ 22, 92.
samaya: 'agreement, contract'.
samarena: 164. An official designation parallel with *tsaṃghina* and *kvemaṃḍhina*. In 387 *samarenaṃmi* is given as an alternative reading for *samasenaṃmi* in the text. There, likewise, the term is used in connection with taxation.
samaho: =*samao*, §§ 28, 92.
samuha: §§ 27, 90.
samṛdhae: § 5.
saṃme: 149, 617. An abbreviation for *saṃvatsare*.
samovada: 'agreement'.

sarachidati: = *sarajitaṃti*, § 27.
sarajitaṃti: = *saṃrañj-*, § 47.
sarġita: 47 *edas̱a goṭha gṛhavasa Apġeyena udaġena sargita* 'His farm and house were flooded with water by Apġeya'; from √*sṛj*, *sarga-*.
sarva: Declension of, § 88.
s̱arvabhavena: § 90.
s̱arvaṣu: Only 422: *s̱arvaṣu Ajiyama av́anaṃnci kilme uthidati....* Obscure.
s̱arvas̱aṃ: 326 *Kam̃aya ni goṭha gṛhavas̱a bhumac̄hetra s̱arvas̱aṃ tena samao.* Read *s̱arvasaṃtena* as one word. 'K.'s farm, house, land along with everything that is his'; cf. s.v. *saṃdena*. For *sarvasanta-* in the sense of 'all one's belongings', cf. Divyāvadāna, p. 439, l. 30.
sarva sṕara: See s.v. *sṕara*.
sarvina: Gen. Plural, § 88.
sali: *syāla-* 'brother-in-law', § 41.
saṃvatsare: § 58.
saṃśaya: See *vera saṃśaya*.
sasteyaṃmi: = '*divasaṃmi*', cf. *sastehi* below.
sastehi: Same as *sasteyaṃmi*. It occurs also in three Kharoṣṭhi inscriptions from N.W. India (*C.I.I.* vol. II, Index). Konow (*ib.* p. 152) explains it as a participle *sasta-* from Iranian *sad-* 'to shine'. The word is not known to occur in this sense in any Iranian dialect that is preserved, but the development of meaning is quite natural; cf. N.Pers. *rōz* from *ruč-* 'to shine'. More difficult to explain is the termination *-hi*. It is less common than *-eyaṃmi*. Since it is the only form that occurs in the (older) inscriptions from India, it is no doubt the original form, while *sasteyaṃmi* represents the analogical introduction of the usual termination of the locative singular. Konow (*loc. cit.*) explains it as instrumental plural, but the syntax is by no means clear.
sahasrahani: §§ 28, 61.
sahini: Epithet of *bhija* 'seed', differentiating it from *juṭhi*, which is equally obscure (see s.v.): 291 *sā aṃna cavala saṃgalitavo, dui bhaġa juṭhi, eka bhaġa sahini, uṭa* 20 20 *tre tre milima nadha kartavo* 'That corn is to be quickly collected, two parts *juṭhi*, one part *sahini*. Forty camels are to be loaded with 3 *milima* each'; 387 *bhuma vikrida bhija sahini vajo khi* 4 3 'He sold land with a capacity for 7 *khi* of *sahini* seed'.
sānapru: 660 (also *sanapru*). Some article consisting of cloth.
s̱ikhi: Epithet of *aṃna* 'corn', 532. Meaning unknown.
siġataṃmi: § 67.
siṃgha: § 47.
sidhalavaṃna: 109. Apparently *siddhalavaṇa-*, meaning some kind of salt. Something corresponding to *sindhu-* or *saindhava- l°* would be more familiar. Saka has *sidaluṃ* translating *saindhova* which is obviously derived from our word.
sima: § 67.

simici: § 77.
siyati: § 42.
sira: Only 140 *si°* 3. Some article.
sukri: Only 74. Epithet of *uṭa* 'camel'.
suji na kirta: Only 318 in a list of objects; Lüders (*Textilien*, p. 31) points out that this word = N.Pers. *sōzankard*. Ar. lw. *sūsanjird* 'embroidery', 'needlework'.
suṭha: = *suṣṭhu* 'very'. The form must correspond to something like **suṣṭham*.
suḍa: or *sutra*; reading uncertain. Epithet of *muli* 'price', e.g. 590 *aṃña sutra muli giḍa* 4 4; 480 *aṃña atǵa suḍa muli giḍa aṃna milima* 1 *khi* 10 (see also *atǵa*). In 714 without *muli* in a list of things sent as tax: ...*croma, aṃña suḍa ekamaṃta*.... The meaning is quite obscure.
suḍi: = (?) 566. *suḍi karna baṃdhana*.
suḍe: 107. Epithet of *draṃgadhare* 'officials'.
sudha: = 'only', § 91. The etymology is not clear.
Supiye: Name of a hostile people always mentioned as engaged in marauding activities, carrying off animals (212) and men (324, 491). They are mentioned as attacking Calmadana (= Cercen) 119, 324, 722, Caḍota 183. There was a garrison at Sāca (Endere) to watch out for them, 133, 578. The *cojhbo* Saṃjaka at Caḍota was not strong enough to oppose them in the field, and locked himself and the inhabitants within the city walls, until they went away. The desert on the north and Khotan in the west being excluded, they must have been tribes in the Kun-Lun mountains to the south-east of that strip of the Shan-Shan kingdom which ran up through Cercen to Niya. In the Saka text published by Leumann (E XVI. 9) they are mentioned as Supīya (which shows that the *i* was long), along with Huns and other invaders who attacked the Kingdom of Khotan. Cf. further Prof. Thomas in *Acta Or.* XII, 54 ff. and *Tib. Texts and Docs.* pp. 78 and 156.
sumiṃna: 'dream', 151.
Suliǵa: Either = 'inhabitant of Kashghar' as Prof. Thomas suggests, or possibly 'Sogdian'. On the form, cf. Gauthiot, *Grammaire Sogdienne*, I, p. vi.
suv́eṭha: (also *suv́eṣṭa*). A title. Nothing very definite about their sphere of activity is to be learned. The *suv́eṭha* Khosa goes on an embassy to Khotan (362). *Suv́eṭhas* act as judges along with *ogus*, *cojhbos*, etc. (506, 709). About nine are mentioned.
suśaǵa: 215. Some class of individuals: *treya suśaǵa eka eka potaǵa giḍaṃti* 'The three *s°*s took one young animal each'. Another possible reading is *vuryaǵa* (see s.v.). The word appears as *sujaǵa* in 387 *sujaǵa rajadhama karemti*. 'Informer' (*sūcaka-*)?
suṣmela: = Skt. *sūkṣmela*, a particular kind of spice ('cardamoms'). On the treatment of *kṣ*, cf. § 48.
suha: = 'well', §§ 27, 91.

s̱e: =*sa*, §§ 12, 22, 80.

seniye: 'soldiers', § 60.

so: =*sa*, § 80.

sokhaliǵa: 665 *sokhaliǵa sarthas̱a* 'The *sokhaliǵa* caravan'. Name of a place (?).

soṃgha: Occurs twice. 637 *aṃña, kālaṣa padamulāde varṣa varṣi rajadhareyana soṃgha pras̱avitaǵa* 'Another thing, *soṃgha* was granted year by year from the feet of the *kȧla* to the employees of the state'; 604 *yaṃ kala Ramakas̱a śitiyaṃmi Caṣǵeya soṃgha anita* 'When Caṣǵeya brought *soṃgha* to the side of (? cf. *śitiyaṃmi*) Ramaka'.

sotira: Apparently a title. 580 *sac̄hi divira Apǵeya sac̄hi sotira tasuca Catata* 'The scribe Apǵeya was a witness, the *sotira tasuca* Catata was a witness'. Possibly an adaptation of the Gk. σωτήρ.

soṃstaṃni: 149. Some article. Probably some piece of apparel because it is mentioned between *kaṃculi* 'girdle' and *kayabaṃdhana*.

stasyati: §§ 41, 99.

stora: =Av. *staora-*, Pahl. *stōr*, N.Pers. *sutūr* 'a large animal' (camel or horse) or simply 'horse'. In 13 *vaḏavi storaṃ ca*, it obviously means 'horse'. In 164 *sada storena, jaṃna samaho*, it means 'animals' as opposed to *jaṃna* 'people'.

storavara: 'riding on a *stora*'. Iranian *-bāra* as in O.Pers. *asabāra-*, etc. Formed with the same suffix are also *aśpavara, uṭavara*, and possibly *Pursavara* (a proper name). In Skt. *aśvavāra* (Epic.).

stovaṃna: Only 399 *tasmartha eta stovaṃnena atra vis̱ajita uṭa prichaṃnaye, yahi eṣa stovaṃna atra eśati, lekha vacitu, tomi stovaṃnas̱a haste uṭa iśa prahadavya* 'Therefore this *stovaṃna* has been sent there to demand a camel, when this *stovaṃna* comes there, having read the letter, a camel is to be dispatched in the hand of the *stovaṃna*'. It is either a proper name, or the name of a particular kind of official that might be used for the purpose.

stri: Declension of, § 68.

Spaniyakȧ: 661. Iranian name (?), cf. *B.S.O.S.* VII, 515. (Av. *spanyah-* 'more holy', Pahl. *spēnāk*.)

sṕara: (also *sṕura*). ='completely'. More often in the phrase *sarva sṕara* (*sṕura*) 'all complete': 272 *praṭha cavala paruvarṣi śuka masu, ima varṣi masu sarva sṕara saṃgalidavya* 'Forthwith last year's dry grapes (?) and this year's grapes are to be quickly collected all completely'. An Iranian word. Saka *uspurra-*, Arm.L.W. *spaṙ*, Pahl. (*u*)*spurr*, (*u*)*spurrik*, N.Pers. *siparī*, cf. *B.S.O.S.* VII, 787.

sṕarna: =*suv́arna*, § 49.

sṕas̱a: 'watch, watching, guard'. Whence *sṕas̱avaṃna* 'guard, watchman'. Iranian **spāsa* and **spāsapāna* (cf. Sogd. *sp*'s 'service', N.Pers. *sipās* 'thanks', both of which have lost the original meaning). The word is discussed in *B.S.O.S.* VII, 512. Cf. § 49. Cf. further Saka *spaśaña* (H. W. Bailey, *Z.D.M.G.* 1936, p. 576).

spura: Cf. *spara*.
spetha: Cf. *suvetha* and § 49.
spora: =*spura*, probably to be read so. Cf. *prochidavo* for *pruchidavo*, etc. and § 4.
Syabala: =*Sīhabala-*, § 28.
sruva: 509. Also *surva*, 524. Only in the phrase *rayaka sruva* (*surva*) *toṃga*, indicating some kind of employment in the royal service (cf. s.v. *toṃga*).
svachaṃtaǵa: 639. ='of their own accord' (*sva-chandas-*). The feminine is *svachaṃdi* at 555.
svachiṃna: 211. =(?).
svaya: §§ 6, 49, 86.
svasavaṃniye: 471. Cf. *spasavaṃna*.
sve: =*svayam*, §§ 6, 86.
sveta: 72. ...*priya sveta Kaṃcaǵa*... seems to indicate some kind of relationship. The same document contains *apru* (see s.v.), which also apparently is a noun of relationship. Neither word appears anywhere else.

H

hachati: Is used both for *siyati* and *bhaviṣyati*, cf. §§ 4, 99, 100. The optative sense is the more usual. The word=Pkt. *acchai*. The *h-* no doubt is from *huda*, *hodi*, *hotu*, etc. Cf. Prof. R. L. Turner in *B.S.O.S.* VIII, 795 ff.
harga: ='tax', or some particular kind of tax. The most usual word for tax is *palpi*. The word is Iranian. The Arm.L.W. *hark* corresponds most closely to it. A different form of the same base is represented by Ar. and N.Pers. *xarāǰ*. For a full discussion, cf. *B.S.O.S.* VII, 788.
hali: Obscure; only 83 *ma iṃci eda hali kariṣyasi*.
haṣga: Word of uncertain meaning: occurs in the phrase *haṣga nikhaleti* (297, 751) 'to remove, take out, a *haṣǵa*'; 297 *haṣga nikhaleti, yatha purva dhaṁa haṣǵa iśa rayadvaraṃmi ativahidavo* 'He takes out the *haṣǵa*...according to the former land the *haṣga* is to be sent over here to the king's court'.

In 542 we have *haṣǵadana* in the sentence: *yatha stri Kaciyae prace, haṣǵadana prace edeṣa vaṃti parihaṣaṃti, eda stri hastagada kareṃti* '...that concerning a woman Kaci, concerning the giving of the *haṣǵa*, they make a claim against (?) him, and take hold of this woman'.
hastama: § 45. ='dispute'. Same as *vivada*. Iranian word *ha*(*m*)-*stamba-*. Cf. *B.S.O.S.* VII, 788.
hiḍiteya: 399. The reading is not certain, but the context demands something corresponding to Skt. *hṛdaya*; a form *hiḍeya* would perhaps be all right.
hinajhasya: Title of Avijita Siṃha king of Khotan, 661. Iranian **hīnāza-*=στρατηγος, cf. *B.S.O.S.* VII, 514, and Konow, *Acta Or.* XIV, 231 ff. The word appears as *hīnāysä* in Saka (*B.S.O.S.* VIII, 791).

huḍiyami: §§ 5, 27. From *bhṛti-*. Only 703 *śarira huḍiyami osuǵa avajidavo* 'Care is to be exercised in the maintenance of your body'.
heḍi: § 28. =*eḍā* 'sheep' (?).
hetuṽena: §§ 29, 71.
hoati: § 96.
hotu: § 98.
hora: An alternative reading for *huve* in 100. Both obscure.

www.ingramcontent.com/pod-product-compliance
Ingram Content Group UK Ltd.
Pitfield, Milton Keynes, MK11 3LW, UK
UKHW042151280225
455719UK00001B/275